'There has always been a risk that the much-need
access and widening participation initiatives may
existing, and unequal, hierarchies of power and the
rich collection shows it is possible to combine rigo᪪   . ᪪᪪᪪᪪᪪᪪ with
critical research and also advocacy and progressive practice.'

**Peter Scott, Professor of Higher Education Studies at the
UCL Institute of Education**

'Rarely does a book come along that so comprehensively addresses
a current need in the equity sector as this one. By bringing together
international perspectives, this book challenges what counts as
"evidence" in the field, critically considering how we frame and
evaluate complex and contested entities associated with "access"
and "widening participation". A must read for not only those
involved in implementing or evaluating equity practice but also
anyone passionate about education and social justice.'

Professor Sarah O'Shea, University of Wollongong

'Thank goodness! A book that moves us beyond what works
to what matters in evaluating equity in higher education. A
book informed by the ontology of widening participation and
a commitment to epistemological equity. Finally, a book that
sets a new platinum standard for educational evaluation to rival
the self-proclaimed and misguided gold standard of RCTs.'

**Trevor Gale, Professor of Education Policy and Social Justice,
University of Glasgow**

Evaluating Equity and Widening Participation in Higher Education

Evaluating Equity and Widening Participation in Higher Education

Edited by Penny Jane Burke,
Annette Hayton and
Jacqueline Stevenson

 is an imprint of

First published in 2018 by the UCL Institute of Education Press, University of London, 20 Bedford Way, London WC1H 0AL

www.ucl-ioe-press.com

British Library Cataloguing in Publication Data:
A catalogue record for this publication is available from the British Library

ISBNs
978-1-85856-703-7   paperback
978-1-85856-858-4   PDF eBook
978-1-85856-864-5   ePub eBook
978-1-85856-865-2   Kindle eBook

Typeset by Quadrant Infotech (India) Pvt Ltd
Printed by CPI Group (UK) Ltd, Croydon, CR0 4YY
Cover image © Hemis/Alamy Stock Photo

Contents

About the contributors

Penny Jane Burke is Global Innovation Chair of Equity and Director of the Centre of Excellence for Equity in Higher Education at the University of Newcastle, Australia. Penny is passionately dedicated to developing methodological, theoretical and pedagogical frameworks that support a critical understanding and the practice of equity and social justice in higher education. She was awarded a full-time Economic and Social Research Council PhD studentship from 1998 to 2001, and upon completion of her PhD (University of London), her first sole-authored book *Accessing Education: Effectively widening participation* was published (2002, Trentham Books), which argued for praxis-based approaches. She has continued to publish extensively in the field of equity and widening participation, including her authored books *Reconceptualising Lifelong Learning: Feminist interventions* (with Sue Jackson, 2007, Routledge), *The Right to Higher Education: Beyond widening participation* (2012, Routledge) and *Changing Pedagogical Spaces in Higher Education* (with Gill Crozier and Lauren Ila Misiaszek, 2016, Routledge). Penny is editor of *Teaching in Higher Education* and was recipient of the UK's prestigious Higher Education National Teaching Fellow award in 2008. Penny has held the posts of Professor of Education at the University of Roehampton and the University of Sussex and Reader of Education at the Institute of Education, University College London.

Annette Hayton is Head of Widening Participation at the University of Bath and has many years of experience in managing activities designed to support successful progression to higher education. She aims to combine theory, research and practice, making praxis the foundation of her work to promote equity and foster progressive change within the education system. She is currently convenor of the Network for Evaluating and Researching University Participation Interventions (NERUPI); Innovative Practice editor for the journal *Widening Participation and Lifelong Learning*; Vice-Chair of the Universities Association for Lifelong Learning; and a member of the International Centre for Higher Education Management at the University of Bath. Her publications include 'Theory, evaluation and practice in widening participation: A framework approach to assessing impact' (with Andrew Bengry-Howell, *London Review of Education*, 2016); 'Who you know, what you know and knowing the ropes: A review of evidence about access to higher education institutions in England' (with Geoff Whitty and Sarah Tang, *Review of Education*, 2015); *Access, Participation and Higher Education: Policy and practice* (with Anna Paczuska, Kogan Page, 2002); and *Tackling Disaffection and Social Exclusion: Issues for education policy* (Kogan Page, 1999).

Jacqueline Stevenson is Professor of Education and Head of Research in the Sheffield Institute of Education, Sheffield Hallam University. She is a sociologist of education with a particular interest in policy and practice relating to equity and diversity in higher education, widening participation, access and student success, pedagogic diversity and the stratification and marketization of higher education. Key areas of focus are the social and academic experiences of religious students, black and minority ethnic students' degree attainment and success, policy and practice relating to the higher education experience of refugees and other forced migrants, and the social and academic experiences of international students. She has undertaken research and evaluation for a range of organizations, including the Higher Education Funding Council for England, the Higher Education Academy, the Social Mobility Commission, the Office for Fair Access, Aimhigher, West Yorkshire Police, and a large number of both voluntary and community organizations and local authority departments. Jacqueline co-convenes the Society for Research into Higher Education's Access and Widening Participation Network and is a member of the Higher Education Race Action Group. She was previously Professor of Higher Education at Leeds Beckett University.

Jessica Abrahams is a Research Fellow at the University of Surrey working on the Eurostudents project exploring contemporary understandings of the university student across Europe. Prior to this she completed a doctorate at Cardiff University focused on the ways in which institutional structures and practices reproduce social class inequalities in education. She has also been a research assistant and consultant on the Paired Peers project looking at social class, and the role of universities in social mobility. Jessie is co-convenor of the British Sociological Association's Bourdieu study group.

Ann-Marie Bathmaker is Professor of Vocational and Higher Education at the University of Birmingham, UK. Her research focuses on questions of equity and inequalities in vocational, post-compulsory and higher education, particularly in relation to issues of social class. Her recent research includes a study of higher education, social mobility and social class (the Paired Peers project), a study of participation in higher education by rural and township youth in South Africa (the Miratho project), and a study of the role and purposes of vocationally oriented University Technical Colleges for 14–19-year-olds in England, as well as research examining constructions of knowledge in general vocational qualifications. She was the specialist adviser to the House of Lords Select Committee on Social Mobility appointed to consider social mobility in the transition from school to work (2015–16). The co-authored book from the project on which chapter 7 in this volume is based was awarded second prize in the Society for Educational Studies book awards in 2017: A.M. Bathmaker, I. Ingram, J. Abrahams, T. Hoare, R. Waller and H. Bradley, *Higher Education, Social Class and Social Mobility: The Degree Generation* (London: Palgrave Macmillan, 2016).

Vikki Boliver is Professor of Sociology in the Department of Sociology at Durham University. She is best known for her research on socio-economic and ethnic inequalities in admission to highly selective universities in the United Kingdom and for her research on patterns and processes of intergenerational social mobility in the UK. Recent articles include 'Exploring ethnic inequalities in admission to Russell Group universities' published in the British Sociological Association's flagship journal *Sociology*. Vikki is Principal Investigator on projects funded by the Economic and Social Research Council and the Nuffield Foundation, which explore the fairness of university admissions policies. She is a member of the Centre for Global Higher Education, where she is leading research into alternative providers of higher education.

Claire Callender is Professor of Higher Education Policy at the Institute of Education, University College London (UCL), and at Birkbeck, University of London. She is Deputy Director of the Centre for Global Higher Education, funded by the Economic and Social Research Council and the Higher Education Funding Council for England, and based at UCL.

Claire's research and writing focus on higher education student finances. She has contributed to some of the most significant UK inquiries into student funding and presented evidence to Parliamentary Select Committees. She was a New Century Fulbright Scholar at the Harvard School of Education from 2007 to 2008. In 2017, she was awarded an OBE in the Queen's New Year's Honours list for services to higher education. Claire is currently conducting research on student loan debt, examining its influence on the enrolment decisions of potential higher education students. She has just started another study exploring the effects and consequences of student loan debt on graduates' employment behaviour and life choices.

Catherine Dilnot is a Senior Lecturer at Oxford Brookes University, where she has run the undergraduate Accounting and Finance suite of programmes. Her teaching focuses on management accounting and research methods. She is a qualified chartered accountant. Catherine's particular research interest is in the role of A-level subject choice and social background in fair access to universities and to leading professions, with a particular interest in the accounting profession. She has devised a typology of A-levels according to their efficacy in access to highly selective universities and uses administrative datasets and anonymized professional firm data in her analysis, working with major graduate employers. She is currently completing a part-time doctorate in the department of Quantitative Social Science at the Institute of Education, University College London.

Nicola Ingram is a Senior Lecturer in Education and Social Justice at Lancaster University and co-founder of the British Sociological Association's Bourdieu study group. Nicola's research is focused broadly on social class inequalities in education and she is particularly interested in how other aspects of identity, such as gender and ethnicity, interweave with the classed dimension. She is co-editor of *Bourdieu: The next generation* and co-author of *Higher Education, Social Class and Social Mobility: The degree generation*. She has published widely in the field of Sociology of Education and her work has strong Bourdieusian theoretical underpinnings. Nicola is co-investigator on the Paired Peers project, which is funded by the Leverhulme Trust and is a longitudinal qualitative inquiry, tracking cohort of working-class and middle-class young people through university from 2010 and into post-graduation destinations in 2017.

Matt Lumb is Praxis Fellow with the Centre of Excellence for Equity in Higher Education (CEEHE) at the University of Newcastle in Australia. Matt's commitment to the field of access to education developed through experiences as a community development professional working on projects in Australia and in parts of Asia and Africa, and as a classroom teacher in Australian high schools. Originally from the mid north coast of New South Wales, he is careful to note that as a white male raised by two educators in a home free from violence, misrecognition or hunger, his capacity to understand and interpret experiences of underrepresentation and marginalization is limited. Since 2011, he has worked at the University of Newcastle as an outreach practitioner and is currently enrolled in a PhD with CEEHE, investigating the concealed impacts of outreach connections. He has an interest in the ways sophisticated participatory methodologies can make evaluative research processes more productive, and deliver contextualized understandings of the underlying dynamics that produce programme impact. His current projects draw on Freirean notions of praxis and employ Nancy Fraser's three-dimensional framework of social justice to collaboratively reimagine university outreach and classroom teaching practices.

Heidi Safia Mirza is Professor of Race, Faith and Culture at Goldsmith's College, University of London. She is known for her pioneering intersectional research on race, gender and identity in education and has an international reputation for championing equality and human rights for black and Muslim young people through educational reform. Her research includes refugee and teacher education, diversity in higher education, religious and cultural difference, including Islamophobia and gendered violence. She advises English Heritage on diversity and established the Runnymede Collection at the Black Cultural Archives, a race relations archive documenting the civil rights struggle for a multicultural Britain. As one of the few female professors of colour in the UK she was awarded the prestigious Eight Women of Colour Awards. She is author of several best-selling books, including *Young, Female and Black*, which was voted among the British Educational Research Association's top 40 most influential educational studies in Britain. Her other publications include *Black British Feminism*; *Race Gender and Educational Desire*; *Black and Postcolonial Feminisms in New Times*; *Respecting Difference: Race, faith, and culture for teacher educators*; and, most recently, *Dismantling Race in Higher Education: Racism, whiteness and decolonising the academy*.

Introduction

Penny Jane Burke

Evaluation is a contested field that raises perplexing challenges for evaluating equity and widening participation (WP). What methodologies, methods and frameworks are appropriate? What is the relationship between research and evaluation? What are the ethical and moral dilemmas raised? The growing demands nationally and globally for 'evidence of impact' frame expectations and discourses of evaluation and are shaped by countless contextual factors. Among the most pressing concerns are that we justify government funding towards particular university-led equity initiatives and understand 'what works' fully enough to ensure that resources are being used appropriately. This is intensified by increasing pressure on public funding.

This book examines evaluation through engagement with equity and WP research and evaluation, largely in the United Kingdom. However, the themes and questions relate to international debates about evaluation in other contexts, such as Australia, where universities are increasingly expected to evaluate their equity initiatives. The book draws on a seminar series that my co-editors, Jacqueline Stevenson and Annette Hayton, and I designed and facilitated over two years from 2014 to 2016. The series aimed to create reflexive spaces of dialogue about how those involved in equity work might develop knowledge and understanding across different national, regional and institutional agendas, various communities of practice (or praxis), and a multitude of projects, programmes and initiatives. We invited seminar participants to explore the value we bring to contested understandings of 'access', 'equity' and 'widening participation' in higher education as a dynamic field of research, evaluation and practice.

Our intention was to bring together the shared and contested views, commitments and values that shape our diverse work and the different methodologies and methods that form our practice. We hope this book will sustain dialogue across the fields of research, evaluation and practice, drawing them together through a framework of praxis: a commitment to critical and reflexive reflection-action-action-reflection. We hope to engage readers in thinking through some of the complex dilemmas that we face in doing equity work. The contributors consider researching and evaluating equity and WP in relation to questions of ethics, power and representation as they seek to address the values, discourses and perspectives at play.

This edited collection aims to orchestrate the voices of those negotiating methodological and ethical challenges and dilemmas. In doing so, the book examines evaluation discourses that construct what counts as 'evidence' and that reduce the focus to measuring what works. Its editors and authors are all aware of the need to tread cautiously when looking for what works and to examine the underpinning values and judgements that might shape evaluative processes at play in higher education policy and practice.

We are of course all evaluators: this is part of how we give meaning to and make sense of the world as social and relational beings. Our everyday experiences are constructed through e-*valu*-ating processes. This book brings attention to the contested values at the heart of these processes and the complex power dynamics that shape *what values* and *whose values* are socially and institutionally legitimated, and through what – and whose – processes, knowledges and practices. The book draws together the rich arena of evaluative work that relates to access, equity and WP and invites you – as a participant in the process of making meaning and judgement – to consider these questions with us.

This collection stems from our shared commitment to promoting social justice though education and our belief in the value of a praxis-based approach to underpin policy formation and inform innovative action. A praxis-based approach embeds reflexivity into equity and WP frameworks, so that reflection-action-action-reflection becomes an integral dimension of policy and practice. This helps us to understand that WP projects are deeply entwined with social formations of difference, power and inequality. Policy developed without cognisance of theory and practice risks limiting its success through partial and often reductive understanding of the problem; and without an understanding of how wider issues and taken-for-granted practices can serve to reinforce existing cultural divisions and social inequalities. Our aim is to create a resource for researchers and evaluators, committed to equity and social justice in higher education and engaged in developing WP strategies and practices, to effect change and transformation at micro-, meso- and macro-levels.

Chapter 1 outlines some key debates in researching and evaluating equity initiatives through the lens of widening participation in higher education in the UK. The authors briefly set out what they regard as some of the key issues, particularly for readers situated in other national contexts, and some of the challenges and ways forward for evaluators.

Chapter 2 attempts to reconceptualize evaluation, by putting it in a social justice framework that emphasizes a praxis-based approach.

Drawing on theories of critical hope, Penny Jane Burke and Matt Lumb seek to redistribute the privilege of evaluation in recognition that we are all researchers and evaluators and to generate evaluation that focuses on social justice and transformation. This helps to recognize the richness of critical theories and research that deepen understanding of the relationships between educational practices and deep-seated and long-standing inequalities. Such praxis-based evaluation offers the possibility of moving dominant and myopic foci from evaluation *products* towards sensitively constructed evaluation *processes*. Burke and Lumb argue that drawing on praxis-based frameworks enables close-up attention to the complex and intricate operations of power at multiple levels across the reflection-action nexus. This requires carefully designed methodological frameworks that focus the evaluative imagination on the multiple dimensions of social justice imperatives as well as on the subtle, micro-level, relational, embodied and insidious workings of power and inequality between and within educational fields and pedagogical spaces.

In chapter 3, Annette Hayton presents an example of using such a framework to inform the planning, provision and evaluation of higher education outreach activities. Using a theoretical perspective derived from the work of Pierre Bourdieu, the NERUPI (Network for Evaluating and Researching University Participation Interventions) framework enables a strategic approach to the planning, provision and evaluation based on five overarching aims grounded in Bourdieu's notions of capitals and habitus. Clear objectives for interventions are organized into five levels, corresponding to students' academic journeys. The praxis-based framework utilizes a structure of broad aims and learning outcomes, providing a common language to make it accessible to practitioners and non-specialists alike. As Hayton explains, while the structure provides a set of overarching aims for measuring impact, it does not restrict research or evaluation methods that facilitate collecting rich sources of data to inform practice; develop institutional reflexivity; improve monitoring; and contribute to theoretical understandings within the field. Initially developed and trialled at the University of Bath, the framework has been used and tested in similar settings through the NERUPI Research Consortium.

In chapter 4, Catherine Dilnot and Vicky Boliver illuminate the importance of interrogating evidence to understand how inequalities continue to play out in the selection of high status degrees in the fields of medicine, dentistry and law. Dilnot and Boliver take the reader through the research process in their assessment of three claims, which they examine through a statistical analysis of applications and admissions data supplied by the Universities and Colleges Admissions Service (UCAS). Their chapter highlights that well-designed and methodical statistical analysis makes a significant contribution to uncovering the ways inequalities might play out in accessing high status degrees. This analysis shows, for example, the impact of facilitating subjects that can compensate for lower grades, subject choice in A levels and school type, quality of personal statements and teacher references. This illustrates the significance of schools in facilitating entry to high status degrees early on and so the methods of statistical analysis translate directly to feeding in to strategies to support students from underrepresented backgrounds.

In chapter 5, Claire Callender outlines her Nuffield-funded research exploring two interconnected policies through the experiences of mothers from low-income backgrounds undertaking part-time university study located in Sure Start Children's Centres. Callender sets out her methodological approaches, including a conceptual framework that aimed to challenge the negative constructions of families and mothers that are underpinned by a 'narrative of disadvantage'. She explores the potentially transformative nature of university participation by thinking about the moral, social and political underpinnings of higher education and the impact on participants in terms of moral reasoning. The mixed methods research involved multiple stages of data collection, providing a 'better understanding of the outcomes of study for the participants than would have been possible from either research approach alone'. By bringing together two different but interconnected policies, widening participation and tackling child poverty, Callender is able to bring to light the potentially transformational and liberating dimensions of participation in higher education. She links this to broader ideas about the role and purpose of higher education in relation to the mothers' lives, the impact on their families and the wider policies that are often examined separately but are deeply intertwined.

Heidi Mirza provides a rich and generative discussion in chapter 6 that helps understand approaches to evaluation that are sensitive to 'affective learning landscapes' or 'eduscapes' and to the complex ways that gender, race, faith and cultural identity play out in higher education spaces. She draws on the concept of 'embodied intersectionality' to explore this and to 'see that different dimensions of social life cannot be separated out into discrete and pure strands'. Mirza explains how this analytical tool is able to knit together the macro-economic, political and social discourses that structure inequities with a complex array of individuated subjectivities that, by imposition, choice or desire, are written on and lived within the body. She illustrates her analytical framework through discussing three case studies so the reader can follow the important insights as a powerful tool of social justice forms of evaluation. Drawing on her notion of racialized institutional flashpoints, Mirza shows that researchers and practitioners need to take the evaluation process seriously by asking themselves about the principles we bring to our antiracist practices and how we come to arrive at those principles.

Chapter 7 presents an analysis of the relationship between social class and university status and employment outcomes, drawing on two case studies from the Paired Peers project funded by the Leverhulme Trust. Nicola Ingram, Jessica Abrahams and Ann-Marie Bathmaker illustrate the power of in-depth Bourdieusian analysis of interview data. Focusing on two female students who had both studied law in the same city but in two different universities, they illustrate how social class trumps university status. Drawing on Bourdieu's interrelated concepts of capital, field and habitus, their analysis explores how middle-class students may be able to maintain their advantages through and beyond higher education into employment. They show through their discussion of the two women's stories how advantage and disadvantage play out through the acquisition, maintenance, development and mobilization of cultural, social and economic resources. Their analysis reveals the power of deep, critical and detailed qualitative data collection and analysis to uncover the workings of the reproduction of classed inequalities.

In the final chapter, Jacqueline Stevenson draws on field notes detailing her research and evaluation work with refugees and asylum seekers to chart her shift from reflective evaluator to reflexive researcher. In doing so she explores how and why she has used storytelling as a methodology and how such an approach has, at times, given rise to a range of methodological and ethical challenges. In the second part of the chapter she describes her approach to data collection, analysis and presentation of findings and how she has used narrative to contribute to findings from a number of evaluation projects. In doing so she draws attention to how the use of stories can add to a more standard evaluative approach and enable a better understanding not just of 'what works' but why it works.

Chapter 1

Key debates in researching and evaluating equity initiatives

Annette Hayton and Jacqueline Stevenson

In this chapter we outline some key debates in researching and evaluating equity initiatives through the lens of widening participation (WP) in higher education in the United Kingdom. As context is a critical factor in equity research and evaluation, we briefly set out what we regard as some of the key issues in the UK, and more specifically England, particularly for those readers situated in other national contexts. While there is a shared commitment to develop policy and interventions that address the entrenched socio-economic divisions inherent within the higher education (HE) sector, there is no agreement on how to measure the impact of these initiatives. In an effort to provide clear evidence of impact, 'cause and effect' approaches to evaluation have been championed as the most rigorous. However, in the complex context of WP, while it is questionable whether attribution of change related to a specific activity will be possible, it is clear that such an approach will not have the same potential to challenge existing attitudes and practices that more reflexive processes offer. Indeed, it is possible that the sector will devote considerable time and resources pursuing a chimera of certainty at the expense of more nuanced approaches to evaluation that have the potential to transform our understandings of the underlying reasons for low participation among particular socio-economic groups. Although this chapter focuses on the UK, the debates are international and extend beyond the specific issue of widening participation to other initiatives concerned with promoting equity and social justice.

The higher education system in the UK is highly stratified. Among HE students, 77 per cent come from professional families (National Statistics Socio-Economic Classification 1–3; HESA, 2015), while 38 per cent of students from private, fee-paying schools progress on to one of the 24 highly select Russell Group universities compared to 11 per cent from state-funded schools (DfE, 2017). In this system, socio-economic inequalities have resulted in stark differences in the participation rates of different geographic localities; for example only 8.5 per cent of 18–19-year-olds from Filwood in Bristol progress to HE as compared with 83.8 per cent in the more prosperous Clifton area of Bristol (maps from the POLAR3 (participation of local areas) classification from the Higher Education Funding Council for England (HEFCE), 10 March 2017). Degree outcomes differ according to socio-economic background and there is also an unexplained but persistent attainment gap between some minority ethnic groups compared to their white counterparts (Richardson, 2015). Finally, the chances of gaining graduate-level employment post-graduation are significantly higher for those from professional families (Milburn, 2012). In a period of ever-shifting global markets and increasing economic inequality in the UK, concerns around social mobility and upskilling the workforce have resulted in a number of widening participation policy interventions designed to increase participation in higher education from groups currently underrepresented in the sector (Whitty *et al.*, 2015; Burke, 2012).

The most notable national initiative was Aimhigher, introduced in England in 2004 under the New Labour government and funded by HEFCE. Largely focused on increasing access to HE, Aimhigher generated a range of new activities to encourage progression of young people belonging to underrepresented groups. Following closure of Aimhigher in 2011 by then coalition government, provision was made for the continuance of WP activity in England, regulated by the Office for Fair Access (OFFA), as part of a new HE funding system based on higher fees and student loans (Burke and Kuo, 2015; Callender and Scott, 2013). WP initiatives in the UK have been largely framed by assumptions based on neoliberal globalization, which individualize responsibility for socio-economic exclusion on the perceived 'deficits' of socially and economically excluded groups (Leathwood and Hayton, 2002; Gewirtz, 2001). Nevertheless the concept of WP remains highly contested and the powerful discourse of neoliberalism has not entirely obscured the equity traditions and working-class and feminist struggles for social justice that have also shaped the UK education system and HE sector (Ross, 2003; Hayton and Paczuska, 2002; Burke, 2002; Rose, 2001). As a result there has been broad public support for WP, at least on a superficial level, based on the belief that the opportunity to participate and benefit from HE should be open to all.

Although inequalities within the sector endure, there have been some positive indicators of change, with data from HEFCE (2010; 2013) and the Universities and Colleges Admissions Service (UCAS, 2016) showing increases in the rate of progression to HE of students from low-participation neighbourhoods and, more recently, in the numbers progressing to the elite 'high tariff' universities. Furthermore, the connections between WP initiatives and increased diversity of the undergraduate population are undertheorized, leaving evaluation of impact as a major challenge for the HE sector (Hayton and Bengry-Howell, 2016). Indeed, widening participation policy and practice itself is largely atheoretical and decontextualized (Burke, 2012), further exacerbating the challenges in developing meaningful evaluation approaches. While there is pressure to demonstrate the impact of WP initiatives, the notion of 'success' for WP is highly contested, differing according to the priorities and values of the various interested groups, which in turn shape the methods used to collect and analyse data and evaluate impact.

Success for an academic researcher might centre on gaining new insights about why students from privileged groups are more likely to progress and succeed in higher education. Over the last 20 years a growing body of research has explored and described the complex cultural contexts that frame individual 'choice' and 'success' (see, for example, Archer and Hutchings, 2003; Ball and Vincent,1998; Bathmaker *et al.*, 2013; Burke, 2009; Reay *et al.*, 2001; Reay *et al.*, 2005; Reay *et al.*, 2009). However, this valuable body of research has rarely made practical suggestions for change and, of more concern, has not generally been used to inform policy.

A key success measure for funding and regulatory bodies, such as HEFCE and OFFA in England (and similar funding and regulatory bodies in other contexts), is a rigorous monitoring system to ensure proper deployment of resources and financial accountability. All higher education institutions (HEIs) in England charging higher fees submit an annual monitoring statement reporting expenditure linked to output measures such as number of participants, and duration and range of activity. In recent years reporting requirements have become more sophisticated, with HEIs expected to evaluate activities and demonstrate their impact. HEFCE's most recent initiative, the National Collaborative Outreach Project (NCOP), will invest £90 million between 2016 and 2018 in 29 collaborative consortia working in particular local areas of England to increase progression to HE. The NCOP represents a very welcome step change in the evaluation of impact, clearly delineating monitoring of activity and expenditure from measurement of success. The latter includes national quantitative analysis, local evaluations, longitudinal tracking, and formative evaluation, as well as 'impact evaluation' conducted by external evaluators. However, the approach is based on the premise that it is possible to demonstrate cause and effect, recommending the use of random control trials (RCTs) for local evaluations and formulating consortia evaluation within a standard 'logic model'. The latter is designed to demonstrate the impact of particular interventions on increasing the number of students from NCOP areas progressing to HE.

The prime success measure for policymakers and senior management teams must be the increased progression of underrepresented groups to HE, a success measure that encapsulates the contradictions and complexities of researching and evaluating the impact of WP policy and practice. Funders and policymakers, quite rightly keen for evidence of value for money, favour empirical evaluation methods, drawn from the medical research tradition, such as RCTs that claim to show a direct causal link between the intervention (often referred to as the 'dosage' or 'treatment') and the prime objective of increased progression to HE. Gorard *et al.*'s evaluation of Aimhigher interventions took this stance:

> Those advocating specific interventions often claim success for them, but most interventions have had no rigorous evaluation. We encountered no randomised controlled trials or similar. This makes it difficult to judge the success, or otherwise, of any attempts to widen participation in the short term. (Gorard *et al.*, 2006: 116)

Ten years on from Gorard *et al.*, the analysis by Crawford *et al.* (2017a) of current institutional practice in evaluating WP outreach activities demonstrates a more nuanced understanding of the context in which interventions are delivered and evaluated. The companion piece setting out 'proposed standards of evaluation practice and associated guidance' (Crawford *et al.*, 2017b) identifies three levels of evaluation based on standards developed by the National Endowment for Science, Technology and the Arts and the Social Innovation Partnerships. Despite the welcome endorsement of a range of approaches and the recognition that innovators are best placed to drive evaluation, the highest of the three standards is described as follows:

> OFFA Level 3: The HEI has implemented an evaluation methodology that provides evidence of a causal effect of an intervention.
>
> Evidence: Quantitative and/or Qualitative evidence of a pre/post treatment change on a treated group relative to an appropriate control or comparison group. (Crawford *et al.*, 2017b: 5)

The complexities of conducting meaningful research of this nature in the context of WP are considerable (Harrison and Waller, 2017). Achieving a robust sample of sufficient size to draw any firm conclusions, combined with the necessity for the intervention to be at least comparable in content and quality, makes attribution a considerable challenge (Doyle and Griffin, 2012). Picciotto warns against the 'lure of the medical model', pointing out that medical RCTs themselves come to different conclusions and that: 'Experimental black boxes are poorly suited to the evaluation of complicated or complex programmes in unstable environments' (Picciotto, 2012: 223). Fendler (2016) draws our attention to challenges in biomedical sciences where pharmaceutical research does not translate as expected into clinical practice; as a result, 'a field called translational science has been invented to concentrate on bridging laboratory finding with clinical experience'.

The place of RCTs in social science evaluation has been much critiqued, largely because versions of 'evidence' of 'what works' rely on models derived from medical science. These are rarely translatable into a social science world, where 'higher education professionals operate in open and messy systems' (Clegg *et al.*, 2016: 2). Despite this messiness, as Morrison argues, the circumstances in which RCTs are judged to operate in education are posited as being context free or context neutral: the reality is 'that "what works" is a matter of judgement rather than data, and that this judgement is imbued with moral and ethical concerns' (Morrison, 2001: 79). However these concerns are rarely articulated, or made visible.

More concerning, as Gale notes in his critique of RCTs, such models of evaluation are (or at least can be) 'premised on students having a problem or "symptoms" that require treatment ... these students are pathologised first by naming their problem (often expressed in terms that match the solutions at hand) and then by being treated with an intervention by some external agency or person' (Gale, 2017: 212).

Our final concern, as we have written elsewhere (Clegg *et al.*, 2016: 2), is that 'what really matters is to know why something works'. However 'knowing' is also neither universal nor neutral. As Gale notes, RCTs 'provide a method for producing knowledge based on a particular view of what counts as knowledge. Specifically, their experimentation is designed to produce knowledge about cause and effect relations, nothing personal' (2017: 214). However, widening participation work is, or at least should be, *based* on the personal. It is the close-up personal work with individuals that creates the conditions in which young people are enabled to make choices and decisions, develop strategies and goals, plan for their futures, and are motivated, inspired and empowered – regardless of how the interventions that lead to these outcomes are measured.

The way to know reality is, instead, through 'stories of relatedness' (Martin 2008: 84). Success for individual participants would be based on very different, highly contextualized criteria related to their interaction with interventions as well as the academy more widely. As we have suggested, 'one of the functions of close-up research with its emphasis on depth and understanding is an attempt to explain why things are as they are and, where we identify wrongs, *ceteris paribus* how we might change them' (Clegg *et al.*, 2016: 3).

Conducting meaningful research that challenges the hegemony of the core practices of the academy, including pedagogies and curricula that constrain successful participation for students from some socio-economic groups, is complex. Nygaard and Belluigi (2011) argue that decontextualized approaches to evaluating learning and teaching are rooted in a static conception of learning based on the acquisition of a fixed body of knowledge. In order to foster active participation and knowledge construction, more creative and flexible pedagogies are required, along with a contextualized model of evaluation that recognizes that relations between individuals and groups 'are determined by context ... each gathering of students and teachers constitutes a unique ongoing system of social relations' (Nygaard and Belluigi, 2011: 659).

Understanding and exploring this complexity is particularly crucial when we are seeking to ensure that students from underrepresented groups are able to participate fully and benefit from HE study. A more productive approach is to consider students' experiences in relation to questions of diversity in praxis-based and reflexive pedagogical spaces that recognize and embrace difference (Burke *et al.*, 2017) and develop approaches to evaluation that support creative pedagogies.

In addition, evaluation of widening participation initiatives should be firmly rooted in ethical practice throughout all the stages of planning, delivery and dissemination of evaluation activities. There is also a lack of involvement of key stakeholders or user groups in much of this process of evaluation and research, and evaluation practice may lack cultural awareness and sensitivity.

Practitioner research and evaluation has, however, great potential. It can offer a unique perspective on the activities and interventions that may often be regarded as peripheral to organizations and academic research, but are nevertheless charged with promoting the cultural changes necessary for widening participation, particularly in the area of access (Burke, 2012).

The action research approach is highly appropriate for WP interventions as it aims to create change within a context or field, rather than changing others 'out there' (Reason and Bradbury, 2008: 1). Grounded in practice, it also avoids the pitfall of much academic research that may provide an excellent description of a problem without offering solutions. When the aim is to challenge the existing culture and practices, as with WP, action research provides the basis for a dynamic, iterative model that promotes reflexivity, described by Somekh and Zeichner as 'interpenetrating reflexive spirals of action research' (2009: 6). However, it is important to guard against the pressure to prove the efficacy of interventions, which can lead to the predetermination of outcomes, overclaiming, or even to results being withheld, distorted or hidden.

In summary, current approaches aiming to measure the impact of WP initiatives do not challenge definitions of what and who is valued and who is empowered to make such judgements. They frequently fail to question what constitutes 'success' and how this (mis)frames educational structures, systems and practices. Confusion about appropriate research and evaluation methodologies is often apparent, with a valorization of decontextualized data and evidence embedded in positivist epistemologies. Within this particular research paradigm, critical and qualitative methodologies and epistemologies are misrepresented as less 'rigorous'. Finally, understandings of the potential for academic research and practice-based knowledge are not used to inform policy and practice.

Copestake argues that the measurement of interventions in complex contexts would be more successful if success were based on the notion of 'reasonableness', with a diverse range of stakeholders specifying what constitutes reasonable evidence of causation. As he explains:

> This falls short of scientific certainty, but in complex situations it is often as much as we can hope for, particularly given the possibility that efforts to aim higher may be counterproductive in terms of cost, timeliness and policy relevance. (Copestake, 2014: 417)

Increasing diversity in the student body and overcoming inequalities in learning and employment are ambitions shared by most, if not all, engaged with WP, albeit for different reasons. To address the enduring inequalities that beleaguer access and parity of participation in HE, we call for a wide-ranging, theoretically grounded ethical approach that draws on a range of methodologies and voices to inform policy and practice, increase our understanding of the underlying issues and contribute to more effective policy formation and practice.

References

Archer, L. and Hutchings, M. (2000) '"Bettering yourself"? Discourses of risk, cost and benefit in ethnically diverse, young working-class non-participants' constructions of higher education'. *British Journal of Sociology of Education*, 21 (4), 555–74.

Ball, S.J. and Vincent, C. (1998) '"I heard it on the grapevine": "Hot" knowledge and school choice'. *British Journal of Sociology of Education*, 19 (3), 377–400.

Bathmaker, A.-M., Ingram, N. and Waller, R. (2013) 'Higher education, social class and the mobilisation of capitals: Recognising and playing the game'. *British Journal of Sociology of Education*, 34 (5–6), 723–43.

Burke, P.J. (2002) *Accessing Education: Effectively widening participation*. Stoke-on-Trent: Trentham Books.

Burke, P.J. (2009) 'Men accessing higher education: Theorizing continuity and change in relation to masculine subjectivities'. *Higher Education Policy*, 22 (1), 81–100.

Burke, P.J. (2012) *The Right to Higher Education: Beyond widening participation*. London: Routledge.

Burke, P.J., Crozier, G. and Misiaszek, L.I. (2017) *Changing Pedagogical Spaces in Higher Education: Diversity, inequalities and misrecognition*. London: Routledge.

Burke, P.J. and Kuo, Y.-C. (2015) 'Widening participation in higher education: Policy regimes and globalizing discourses'. In Huisman, J., de Boer, H., Dill, D.D. and Souto-Otero, M. (eds) *The Palgrave International Handbook of Higher Education Policy and Governance*. Basingstoke: Palgrave Macmillan, 547–68.

Callender, C. and Scott, P. (eds) (2013) *Browne and Beyond: Modernizing English higher education*. London: Institute of Education Press.

Clegg, S., Stevenson, J. and Burke, P.-J. (2016) 'Translating close-up research into action: A critical reflection'. *Reflective Practice*, 17 (3), 233–44.

Copestake, J. (2014) 'Credible impact evaluation in complex contexts: Confirmatory and exploratory approaches'. *Evaluation*, 20 (4), 412–27.

Crawford, C., Dytham, S. and Naylor, R. (2017a) *Improving the Evaluation of Outreach: Interview report*. Bristol: Office for Fair Access.

Crawford, C., Dytham, S. and Naylor, R. (2017b) *The Evaluation of the Impact of Outreach: Proposed standards of evaluation practice and associated guidance*. Bristol: Office for Fair Access.

DfE (Department for Education) (2017) *Revised Destinations of Key Stage 4 and Key Stage 5 Students, England, 2014/15* (SFR 01/2017). London: Department for Education.

Doyle, M. and Griffin, M. (2012) 'Raised aspirations and attainment? A review of the impact of Aimhigher (2004–2011) on widening participation in higher education in England'. *London Review of Education*, 10 (1), 75–88.

Fendler, L. (2016) 'Ethical implications of validity-vs-reliability trade-offs in educational research'. *Ethics and Education*, 11 (2), 214–29.

Gale, T. (2017) 'What's not to like about RCTs in education?'. In Childs, A. and Menter, I. (eds) *Mobilising Teacher Researchers: Challenging educational inequality*. London: Routledge, 207–23.

Gewirtz, S. (2001) 'Cloning the Blairs: New Labour's programme for the re-socialization of working-class parents'. *Journal of Education Policy*, 16 (4), 365–78.

Gorard, S., Smith, E., May, H., Thomas, L., Adnett, N. and Slack, K. (2006) *Review of Widening Participation Research: Addressing the barriers to participation in higher education: A report to HEFCE by the University of York, Higher Education Academy and Institute for Access Studies*. Bristol: Higher Education Funding Council for England.

Harrison, N. and Waller, R. (2017) 'Success and impact in widening participation policy: What works and how do we know?'. *Higher Education Policy*, 30 (2), 141–60.

Hayton, A. and Bengry-Howell, A. (2016) 'Theory, evaluation, and practice in widening participation: A framework approach to assessing impact'. *London Review of Education*, 14 (3), 41–53.

Hayton, A. and Paczuska, A. (eds) (2002) *Access, Participation and Higher Education: Policy and practice*. London: Kogan Page.

HEFCE (Higher Education Funding Council for England) (2010) *Trends in Young Participation in Higher Education: Core results for England* (Issues Paper 2010/03). Bristol: Higher Education Funding Council for England. Online. www.hefce.ac.uk/media/hefce/content/pubs/2010/201003/10_03.pdf (accessed 10 December 2017).

HEFCE (Higher Education Funding Council for England) (2013) *Trends in Young Participation in Higher Education* (Issues Paper 2013/28). Bristol: Higher Education Funding Council for England. Online. www.hefce.ac.uk/media/hefce/content/pubs/2013/201328/HEFCE_2013_28.pdf (accessed 10 December 2017).

HESA (Higher Education Statistics Agency) (2015) 'Table T1b: Participation of under-represented groups in higher education: UK domiciled young full-time undergraduate entrants 2013/14'. Online. www.hesa.ac.uk/data-and-analysis/performance-indicators/releases/2013-14-widening-participation (accessed 10 December 2017).

Leathwood, C. and Hayton, A. (2002) 'Educational inequalities in the United Kingdom: A critical analysis of the discourses and policies of New Labour'. *Australian Journal of Education*, 46 (2), 138–53.

Martin, K. (2008) *Please knock before you enter: Aboriginal regulation of outsiders and the implications for researchers*. Teneriffe, Queensland: Post Pressed.

Milburn, A. (2012) *University Challenge: How higher education can advance social mobility: A progress report by the Independent Reviewer on Social Mobility and Child Poverty*. London: Cabinet Office.

Morrison, K. (2001) 'Randomised controlled trials for evidence-based education: Some problems in judging "what works"'. *Evaluation and Research in Education*, 15 (2), 69–83.

Nygaard, C. and Belluigi, D.Z. (2011) 'A proposed methodology for contextualised evaluation in higher education'. *Assessment and Evaluation in Higher Education*, 36 (6), 657–71.

Picciotto, R. (2012) 'Experimentalism and development evaluation: Will the bubble burst?'. *Evaluation*, 18 (2), 213–29.

Reason, P. and Bradbury, H. (2008) 'Introduction'. In Reason, P. and Bradbury, H. (eds) *The SAGE Handbook of Action Research: Participative Inquiry and Practice*. 2nd ed. London: Sage, 1–10.

Reay, D., Crozier, G. and Clayton, J. (2009) '"Strangers in paradise"? Working-class students in elite universities'. *Sociology*, 43 (6), 1103–21.

Reay, D., David, M.E. and Ball, S. (2005) *Degrees of Choice: Class, race, gender and higher education*. Stoke-on-Trent: Trentham Books.

Reay, D., Davies, J., David, M. and Ball, S.J. (2001) 'Choices of degree or degrees of choice? Class, "race" and the higher education choice process'. *Sociology*, 35 (4), 855–74.

Richardson, J.T.E. (2015) 'The under-attainment of ethnic minority students in UK higher education: What we know and what we don't know'. *Journal of Further and Higher Education*, 39 (2), 278–91.

Rose, J. (2001) *The Intellectual Life of the British Working Classes*. New Haven: Yale University Press.

Ross, A. (2003) 'Higher education and social access: To the Robbins Report'. In Archer, L., Hutchings, M. and Ross, A. (eds) *Higher Education and Social Class: Issues of exclusion and inclusion*. London: RoutledgeFalmer, 21–44.

Somekh, B. and Zeichner, K. (2009) 'Action research for educational reform: Remodelling action research theories and practices in local contexts'. *Educational Action Research*, 17 (1), 5–21.

UCAS (Universities and Colleges Admission Service) (2016) *End of Cycle Report 2016: UCAS analysis and research*. Cheltenham: Universities and Colleges Admission Service.

Whitty, G., Hayton, A. and Tang, S. (2015) 'Who you know, what you know and knowing the ropes: A review of evidence about access to higher education institutions in England'. *Review of Education*, 3 (1), 27–67.

Researching and evaluating equity and widening participation: Praxis-based frameworks

Penny Jane Burke and Matt Lumb

This chapter draws on a praxis-based framework for widening participation research and evaluation currently being developed by the Centre of Excellence for Equity in Higher Education (CEEHE). This framework brings theory and practice together in cycles of reflection-action and action-reflection, with the dialogic relationship between critical reflection and critical action strengthened through participatory methodologies and practices. A process of ongoing exchange aims to sensitize participants to the multiple layers, contexts and challenges that characterize the fields of equity in higher education. These methods help us to question and disrupt entrenched and historical inequalities that are often sustained by taken-for-granted assumptions.

The underpinning principle is that equity and widening participation (EWP) is part of a wider project of social justice and transformation in, through and beyond higher education (Burke, 2012). Drawing on theories of critical hope (Freire, 2004; Zembylas, 2014; Bozalek *et al.*, 2014), we seek to redistribute the privilege of evaluation in recognition that we are all researchers and evaluators (Sayer, 2011) and that we have a 'right to research' (Appadurai, 2006). This approach generates research and evaluation that 'theorizes the relationship among the pedagogical, the affective, the political and the ethical sensibilities in educational practices that attempt to instil critical hope and transformation' (Bozalek *et al.*, 2014: 4). Such praxis helps to recognize the richness of critical theories and research that deepen understanding of the relationships between educational practices and deep-seated and long-standing inequalities. It also provides the possibility of moving dominant and myopic foci from evaluation *products* towards sensitively constructed evaluation *processes*.

Creating praxis-based frameworks demands that access and participation are not determined within individualist, meritocratic frameworks that reduce the problem of widening participation to changing the attitudes and dispositions of disadvantaged individuals. These frameworks redress the problematic historical condition that EWP (equity and widening participation) policy and practice in higher education have largely been 'atheoretical' (L. Archer *et al.*, 2003) and situated at the peripheries of university structures and priorities (Jones and Thomas, 2005; Burke, 2012). They also draw attention to *processes of widening* – rather than simply *increasing* – participation through redistributing opportunities to those who continue to be excluded, misrecognized or misrepresented in higher education. The focus at the pre-access and entry stages of the student life cycle often tends to overlook the lived, embodied experiences of university participation as a key dimension of equity in higher education. The CEEHE framework draws on the multi-dimensional theorization of social justice by Nancy Fraser (1997; 2003) to capture the economic, cultural and political spheres of equity in higher education. It also draws on critical, feminist and post/structural theories of embodiment, subjectivity and embodied practice to bring attention to the ways inequalities are experienced and felt through complex formations of personhood (Burke, 2012).

Our aim in this chapter is to bring to light and challenge some of the assumptions that currently frame research and evaluation approaches across the international field of EWP in higher education. A key concern is the ways that 'evidence-based' policy and practice have gained hegemony without interrogating the discourses and methods that constitute these approaches. The dominance of 'evidence based' as the driving force of EWP research, evaluation and practice foregrounds notions of 'generalizability' and 'objectivity', with a strong emphasis on the measurable (Harding, 1986; Lather, 1991). Yet, in communities of critical methodological researchers such 'evidence-based' frameworks have been extensively critiqued as embedded in an objectifying, paternalistic and colonizing set of technologies that work to construct 'the disadvantaged' in pathologizing ways (Smith, 1999; Mirza, 2015). These technologies regulate, narrow and discipline our imaginations of who is seen as having the right to higher education (Burke, 2012). Critical methodologies disrupt the positioning of the social scientist as the dispassionate researcher measuring the world as it is. Indeed, there is no one 'truth' to be discovered or claimed by the dispassionate researcher; rather, there are multiple 'truths', which are contested and tied to complex relations of power and inequality (Rich, 1979; Lather, 2000). The critical researcher aims to pay particular attention to the truths of those who have been subjected to the colonizing, regulating, normalizing and paternalistic gaze of hegemonic forms of social science research and policy (Harding, 1986).

It is important that we collect higher education data that identify and reveal unequal patterns of access, participation, impact and outcomes. However, these data need to be gathered and analysed within broader methodological frameworks that seek to capture the many contextual, intersecting, and often contradictory layers of inequality. Such approaches are sensitive to the social differences and systems that interact to form participatory possibilities. Critical research methodologies embedded in praxis are attuned to the explicit forms of inequality at play but also to the processes by which inequalities are *unwittingly reproduced through taken-for-granted methods, practices or assumptions* (Burke, 2012). Equity practice that is developed *in dialogue* with critical research and evaluation aims to ensure that those taken-for-granted meanings are challenged and interrogated. Generating knowledge and insight about the ways that insidious inequalities work requires a range of fine-tuned research and evaluation methodologies shaped by praxis-based frameworks (Freire, 1972). These methodologies must also be carefully designed to capture how inequality is located in complex social and power relations, and is contextual and emotional, as well as to map patterns of inequality that are multiple and relational (Weedon, 1999; Burke, 2012). Attention to the different and contradictory ways that inequalities play out in local, institutional, disciplinary, subject-based, regional, national and global contexts is key to such approaches. Ultimately, EWP praxis is needed to develop deep understandings that draw together critical theories of inequalities in higher education, practice-based perspectives and lived and embodied educational and pedagogic experiences.

Sayer, in *Why Things Matter to People* (2011), argues for a new conception of social science that takes into account the ways in which normative reasoning might complement critical theory's attempts to provide adequate accounts of human capacity, vulnerability and flourishing. We acknowledge that the time needed for reflection requires 'distance from necessity' (Bourdieu, 2000). However, we also believe that redistributing access to conceptual tools through widening participation in theory-driven evaluation will produce more nuanced understandings of the dynamics operating within programmatic contexts. To acquire the conceptual tools for this endeavour, we will consider and interpret the depth ontology presented by realism later in this chapter.

Reconceptualizing widening participation:
A praxis-based framework

In contemporary societies people participate in a 'dynamic regime of ongoing struggles for recognition' (Fraser, 2003: 57), although not everyone will have access to the resources needed or the social esteem and status required to participate fully and at the same level as other participants. Nancy Fraser's social justice framework provides a powerful set of conceptual tools to grasp the multi-dimensions and intersections of redistribution, recognition and representation. Her conceptual framework is particularly fruitful for refocusing on questions of 'participation' that have often been untheorized or taken for granted in 'evidence-based' research and evaluation. The framework demands that researcher-practitioners and practitioner-researchers grapple with the tensions and dilemmas posed by the imperatives of 'equity' policy and practice. These commonly attempt to treat persons 'equitably' through standardized mechanisms devised on notions of 'sameness'. Fraser instead provides the tools to recognize and represent 'difference' in ways that understand power relations as an inevitable part of social life but that simultaneously reject regulatory technologies that operate to exclude those who do not fit in or conform to the hegemonic way of being (Chawla and Rodriguez, 2007). This might point, for example, to problematizing the ways in which social inclusion operates as a disciplinary technology to 'transform' the individual in relation to hegemonic discourses that narrowly constitute 'aspiration', 'potential', 'resilience' and 'capability'. The result can be to reproduce misrecognitions and misrepresentations in higher education practices, including practices of research and evaluation.

Redistribution requires detailed and close attention to the targeting methodologies through which equity groups and institutional categorizations are created. Praxis-based principles guide targeting to focus on redistributing resources to those groups who have suffered long-standing forms of social, educational and economic inequalities. To develop strategies for redistribution, it is important to carefully identify structural and material inequalities, such as those operating through socio-economic status, and to examine them in relation to symbolic and cultural formations of (mis) recognition. These inequalities are intersecting, embodied formations that simultaneously operate at symbolic, cultural and affective levels. Therefore, in order to develop methods of redistribution connected to socio-economic inequalities, it is important to analyse their intimate relationship to other formations of difference, such as gender, ethnicity and race, which are also tied to the politics of misrecognition and misrepresentation. Methodological considerations are vital to address these complexities and to generate mechanisms for broader equity and social justice processes and practices.

A praxis-based framework focuses researchers' analytical powers on the complex relationship between redistribution, recognition, representation and subjective formation. This framework sheds light on the implications of taking a decontextualized, individualized and disembodied perspective, which tends to reproduce assumptions of deficit through discourses such as 'raising aspirations'. This objectifying gaze tends to misconstrue material poverty with a presumed 'poverty of aspiration', placing the analytic lens on the individual 'with potential' who however 'lacks aspiration'. The presentation of atheoretical, decontextualized data dehumanizes questions of access and participation and makes no connection with lived experiences of misrecognition and misrepresentation. We argue for research and evaluation that is carefully designed, drawing on the insights of social science. Critical perspectives can highlight the ways in which inequalities are not only sets of measurable indicators but are internalized, lived and embodied subjectivities.

Fraser's multi-dimensional approach illuminates the institutional structures and practices that are implicated in reproducing inequalities at intersecting cultural, symbolic, discursive and structural levels. Fraser explains:

> When misrecognition is identified with internal distortions in the structure of the self-consciousness of the oppressed, it is but a short step to blaming the victim ... Misrecognition is a matter of externally manifest and publicly verifiable impediments to some people's standing as full members of society. To redress it, means to overcome subordination. *This in turn means changing institutions and social practices.* (Fraser, 2003: 31, emphasis added)

A praxis-based approach to researching and evaluating widening participation opens up spaces for analysis of the 'forms and levels of economic dependence and inequality that impede parity of participation' and emphasizes the importance of a dialogical approach to participation, in a 'democratic process of public deliberation' (Fraser, 2003: 36 and 43). There is, however, a dilemma in the circularity of this argument:

> To make a recognition claim one must first have a recognizable identity, and this identity must be 'proper': that is, it must have recognizable public value. This immediately presents a problem

for those who are not considered to have 'proper' identities and are continually misrecognized; it also presents a problem for those who are forced to inhabit an identity category not of their own making, as well as those who are forced to be visible in order to be seen to have a recognizable identity. (Skeggs, 2004: 178)

We argue that it is through the analytic tools we have described that dilemmas and challenges become more visible. This is key to the aim of developing praxis-based frameworks for EWP research and evaluation. Through analysis of this kind, the imperative to develop institutional tools of representation *across* different groups and communities, while recognizing differences *within* them, becomes clear. For example, it is important to redistribute resources and opportunities to those communities that have been denied such opportunities through forms of institutionalized racism in schools and in higher education (Gillborn, 2008). It is also important to recognize and value the different perspectives and knowledges those communities bring to higher education and to provide genuine opportunities for representation of different experiences and histories (Burke and Jackson, 2007). However, homogenizing those communities (for example, through policy categorizations such as 'black and minority ethnic') often perpetuates a pathologizing, neocolonial gaze while ignoring differences *within* as well as between communities. Thus, research and evaluation methodologies must be highly sensitive and fine-tuned to the formations of difference in different communities and to understand this in relation to the complex intersectionalities that form subjectivities, ontologies and epistemologies (Mirza, 2015). Although there are important differences between groups often 'targeted' by higher education policies to widen participation, these principles are also important in their application not only to policy categorizations such as 'black and minority ethnic', but also to those of 'low socio-economic groups', 'mature' and 'part-time' students, 'students with disabilities' and other such 'equity groups'.

Care must be taken, however, when working across 'difference', as it is important to pay close attention to the subjective and emotional dimensions of misrecognition. Without this attention, researchers might limit their analysis of misrecognition 'primarily as externally imposed injuries rather than as lived identities' (McNay, 2008: 150). The imperative of praxis-based research and evaluation is to illuminate how actions are always shaped by a person's representations and understandings of the world, although 'the visible, that which is immediately given, hides the invisible which determines it' (Bourdieu, 1990: 126–7, cited in McNay,

2008: 181). A praxis-based framework for developing EWP practices must enable the more subtle, sometimes invisible, and insidious inequalities at play in higher education (which are always connected to wider social relations and contexts) to come into view, and to be linked to the level of the embodied context of action and practice.

Towards a praxis-based framework

Praxis emphasizes the dialogic relationship between critical reflection and critical action. Drawing on collaborative and participatory approaches, 'praxis' promotes iterative and cyclical processes of reflection-action and action-reflection (Lather, 1991). A guiding principle is that EWP practice should be informed by research, including critical perspectives that deconstruct taken-for-granted assumptions, and EWP research and evaluation should be informed by practice. Through this process of ongoing, reciprocal exchange, new approaches are formed that are deeply sensitive to the multiple layers, contexts and challenges that characterize this field in higher education. An overarching aim of this praxis-based framework is to find ways to challenge and disrupt entrenched and historical inequalities that are often tied to taken-for-granted practices and assumptions.

Higher education is never neutral but is always a site of struggle over meaning making, identity formation and knowledge production (Lather, 1991; Burke, 2012). It is a potential space for personal, social and cultural transformation, yet it is also an institution of reproduction, regulation, disciplinary control and marginalization. Researching and evaluating EWP by drawing on praxis-based frameworks that bring critical tools to bear on its multiple dimensions can illuminate both explicit and subtle processes of distribution, recognition and representation as well as subjective formation (of both personhood and knowledge). In order to study these processes, and to develop practices to challenge inequalities, it is paramount to draw on praxis-based frameworks to examine the intricate operations of power in the reflection-action nexus. Praxis requires carefully designed methodological frameworks that pay close attention to the many dimensions of social justice imperatives as well as to the subtle, micro-level, relational, embodied and insidious workings of power and inequality in educational fields and pedagogical spaces.

Pedagogical and educational spaces are precarious contexts in which shifting, complex and discursively produced power relations are at play in the formation of personhood and knowledge and in the privileging of particular epistemological and ontological perspectives (Narismulu, 2016: 87–99). For example, the privileging of evidence-based EWP reproduces certain values and assumptions about how and why the 'problem' is measurable, and what should be measured. Simultaneously, claiming a policy or practice as 'evidence based' tends to conceal the underpinning values and dynamics that produced the evidence. Evaluation is ultimately about social values, and the frameworks that are used often work to reinforce the values of the researcher-evaluator. For example, the belief that aspiring to higher education is the appropriate form of aspiration (for those deemed to be capable of university study) is a value judgement. The tools of evaluation are underpinned by the hidden values of those conducting the research and the evidence produced is shaped by those values. This is problematic as it privileges particular dispositions and not others. This process reproduces particular value judgements and generates an array of 'evidence-based' misrecognitions that perpetuate rather than challenge wider social inequalities, driven by a series of 'equity practices' designed to widen participation. 'Challenging assumptions about the assignment of value is central to tackling the chauvinisms and bigotry that are still rife in our society and the world' (Narismulu, 2016: 88).

The 'problem' of who participates in higher education, and who does not, has largely been constructed through research and evaluation that collects 'hard' data to measure patterns of higher education participation of different social groups. As part of this 'evidence-based' technology, classifications are constructed that reproduce histories of mis/recognition of 'the disadvantaged'. These classifications are used by institutions to create 'objective' methods that target certain persons in ways that are seen to have been evaluated as 'effective'. The problematic way that this might *reproduce* inequalities through homogenizing technologies and dividing practices is hidden as there is no framework for interrogating the assumptions informing such technologies in the first place.

Without praxis-based research and evaluation to interrogate such processes, a vicious circle is unwittingly put into place in which resources specifically intended to create greater equity become complicit in the reproduction of social, cultural and symbolic inequalities. Without critical analysis, the reduction of EWP research and evaluation to methods of measurement is in danger of reconstructing technologies that operate to divide and classify people. Some groups are marked out as 'included' or 'advantaged' and other groups as 'excluded' or 'disadvantaged'. Drawing on the insights of a Fraserian social justice framework helps to examine the implications of technologies of classification, including the ways classification homogenizes people, often in derogatory ways. Classifications are useful and important to provide researchers with variables to produce datasets and to analyse them, thus providing some of the tools for formulating policy and practice. However, they are simultaneously problematic in the constructions they produce and reproduce – narrowing, reducing and dehumanizing personhood. Classifications often frame and constrain the ways we think about questions of access, equity and participation as they are always tied to power relations and the politics of difference (Weedon, 1999). Research and evaluation as separate but linked processes thus require classifications but also together need the tools to deconstruct and problematize them.

Praxis-based methodologies challenge hegemonic perspectives that research and evaluation are only valid if they aim for objectivity, generalizability and neutrality. EWP research and evaluation, with their commitment to revealing and challenging educational inequalities, misrecognitions and misrepresentations, must then explicitly address relations of power and (micro) politics. Representations of the social world as decontextualized sets of evidence must therefore be interrogated. Praxis-based methodologies expose the ways knowledge and power are inextricably connected and are not reducible to measurable facts. These approaches help to get beneath taken-for-granted assumptions and to identify the ways that some values are foregrounded, while others are discounted. Praxis-based methodologies involve close consideration of the different and contested values at work across participant communities, making this explicit and part of the process of creating understanding and knowledge about 'the fields' in which participants are differently and unequally positioned and represented. This requires acknowledging and addressing difference as part of the process of widening participation research, evaluation and practice.

Drawing on Fraser, praxis-based methodological frameworks emphasize notions of 'parity of participation', seeking to 'empower those involved in change' as well as in critically understanding the social world (Lather, 1991: 3). Praxis helps to deepen engagement with the many dimensions of EWP practices, so that participants subject their assumptions and perspectives to interrogation by engaging with difference. As Buker explains, the 'requirements of praxis are theory both relevant to the world and nurtured by action in it', theory that emerges from 'practical political grounding' (E. Buker, quoted in Lather, 1991: 11–12).

Praxis demands that explicit connections are made between research, evaluation and practice, including engagement with critical theoretical and conceptual perspectives, and reflexive tools that help illuminate complex relations of inequality in and through higher education. Research praxis creates challenging spaces for researchers/evaluators and practitioners to work together to critically interrogate and further develop their work. Praxis underscores the urgency of enabling dialogue to inspire the methodological and pedagogical imagination in ways that explicitly challenge inequalities, misrecognitions and exclusions.

Pedagogical methodologies

Pedagogical methodologies (PMs) are premised on an aim to provide parity of participation (Fraser, 1997) through praxis-based approaches (Burke *et al.*, 2017). The purpose is to create and open up collaborative, collective, dialogical and participatory methodologies and spaces that engage participants in processes of collaborative sense and meaning making. Such spaces create opportunities for resistance and doing things differently, provoking our pedagogical imaginations. PMs help to broaden the ways we think about 'pedagogies' in higher education. Pedagogies are conceptualized not as methods of teaching and learning but as relational spaces through which we engage the politics of difference (Weedon, 1999) and the circle of knowledge (Freire, 2004). Participants work together to challenge those exclusionary processes that regulate practices and personhood. Through the circle of knowledge, participants co-produce meaning and explicitly examine the values circulating in particular pedagogical spaces and contexts.

Research and evaluation drawing on PMs require participants to consider deeply their values and the histories of those values in relation to power and inequality, and to identify collectively those that support equity, parity of participation and social justice. PMs move beyond thinking in terms of 'evidence' or 'data collection' to consider the social and cultural relations that are created and recreated through the pedagogical, research and evaluation processes in which participants engage. Developing pedagogical spaces through PMs attends to the complex ways in which (iterative) processes shape our sensibilities of self and personhood through the meaning-making spaces of research and evaluation, and the impact on what is imagined and what is seen as possible. The meanings we produce are part of a circle of knowledge (Freire, 2004), enabled through participation in the research and evaluation process and through the relationships between pedagogy, identity formations and difference (Burke *et al.*, 2017). PMs allow for meaning making to be refined through participatory practices, creating spaces of praxis both through and *beyond* the research. They facilitate new ways of knowing and understanding that otherwise might be unavailable or closed down:

> research *becomes* a form of pedagogy, as part of the process of
> meaning-making, learning and making sense of ourselves and our

relation to others. This engages research participants in relational processes in which we, as the researchers, learn and in which the participants in our study also have opportunities to learn; this ultimately is manifested in the way the research is iteratively understood, and how it is shaped/formed/developed. (Burke *et al.*, 2017: 53)

PMs disrupt constructions of widening participation as a form of individual transformation, embedded in problematic discourses of 'inclusion' that narrowly standardize and regulate personhood. They embrace notions of praxis within a framework of participation that understands transformation as a project of social justice. Methodological approaches are demanded that address issues of power, ethics, inclusion and exclusion within the overall design of research, aiming to develop opportunities for research praxis. Furthermore, research must be accessible to a broad range of participants, including scholars in the field, but also those who are committed to developing transformative practices of equity and widening participation.

There is an extensive body of research and literature that theorizes and exposes the complex ways in which inequalities in education are produced and reproduced through our everyday practices (e.g., among many others, Apple, 1986 and 2006; Ellsworth, 1992; Mirza, 2009; Reay, 2001; Reay and Ball, 1997; Reay *et al.*, 2001; Skeggs, 1997; Youdell, 2006). Importantly, the literature shows that the reproduction of inequalities is not always intended or explicit but that the processes and practices are often subtle, insidious and unwitting (Burke and McManus, 2009; Burke, 2012). However, the literature is often written in exclusive ways that demand specialist theoretical knowledge in order to decode the arguments and points being made. This scholarly positioning of critical knowledge and understanding is problematic and, due to the academic and performative frameworks in which researchers (are compelled to) disseminate their work, renders it unavailable to those who could draw on it to make a difference to higher education practices and cultures. Praxis-based PMs require that such theoretical work should be accessible to practitioners, policymakers, leaders and managers, as well as academics and scholars in the field. PMs might comprise strategies including more than just scholarly publications, such as facilitating forums, workshops and seminars, as well as producing resources underpinned by the principles of critical praxis. Two such examples are is are CEEHE's Equity, Capability and Belonging resources (https://www.equityhe.com) and the *Teaching Inclusively: Changing pedagogical spaces* resource pack produced by Burke and Crozier (2016). Presenting a series of 'think pieces' and 'reflective activities', this resource pack aims to:

> ... challenge those dominant assumptions, discourses and practices in higher education that often exacerbate and reproduce inequalities in such subtle ways that they are difficult to make sense of in the context of our everyday, taken-for-granted experiences of teaching and learning. The think pieces aim to contribute to inclusive teaching practices whilst acknowledging the on-going complexity of power, difference and identity formation in pedagogical relations and encounters. (Burke and Crozier, 2016: 4)

EWP practitioners are often expected to conduct evaluation without access to methodological resources and tools, recognition of knowledge and expertise, or representation in the academic field of EWP research. Furthermore, those immersed in this academic field often have not had the benefit of access to the knowledge and understanding of those working from the perspectives of practice. A framework that stands in opposition to this atheoretical trend is that built by Annette Hayton and Andrew Bengry-Howell (2016) in the UK context. Hayton, a highly experienced widening participation practitioner-researcher, manager and academic, collaborates with Bengry-Howell to draw on Bourdieu's capitals to construct a framework providing explicit support to practitioners and managers while offering theoretical depth to programme design and evaluation. Research and evaluation allow pedagogical spaces to be opened up for understanding, sense-making and meaning-making processes, yet the absence of redistributive mechanisms operating in this nexus limits both research and practice possibilities. Praxis-based frameworks aim to ensure that all participants engaged in the research/practice nexus, and indeed all working in higher education, have access to the theoretical, methodological and conceptual tools and resources to enable the complexity of inequalities to be illuminated and examined, as well as then translated for practice and 'making a difference' (Clegg *et al.*, 2016). Praxis-based PMs provide a framework for developing more sensitivity to issues of power in relation to questions of redistribution, recognition, representation and embodied subjectivities. Indeed, researchers conducting evaluation of widening participation initiatives and strategies must have a firm understanding of the difference between methods, which are simply tools of enquiry, and methodology, which includes attention to epistemology, ontology and theory as well as method. A praxis-based PM framework brings all participants together in dialogue, and opens up pedagogical spaces to deepen levels of understanding from multiple perspectives and dimensions.

Ontological depth and social dynamics

Meta-theoretical perspectives directly shape evaluative paradigms and have been the subject of debate over many decades. It is in the interest of critically hopeful, progressive research and evaluation of EWP initiatives that we seek to account for the ways in which observational 'evidence' alone is insufficient for sophisticated understandings of equity practices and programme impact. Commonly absent from research and evaluation methodologies are the crucial entities connecting 'inputs' and 'outputs' operating in social systems; entities that cannot simply be presented as variables yet are vital to understanding impact.

Praxis-based approaches to PMs are supported by notions of 'ontological depth' as developed by critical and social realist conceptions of the world. In drawing on the concept of 'ontological depth', we do not necessarily locate our position as 'realist' researcher-practitioners or practitioner-researchers. We do, however, contend that EWP programmes and practices are always shaped by their contexts and that ongoing programme formation requires sensitivity to the social norms, rules, interrelationships and values that can set limits on the efficacy of mechanisms. A challenge, therefore, is to make sense of how these structures, interrelationships and values impact on the intended processes of transformation through equity work. We argue that PMs that recognize and address ontological depth and the existence of underlying and generative mechanisms can provide the space and time for hopeful theorization about the channelling of resources, relationships and choice-making processes that can lead to sustained change underpinned by a collective sense of value.

The influential scholar Roy Bhaskar (1978), starting from the question of what the world must be like for science to be possible, reasons that there are three interwoven levels of a stratified reality: mechanisms (the real), events (the actual), and experiences (the empirical). This stratified reality (or 'depth ontology') – a world divided into emergent, explanatory levels – establishes a platform for investigation that operates by identifying generative, underlying mechanisms that are 'real' in that they give rise to 'outcomes', 'impact' and 'results'. These mechanisms are not some additional variable; they actually constitute the relationship between programme resources and programme impacts. An important tenet of realism with implications for evaluation is that observational evidence alone is insufficient to provide satisfactory explanations of the relationships between what are usually understood as 'variables' in a given context. It is not the aim of this chapter to provide a complete treatment of realist conceptions of 'regularity' and 'causation'; these can be understood better, however, by engaging with, for example, Pawson and Tilley's comparison of 'successionist' and 'generative' models of causation (1997). It is clear, though, that a meta-theoretical commitment to unobservable mechanistic forces has implications for applied research and can be found, for example, in the work of Hesse (1974), Sayer (1984), Boudon (1998) and Pawson (1989 and 2013). There are inevitably contested views within this realist paradigm. Different perspectives might be understood, for example, by examining the differences between a 'critical realism' (e.g. Bhaskar, 1978; Bhaskar, 1979) versus a 'scientific realism' (e.g. Pawson, 1989).

Importantly for understanding complex formations of difference and inequality, Bhaskar (1979) argues that the closed system and experimental controls available to the natural scientist are not achievable in social research. This is largely because of our unique and unceasing human capacity to have an impact on the circumstances in which we live. Due to this ever-present *emergence*, and as a 'substitute' for closed system empirical enquiry, Bhaskar (1979) suggests abstract *a priori* reasoning and the acceptance of a moral lens through which to critically evaluate human action. This focus on the moral and ethical are key aspects of equity agendas (Burke and Hayton, 2011) and complement critical theories of social justice, such as the work of Freire (2004) and Fraser (1997 and 2003). Pawson (2013) offers further insight through his more pragmatic argument that no scientific investigation (physical or social) depends on the achievement of closed systems. He also maintains that there are no decisive experiments (including the supposed 'gold standard' randomized control trials) that can supply social laws, that natural science only ever makes gradual and imperfect progress.

Realist accounts of social change mostly agree with Archer's (1995) explanation regarding the way 'impact' is constructed via collective and constrained decision making. This explanation of change involves choices made by people that are conditioned by pre-existing social structures. In this account, we are all constrained in our actions, yet, with agency, we have degrees of choice to attempt to change the conditions we experience. These choices interact with structures and can change institutions. In this way, our collective present decisions form the new systems and pre-existing conditions that enable and constrain choices for the next generation. There are significant differences in terms of where realists locate the precise locus of that change. Bhaskar (1978) sees causal mechanisms primarily residing in the power and resources that lie with the great institutional forms of society, whereas Pawson and Tilley (1997) believe mechanisms are identified at the level of human reasoning. It is important for research and evaluation of EWP initiatives to engage with such debates and to note that mechanisms can have different meanings depending on the scope of the intended explanation.

The framework promoted by Pawson and Tilley (1997) does provide ground on which to consider the importance of evaluation of theory and ongoing theorization. Specifically, they suggest theorization of *context-mechanism-outcome pattern configurations*: ideas about the variety of ways these configurations can operate, arguing for specification rather than generalization. To clarify these relationships, they provide an instructive 'logic of realist explanation':

> The basic task of social inquiry is to explain interesting, puzzling, socially significant regularities. Explanation takes the form of positing some underlying mechanism which generates the regularity and thus consists of propositions about how the interplay between structure and agency has constituted the regularity. Within realist investigations there is also investigation of how the workings of such mechanisms are contingent and conditional, and thus only fired in particular local, historical or institutional contexts. (Pawson and Tilley, 1997: 71)

There are, unsurprisingly, many conceptions of what constitutes a 'mechanism' in the context of realist forms of research and evaluation. The use of 'mechanism' in evaluative research is not new. Chen and Rossi (1987) were among the first to use the term to describe the production of regularities in social contexts as a result of programmatic mechanisms. Weiss (1997) helps us to understand the important differences between implementation theory and programme theory in relation to mechanisms of change. In Weiss's explanation, implementation theory can be conceptualized as the often cited 'logic model' in evaluation, whereas programme theory relates to the mechanisms operating between 'delivery' and 'outcomes', often focused on human responses to resources provided. In this, 'mechanism' is therefore not the programme service but the response generated. Commonly, the term 'firing' is used to denote the activation of a mechanism in the context of a social programme that is understood to be producing observable impacts or outcomes. An important extension of the notion of mechanisms 'firing' in social science research is provided by Dalkin *et al.* (2015) with a discussion relating to how this binary mode of thought, with its on/off switch, might stifle realist thinking. Instead, the importance of conceptualizing mechanisms as operating on a continuum is underlined.

We are concerned about this increasingly ubiquitous deployment of the term 'mechanism' to describe the depiction of such fierce, emergent, relational and unpredictable social forces operating to produce consequences that can be deeply felt by humans in communities. Bygstad and Munkvold (2011) explain that the term 'mechanism' has caused much consternation, often to do with its insinuation of a linear causality. While critical realists explain the contextual nature of any regularity, or 'contingent causality' (M.L. Smith, cited in Bygstad and Munkvold, 2011), the ongoing commitment to this word appears to be linked to the notion of these underlying mechanisms having impact in direct and material ways. We thus advocate an alternate term to 'mechanism'. We do so in recognition of the power of language and in search of a term that better represents the emergent, generative nature of social processes under collective theorization. We do so in an attempt to find a term more capable of incorporating, throughout processes of discussion and collective conception, the power relations inherent in all social interaction and change. We recoil linguistically from the militaristic connotations of mechanical 'firing', or the sporting analogies of mechanisms 'being in play'. We seek to move in a direction that is less technocratic, more hopeful and human. We thus suggest the term *dynamic*, a term that is not new but which captures the unpredictable, the changeable and the multifarious nature of human behaviour and experience

In our understandings, it is the underlying social *dynamics* – the nuanced, hopeful, collective theories of possible change – that constitute the explanation of the relationship between programme resources and programme impacts. With historical links to musical notation, this term with its attendant meanings also provides a new possibility of conceiving the way that social dynamics rise or fall to a 'crescendo' or 'diminuendo' in close concert with contextual conditions. Dynamics are not mechanical, nor are they predictable. Dynamics might help us to explain impact, but are always becoming, always fluid, always shifting. They are an important tool for praxis.

Clegg (2016) explains how a depth ontology can be a productive framework for thinking and theorizing. It is in this process of positing that praxis-based PMs, enacted through sophisticated participatory principles and taking into account ontological conceptions, can become most fruitful. In this process of theorization, it is important to remain aware that, as mentioned earlier, *dynamics* are not some additional variable; they constitute the relationship between programme 'inputs' and impacts.

Therefore, participants at multiple levels have critical insight into the operation of these dynamics from various perspectives and through space-time. In this context, PMs can improve the admirable realistic evaluation question – 'What *works*, for whom, in what circumstances, over what duration, and why?' – via a prior question, 'What is *valued*, by whom, in what circumstances, over what duration, and why?'

This new question sets up an amended evaluative cycle that goes beyond the scientific realism iterations of theorize, hypothesize, observe, specify, theorize, and moves towards working in dialogue with diverse participants through the following stages:

- *theorizing* the contexts, dynamics (including power relations) and impact in ways that are inclusive of 'everyday' theory, programme theory and conceptual theory;
- *critically questioning* what might 'work', for whom, in what circumstances or conditions, over what duration, and how;
- *investigating* via multi-method data collection and analysis the dynamics, contexts and impact and outcomes;
- *specifying* what might 'work' for whom, in what circumstances or conditions, over what duration, and how;
- before moving back to ongoing *theorization* of emerging configurations.

This approach enables a progressive evaluation process to collectively 'unveil opportunities for hope, no matter what the obstacles may be' (Freire, 2004: 3). It acknowledges the ways in which our relation to the world is one of concern; in which 'we don't just do things and interpret one another. Things matter to us' (Sayer, 2011: 20). And it is an approach that offers an escape from the 'abstracted empiricism' C. Wright Mills outlines in *The Sociological Imagination,* which can produce a 'thinness of result' (2000: 71) whereby quantitative techniques are impressed upon the social world, starting from a concern with measurement, regardless of the nature and dynamics of the context. As Law explains, methods 'produce the reality they understand' (2004: 5). It is through a careful consideration of a depth ontology that we can co-theorize dynamics in relation to programmatic contexts and impact through the acceptance of a stratified reality, for the purposes of nuanced EWP research and evaluation.

Final reflections

Praxis-based PM frameworks emphasize the importance of critical reflexivity and depth ontology in research and evaluation processes, with attention to complex relations of power and formations of difference. These frameworks aim to develop ethical, inclusive and participatory dynamics and practices in higher education that build sustainable and equitable relationships. Nancy Fraser's conceptualization of social justice, together with insights from critical, feminist, realist and poststructural work about the ways that inequalities are embodied and lived through practice, is particularly insightful and important in developing such reflexive, praxis-based frameworks. A deeply transformative reorientation to the EWP project is called for, which engages those in the most privileged nations, institutions and social groups in subjecting themselves to change. This challenges the current context, which focuses on the 'disadvantaged' becoming more like the advantaged (Gewirtz, 2001; Archer *et al.*, 2003). A re-visioning of equity and widening participation must, however, also involve a broadening of the focus on participation in higher education to examine participation beyond it. This allows consideration of other interconnected realms, with particular detailed attention to the politics of redistribution, recognition and representation, and constructions of different forms of learning, students and education. Processes of remembering are required in making connections between Fraser's framework for social justice and the silenced histories that have been key in shaping current unequal relations in different social, cultural and global contexts (Livingstone, 2009). Reconceptualizing equity and widening participation requires participants (including educational leaders and managers, policymakers, equity practitioners, students and teachers) to problematize and reconstitute their practices in all dimensions of education, including approaches to teaching, assessment, curriculum, quality, management and leadership, by challenging discourses of difference and inequality (Burke and Jackson, 2007). Research and evaluation can create the time and space for such processes when they are embedded in praxis-based PMs.

As Patti Lather states in relation to the struggle for social justice in education, 'the conjunction in critical social theory of the various feminisms, neo-Marxisms and poststructuralisms feels fruitful ground for shifting us into ways of thinking that can take us beyond ourselves' (1991: 164). Those of us committed to the struggle for social justice in higher education have the fruits from such theoretical perspectives to draw on to move us beyond narrow and regulating technologies that reinforce individualism and deficit. Rather, such critical resources move research and evaluation participants towards practices aiming to transform institutional, pedagogical, and local cultures and practices for equity and parity of participation both in and beyond higher education. Reconsidering EWP research and evaluation from a social justice and praxis-based perspective demands that access and participation are not determined within individualist, meritocratic frameworks that reduce the problem of widening participation initiatives to changing the attitudes and dispositions of disadvantaged individuals. Equity and widening participation is ultimately about deeply valuing and recognizing the significant contribution of higher education to social justice and the public good, to the processes of knowledge construction and learning, and to the ongoing development of different social groups and societies in the context of a long-term commitment to eradicating social inequalities. This requires multiple strategies and approaches, including the redistribution of privileged resources and opportunities, reflexive attention to the politics of recognition and representation, and praxis that draws together the insights of critical, feminist, realist and poststructural theories with embedded, transformative and participatory practices in higher education.

PMs address ontological depth and the existence of 'real' dynamics, which has implications for theorizing programme impact. In the Centre of Excellence for Equity in Higher Education we are developing research and evaluation frameworks as a form of meta-dynamic. Through this, CEEHE is generating a range of conceptual tools and programmes operating in open and constantly emergent sets of stratified social realities to produce the possibility of parity of participation in equity and widening participation research and evaluation that makes a difference.

References

Appadurai, A. (2006) 'The right to research'. *Globalisation, Societies and Education*, 4 (2), 167–77.

Apple, M.W. (1986) *Teachers and Texts: A political economy of class and gender relations in education*. New York: Routledge and Kegan Paul.

Apple, M.W. (2006) *Educating the "Right" Way: Markets, standards, God, and inequality*. 2nd ed. New York: Routledge.

Archer, L., Hutchings, M., Leathwood, C. and Ross, A. (2003) 'Widening participation in higher education: Implications for policy and practice'. In Archer, L., Hutchings, M. and Ross, A. (eds) *Higher Education and Social Class: Issues of exclusion and inclusion*. London: RoutledgeFalmer, 193–202.

Archer, M.S. (1995) *Realist Social Theory: The morphogenetic approach*. Cambridge: Cambridge University Press.

Bhaskar, R. (1978) *A Realist Theory of Science*. 2nd ed. Hassocks: Harvester Press.

Bhaskar, R. (1979) *The Possibility of Naturalism: A philosophical critique of the contemporary human sciences*. Brighton: Harvester Press.

Boudon, R. (1998) 'Social mechanisms without black boxes'. In Hedström, P. and Swedberg, R. (eds) *Social Mechanisms: An analytical approach to social theory*. Cambridge: Cambridge University Press, 172–203.

Bourdieu, P. (1990) *In Other Words: Essay towards reflexive sociology.* Cambridge: Polity.

Bourdieu, P. (2000) *Pascalian Meditations.* Trans. Nice, R. Stanford: Stanford University Press.

Bozalek, V., Leibowitz, B., Carolissen, R. and Boler, M. (eds) (2014) *Discerning Critical Hope in Educational Practices.* London: Routledge.

Burke, P.J. (2012) *The Right to Higher Education: Beyond widening participation.* London: Routledge.

Burke, P.J. and Crozier, G. (2016) *Teaching Inclusively: Changing pedagogical spaces.* 2nd ed. Newcastle, NSW: Centre of Excellence for Equity in Higher Education, University of Newcastle, Australia.

Burke, P.J., Crozier, G. and Misiaszek, L.I. (2017) *Changing Pedagogical Spaces in Higher Education: Diversity, inequalities and misrecognition.* London: Routledge.

Burke, P.J. and Hayton, A. (2011) 'Is widening participation still ethical?'. *Widening Participation and Lifelong Learning*, 13 (1), 8–26.

Burke, P.J. and Jackson, S. (2007) *Reconceptualising Lifelong Learning: Feminist interventions.* London: Routledge.

Burke, P.J. and McManus, J. (2009) *Art for a Few: Exclusion and misrecognition in art and design higher education admissions.* London: National Arts Learning Network.

Bygstad, B. and Munkvold, B.E. (2011) 'In search of mechanisms: Conducting a critical realist data analysis'. Paper presented at the 32nd International Conference on Information Systems (ICIS), Shanghai, 4–7 December 2011.

Chawla, D. and Rodriguez, A. (2007) 'New imaginations of difference: On teaching, writing, and culturing'. *Teaching in Higher Education*, 12 (5–6), 697–708.

Chen, H.-T. and Rossi, P.H. (1987) 'The theory-driven approach to validity'. *Evaluation and Program Planning*, 10 (1), 95–103.

Clegg, S. (2016) 'Critical and social realism as theoretical resources for thinking about professional development and equity'. In Leibowitz, B., Bozalek, V. and Kahn, P. (eds) *Theorising Learning To Teach in Higher Education.* London: Routledge, 141–56.

Clegg, S., Stevenson, J. and Burke, P.-J. (2016) 'Translating close-up research into action: A critical reflection'. *Reflective Practice*, 17 (3), 233–44.

Dalkin, S.M., Greenhalgh, J., Jones, D., Cunningham, B. and Lhussier, M. (2015) 'What's in a mechanism? Development of a key concept in realist evaluation.' *Implementation Science*, 10 (1), 49.

Ellsworth, E. (1992) 'Why doesn't this feel empowering? Working through the repressive myths of critical pedagogy'. In Luke, C. and Gore, J. (eds) *Feminisms and Critical Pedagogy.* New York: Routledge, 90–119.

Fraser, N. (1997) *Justice Interruptus: Critical reflections on the 'postsocialist' condition.* New York: Routledge.

Fraser, N. (2003) 'Social justice in the age of identity politics: Redistribution, recognition, and participation'. In Fraser, N. and Honneth, A. *Redistribution or Recognition? A political- philosophical exchange.* Trans. Golb, J., Ingram, J. and Wilke, C. London: Verso, 7–109.

Freire, P. (1972) *Pedagogy of the Oppressed.* Trans. Ramos, M.B. Harmondsworth: Penguin Books.

Freire, P. (2004) *Pedagogy of Hope: Reliving Pedagogy of the Oppressed.* Trans. Barr, R.R. Originally 1992. London: Bloomsbury.

Gewirtz, S. (2001) 'Cloning the Blairs: New Labour's programme for the re-socialization of working-class parents'. *Journal of Education Policy,* 16 (4), 365–78.

Gillborn, D. (2008) *Racism and Education: Coincidence or conspiracy?* London: Routledge.

Harding, S. (1986) *The Science Question in Feminism.* Ithaca, NY: Cornell University Press.

Hayton, A. and Bengry-Howell, A. (2016) 'Theory, evaluation, and practice in widening participation: A framework approach to assessing impact'. *London Review of Education,* 14 (3), 41–53.

Hesse, M. (1974) *The Structure of Scientific Inference.* Berkeley: University of California Press.

Jones, R. and Thomas, L. (2005) 'The 2003 UK Government Higher Education White Paper: A critical assessment of its implications for the access and widening participation agenda'. *Journal of Education Policy,* 20 (5), 615–30.

Lather, P. (1991) *Getting Smart: Feminist research and pedagogy with/in the postmodern.* New York: Routledge.

Lather, P. (2000) 'Drawing the line at angels: Working the ruins of feminist ethnography'. In St Pierre, E.A. and Pillow, W.S. (eds) *Working the Ruins: Feminist poststructural theory and methods in education.* New York: Routledge, ch. 14.

Law, J. (2004) *After Method: Mess in social science research.* London: Routledge.

Livingstone, G. (2009) *America's Backyard: The United States and Latin America from the Monroe Doctrine to the War on Terror.* London: Zed Books.

McNay, L. (2008) *Against Recognition.* Cambridge: Polity Press.

Mills, C.W. (2000) *The Sociological Imagination.* Originally 1959. New York: Oxford University Press.

Mirza, H.S. (2009) *Race, Gender and Educational Desire: Why black women succeed and fail.* London: Routledge.

Mirza, H.S. (2015) 'Decolonizing higher education: Black feminism and the intersectionality of race and gender'. *Journal of Feminist Scholarship,* 7–8, 1–12.

Narismulu, P. (2016) 'A heuristic for analysing and teaching literature dealing with the challenges of social justice'. In Burke, P.J. and Shay, S. (eds) *Making Sense of Teaching in Difficult Times.* London: Routledge, 87–99.

Pawson, R. (1989) *A Measure for Measures: A manifesto for empirical sociology.* London: Routledge.

Pawson, R. (2013) *The Science of Evaluation: A realist manifesto.* London: Sage.

Pawson, R. and Tilley, N. (1997) *Realistic Evaluation.* London: Sage.

Reay, D. (2001) 'Finding or losing yourself? Working-class relationships to education'. *Journal of Education Policy,* 16 (4), 333–46.

Reay, D. and Ball, S.J. (1997) '"Spoilt for choice": The working classes and educational markets'. *Oxford Review of Education,* 23 (1), 89–101.

Reay, D., Davies, J., David, M. and Ball, S.J. (2001) 'Choices of degree or degrees of choice? Class, "race" and the higher education choice process'. *Sociology*, 35 (4), 855–74.

Rich, A. (1979) *On Lies, Secrets, and Silence: Selected prose, 1966–1978.* New York: W.W. Norton.

Sayer, A. (1984) *Method In Social Science: A realist approach.* London: Hutchinson.

Sayer, A. (2011) *Why Things Matter to People: Social science, values and ethical life.* Cambridge: Cambridge University Press.

Skeggs, B. (1997) *Formations of Class and Gender: Becoming respectable.* London: Sage.

Skeggs, B. (2004) *Class, Self, Culture.* London: Routledge.

Smith, L.T. (1999) *Decolonizing Methodologies: Research and indigenous peoples.* Dunedin: University of Otago Press.

Weedon, C. (1999) *Feminism, Theory and the Politics of Difference.* Oxford: Blackwell.

Weiss, C.H. (1997) 'Theory-based evaluation: Past, present, and future'. In Rog, D.J. and Fournier, D. (eds) *Progress and Future Directions in Evaluation: Perspectives on theory, practice, and methods* (New Directions for Evaluation 76). San Francisco: Jossey-Bass, 41–55.

Youdell, D. (2006) *Impossible Bodies, Impossible Selves: Exclusions and student subjectivities.* Dordrecht: Springer.

Zembylas, M. (2014) 'Affective, political and ethical sensibilities in pedagogies of critical hope: Exploring the notion of "critical emotional praxis"'. In Bozalek, V., Leibowitz, B., Carolissen, R. and Boler, M. (eds) *Discerning Critical Hope in Educational Practices.* London: Routledge, 11–25.

Chapter 3

NERUPI: A praxis-based framework

Annette Hayton

Introduction

The wider socio-economic divisions that are a ubiquitous feature of United Kingdom society are, unsurprisingly, reflected in the higher education (HE) system. Stark differences related to social class, income, ethnicity, locality and gender are reflected in levels of participation in subjects studied, higher education institutions (HEIs) attended and postgraduate outcomes (Whitty *et al.*, 2015; Callender and Scott, 2013; P. Burke, 2012; Hayton and Paczuska, 2002). Generally known under the broad heading of Widening Participation (WP), a number of government-led initiatives designed to address these inequalities have been introduced in the UK over the last 15 years. Widening participation encompasses national, local and institutional policies and practices in three broad areas: access to HE (recruiting underrepresented groups); student success (supporting students during their HE studies); and progression (ensuring that students progress to graduate employment or postgraduate study) (BIS, 2014).This chapter is concerned with the access element of this trio, WP outreach activities, and focuses on interventions for school and college students and their communities. WP outreach activities can take many forms, including residential summer schools, subject taster days, in-school workshops and tutoring, extended supplementary programmes and simple campus visits (the range of activity on offer is described in OFFA, 2017a). Data from the Higher Education Funding Council for England (HEFCE, 2010 and 2013) and the Universities and Colleges Admissions Service (UCAS, 2016) show a steady increase in the rate of progression to HE of students from low-participation neighbourhoods and, more recently, in the numbers of these students progressing to the elite 'high tariff' universities (figure 3.1, based on POLAR3 (participation of local areas)).

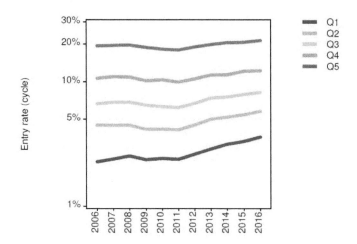

Figure 3.1: English 18-year-olds, entry rates to higher tariff providers by POLAR3 groups (Q5 = advantaged) (logarithmic scale)
Source: UCAS (2016), figure 52.

However, the link between initiatives designed to widen participation and this increased diversity in the student population has been, and remains, contested (Gorard *et al.*, 2006; Hayton and Bengry-Howell, 2016), and pressure from government and funders for effective evaluation gathers pace (OFFA, 2016). At the same time, an increasing body of academic research has explored how the experience of progressing to and participating in higher education differs according to socio-economic background. While these findings can provide illuminating descriptive insights, they rarely include recommendations to address the issues. Policymakers and practitioners alike are often unaware of the research undertaken by academic colleagues. Similarly, academic researchers are often unfamiliar with WP policy developments or the increased sophistication and volume of the WP outreach activities on offer. Theory, policy and practice continue to operate largely in their separate spheres driven by the imperatives of their own agendas, leaving little capacity for productive cooperation.

The Network for Evaluating and Researching University Participation Interventions (NERUPI) framework described in this chapter seeks to overcome some of the divisions between theory, policy and practice and provide a collaborative space to address some of the underlying issues impeding progress in widening participation. Drawing largely on the work of Pierre Bourdieu (1986; 1990; 2003; Bourdieu and Passeron, 1979; Bourdieu and Wacquant, 1992) to identify the dynamics of social and cultural inequalities, the chapter outlines the development and application of a theoretically informed framework for the design and evaluation of

WP outreach activities. While the NERUPI framework is underpinned by a number of Bourdieu's key theoretical concepts, like Thatcher *et al.* it 'unashamedly celebrate[s] the use of Bourdieu's thinking tools in ways which he himself did not use' (Thatcher *et al.*, 2016: 1).

While Bourdieu's theories are useful in explaining how cultural differences translate into structural inequalities at a societal level, he does not set out to recommend practical strategies for change or address individual processes for developing and mobilizing capitals. Therefore a number of related theoretical concepts also informed the development of the framework, most notably Freire's (1972) concept of praxis, which provides a theoretical basis for combining insights from the expertise of the practitioners who plan and deliver outreach programmes with academic research into the reasons for differential participation.

Theory, policy and practice

Economic factors are often cited to explain the socio-economic disparities in HE participation, and their importance should not be underestimated. However, finances alone cannot explain differences in participation as these were also present when UK students benefited from non-repayable grants and free tuition (Kelly and Cook, 2007). Over the last 50 years a growing body of educational research has explored the significance of cultural factors in explaining differences in educational achievement and participation in HE between socio-economic groups. The 1997 New Labour government recognized this and introduced a number of high profile initiatives designed to reduce socio-economic inequality and build 'cultural capital'. Aimhigher, a national initiative launched in 2004, was designed specifically to increase the number of students from underrepresented groups progressing to HE. This concern with cultural aspects of social exclusion represented an important political and policy shift on the part of New Labour, in marked contrast to the previous government whose prime minister, Margaret Thatcher, denied the very existence of 'society' (Hayton, 1999: 3). Aimhigher, along with other initiatives, opened up opportunities for innovative interventions and cross-sectoral working, providing practical support for the most disadvantaged. However, New Labour's policies were based on a particular interpretation of social and cultural capital that tended to endorse middle-class values, thus situating problems firmly with the perceived 'deficits' of socially and economically excluded groups (Gamarnikow and Green, 1999; Leathwood and Hayton, 2002; Gewirtz, 2001). Policy and practice were defined by this approach, with, for example, 'aspiration raising' becoming a key tenet of

Aimhigher, reinforcing the idea that lack of aspiration among 'deprived' groups was one of the main reasons for low levels of participation in HE.

Bourdieu's theories of capital, habitus and field

In contrast, Pierre Bourdieu's approach to cultural and social capital makes it possible to circumvent the trap of understanding educational disparities through a 'deficit model' by bringing the focus back to the socio-economic systems and power relationships that produce inequalities. Bourdieu employed a number of concepts that he described as 'thinking tools' to analyse the power relationships that produce inequalities in socio-economic systems. His central concepts of 'capitals', 'habitus' and 'field', explored in more depth in this chapter, are used here to analyse the forces that lead to differential participation in HE. Bourdieu describes capital as presenting 'itself under three fundamental species (each with its own subtypes), namely economic capital, cultural capital and social capital' (Bourdieu and Wacquant, 1992: 119). Social capital concerns the nature of social networks or connections and, while all socio-economic groups have social capital, their value is dependent on context. For example, a young person applying to HE who has a social circle that includes a high proportion of graduates is more likely to have access to information and support denied to others (Macrae and Maguire, 2002; Reay *et al.*, 2005). Similarly, Bourdieu's formulation recognizes that all individuals possess cultural capital, that is cultural competence within a specific context, but argues that certain forms of cultural capital are assigned greater value (symbolic capital) by groups with power. Along with economic capital, social and cultural capital are critical factors in the maintenance of privilege for some groups and the exclusion of others.

In order to understand how socio-economic systems operate, Bourdieu also uses the concepts of 'habitus' and 'field'. Ciaran Burke draws our attention to the interaction of the different elements of Bourdieu's theories: 'Bourdieu provides an – albeit misleadingly – simplistic but concise account of how these three conceptual tools operate: "[(habitus) (capital)] + field = practice" (1984: 101). Habitus and capital interact together within a dynamic context, engendering practice or strategic agency' (C. Burke, 2016: 10). A habitus can be described as a set of dispositions formed through the active embodiment of cultural, emotional and material circumstances, with those acquired in early childhood being particularly enduring. Bourdieu's concepts were developed over several decades and his early formulations of habitus have been criticized for appearing to deny individual agency. However, if habitus is not regarded as fixed but as dynamic, it becomes a useful concept for analysing and understanding the complexity of the interplay between an individual and a particular context (Reay, 2004). Bourdieu writes that habitus is only difficult to understand if 'one remains locked in the usual antinomies – which the concept of the *habitus* aims to transcend – of determinism and freedom, conditioning and creativity, consciousness and the unconscious, or the individual and society' (1990: 55). By moving beyond crude dualities of structure and agency, habitus offers us a tool to describe how an individual is shaped, and has the capacity to shape, their environment. Bourdieu's concepts of social and cultural capitals and habitus have been used to provide a theoretical basis for the five aims of the NERUPI evaluation framework and are discussed in more depth later in this chapter.

A sometimes overlooked but critical element of Bourdieu's toolbox is the concept of field, which distinguishes his work from other cultural and social capital theorists such as J.S. Coleman and R.D. Putnam (Gamarnikow and Green, 1999). At its most basic level, Bourdieu's use of field is similar to everyday usage in expressions such as the 'field of high finance' or the 'field of medical research'. A field can be viewed as a dynamic space where actors, with capitals and habitus, interact. 'In a field, agents and institutions constantly struggle ... with various degrees of strength and therefore diverse probabilities of success, to appropriate the specific products at stake in the game' (Bourdieu and Wacquant, 1992: 102). Within a particular field, those with privilege are in a stronger position to define what is 'valuable', making the worth of an individual's particular form of capital or habitus dependent on the context, or field, they are operating in at any point in time. Without field, habitus and capitals become merely cultural arbitraries reflecting dominant cultural values.

The field of higher education progression

Bourdieu (2003) defined the field of higher education in order to analyse and explain how historical privilege in the academy is renewed and contested through its organizational and cultural traditions. In the UK, the role of HEIs as gatekeepers that select students is a particularly powerful factor in the retention of HE's exclusivity, as examination success in school or college does not result in automatic acceptance on to a degree. Higher education progression, with 'its own logic, rules and regularities' (Bourdieu and Wacquant, 1992: 104), can usefully be regarded as a field (or a subfield of HE, see figure 3.2), providing a context for exploration of the complex interactions between the HEIs, schools, colleges, students and their communities through an analysis of the power relations, objective structures and the habitus of these areas (Bourdieu and Wacquant, 1992: 105). This section draws on previous research and analysis to set out the main features of the field of higher education progression.

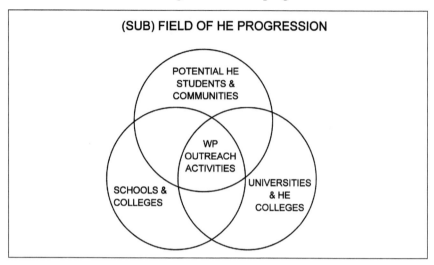

Figure 3.2: (Sub)field of higher education progression

Higher education institutions

As providers of, and gatekeepers to undergraduate degrees with high symbolic value, all HEIs hold a position of power in relation to schools, colleges and individuals. The relative status of HEIs within the HE sector is based on a variety of factors but selectivity, signified by the examination grades required for admission, is a major indicator, with the 'high tariff institutions' that ask for the highest grades regarded as higher status in the 'league tables' (see Complete University Guide, 2017). The distinction between 'recruitment' and 'widening participation' activities is less marked in HEIs with a more diverse range of students whereas 'high tariff' universities, often struggling to increase the intake of students from state schools, tend to run discrete and highly targeted programmes.

All HEIs in England charging fees above the minimum set by government are required to set out a range of measures to widen participation as part of an Access Agreement regulated by the Office for Fair Access (OFFA). This has led to an increase in WP outreach activities offered by HEIs and a growth in the number of WP practitioner staff to develop and deliver them. Outward-facing and delivering to government-led social mobility priorities, WP units and staff often fit uneasily into traditional university organizational structures occupying a liminal space on the borders of the institution. Nevertheless, the emerging profession of WP practitioners plays a pivotal role in interpreting policy through the development and delivery of activities (Wilkins and Burke, 2015).

Within HEIs, academic staff researching social inequalities generally operate separately from WP practitioners, who are normally based in professional service departments. The involvement in WP outreach activities of academic staff with subject specialisms can be extremely valuable, opening up opportunities for curriculum-focused activities and providing access to specialist resources. Recent OFFA guidance (OFFA, 2015; OFFA, 2016; OFFA, 2017b) has stressed the importance of developing activities to support attainment-raising activities, so increased engagement from academic staff will be essential. However, working with younger age groups often presents pedagogical challenges for lecturers whose main teaching experience lies with university students.

Current students who support the delivery of activities, often known as student ambassadors, can provide an effective bridge between age groups and be one of the most important factors for enabling younger students to imagine themselves as undergraduates and access accurate 'hot knowledge' (Ball and Vincent, 1998) not available within their own social networks. Equally, ambassadors without awareness and understanding of the reasons for differential participation can be off-putting and reinforce participants' perception that they won't 'fit in' in an HE context (Gartland, 2015).

Schools, colleges and students

While schools and colleges can be powerful vehicles for challenging socio-economic inequality (Mills, 2008), they are grounded in an unequal system and often reflect and reproduce socio-economic inequalities. The research of Reay *et al.* (2013) demonstrated the value that middle-class parents place on a 'good school' and how they mobilize their already considerable economic and cultural capital to secure places at the state schools of their choice and thus serve to maintain the distinction between 'good' and 'bad' schools. In terms of HE progression, achieving good grades in General Certificate of Secondary Education (GCSE) school examinations at the age of 16 is the main indicator for subsequent entry to university, regardless of social class, ethnicity or gender (Crawford, 2014). However, those from higher social classes (NS-SEC 1–3) are more likely to gain the grades required to be successful in post-16 education and progress to HE, in particular to the elite 'higher tariff' universities. Belief in the link between attainment and fixed, measurable individual 'intelligence' is still a prevailing discourse that shapes national and institutional policies, such as recent proposals in the UK to reintroduce selective education (Millar, 2016). The reasons for academic underachievement and success require a more complex explanation than that offered by simplistic notions of intelligence. Bourdieu's concepts of capitals and habitus provide a different perspective for exploring the interplay between an individual's dispositions, capacities, actions and background and how this affects their relationship to schooling and attainment in public examinations such as GCSE and A Levels, as Ball explains:

> Resource differences and collective efforts and investments made or not within families become translated into individual 'ability' ... identities become tied to routes and programmes inscribing social barriers and academic boundaries which are constantly re-privileged within education policy and schools ... children and their performances are essentialised rather than seen as socially, culturally and economically 'made up'. (Ball, 2010: 162)

In this way an individual's capacities are nurtured or crushed through the active embodiment of cultural, emotional and material circumstances and the situation in which they find themselves, with any 'natural' dispositions or talents becoming virtually indistinguishable from their cultural context.

In relation to HE progression, Reay *et al.* (2005) apply Bourdieu's concept of habitus to higher education choice, identifying two 'ideal types' of HE applicant: 'embedded' choosers who possess the economic, social and cultural capital to support progression to university, and 'contingent' choosers who do not have these advantages. Contingent choosers often perceive HE culture as quite alien, feeling like 'fish out of water' (Bourdieu and Passeron, 1979), and a now considerable body of research describes the negative impact on these students and the challenges they face in progressing to and participating in HE (e.g. Archer *et al.*, 2003; Bathmaker *et al.*, 2013; Reay *et al.*, 2009). In schools and colleges where the majority of students continue on to HE, progression activities are integral elements of the institutional habitus (Reay *et al.*, 2001). These can include well-developed links with HEIs and a sophisticated programme of advice and support, often utilizing staff who are alumni of prestigious universities themselves. This expertise, built up over time, is difficult to replicate in schools and colleges with lower rates of progression. Engaging with university-led outreach activities can be a lower priority and more challenging when the imperative must be to prioritize success in public examinations and meet the more demanding support needs of their students (Hayton *et al.*, 2015: 1258–76).

Widening participation activities

The growth in WP outreach activities has been largely driven by government WP policy, which Hart describes as an interventionist strategy: 'In the context of Bourdieu's concept of field, WP policy in England can be viewed very much as an interventionist strategy in the sense that it attempts to go against the natural order of dominant fields of power and education' (Hart, 2013: 57). WP outreach activities are the heart of this strategy, setting out to disrupt the expected progression trajectory of groups underrepresented in HE by providing opportunities to engage with HE culture and practices. In their survey of WP activities, commissioned by the Department for Education, Thornton *et al.* (2014) found that a sustained approach, where students engaged with universities on a number of occasions, was most effective in promoting HE progression. However, the importance of the content and quality of the activities themselves is often overlooked, and merely offering a number of similar activities can be counterproductive, as one student explained: 'Every single one [visit] I have been to is pretty much a tour of the campus and then lectures on student finance and UCAS applications when you get bored' (section 3.12.1).

In order to develop, deliver, and engage with successful activities, individuals and organizations are required to operate outside their normal spheres, challenging personal and institutional habituses. Universities are required to focus on the needs of the school and college sector and its students, schools need to review their approaches to supporting HE progression, and student participants have to face the challenge of engaging with the often alien environment of HE. The NERUPI framework actively recognizes that groups underrepresented in HE face a greater cultural challenge in progressing to HE and that offering 'equal opportunity' is not sufficient when familial and school habituses cannot develop the capabilities necessary for successful engagement (Sen, 2005). The NERUPI framework sets out to provide a basis for developing activities that build both institutional and individual capacities to support progression to HE, utilizing the cross-sectoral nature of the work to provide a 'third space' (Bhabha, 2004) where assumptions and preconceptions can be challenged, new partnerships forged and innovative practices developed.

The NERUPI framework

The NERUPI framework sets out to maximize the impact of interventions in three ways:

- providing a robust theoretical and evidence-based rationale for the types of intervention that are designed and delivered;
- setting out clear aims and learning outcomes for interventions, enabling more strategic and reflexive design and delivery;
- rationalizing and integrating evaluation processes across programmes of interventions to improve data quality, ensure utility and more effectively demonstrate impact using a range of indicators. (Hayton and Bengry-Howell, 2016)

WP outreach activities have been positioned as potential 'critical actions' with the capacity to disrupt the expected progression pathways of students from underrepresented groups by supporting their access to HE. Freire's (1972) concept of praxis underpinned the framework's development. As Burke and Lumb explain in chapter 2 of this volume, praxis 'emphasizes the dialogic relationship between critical reflection and critical action'. The framework was initially developed at one university (University of Bath) to provide a bounded context where practice and theory could be tested against each other at every stage of development. WP outreach activities were mapped against the theoretical concepts of habitus, cultural capital and social capital, revealing both synergies and omissions. At the same time, the theoretical concepts were interrogated in the context of the activities, and while the validity of the theoretical basis was affirmed, some adaptations were made. The most notable are the conjoining of social capital with academic capital and the creation of a new category of skills capital. This reflexive process resulted in the formulation of five overarching aims with the capacity to encompass all activities in the programme. Table 3.1 summarizes the aims and their theoretical underpinning and these will be described in more detail.

The framework sets out to provide a common language for operationalizing complex theoretical insights clearly representing the concepts of social and cultural capital and habitus in relation to practical aims. Key areas are also translated into the generally more accessible language of education through use of the term 'curriculum' to signify the importance of the design and content of the WP outreach activities. This approach is reinforced in the formulation of the objectives that use the language of learning outcomes to place responsibility for successful delivery with the HEI. To encourage practitioners and academics to employ active pedagogies in the design and delivery of WP outreach activities, active terms such as 'explore', 'discover' and 'understand' have been embedded into the language used in the aims and objectives of the framework.

Table 3.1: Outline of the NERUPI framework

SOCIAL AND ACADEMIC CAPITAL		HABITUS	SKILLS CAPITAL	INTELLECTUAL CAPITAL
PROGRESSION CURRICULUM		STUDENT IDENTITIES	SKILLS CURRICULUM	KNOWLEDGE CURRICULUM
KNOW	CHOOSE	BECOME	PRACTISE	UNDERSTAND
Develop students' knowledge and awareness of the benefits of higher education and graduate employment	Develop students' capacity to navigate higher education sector and make informed choices	Develop students' confidence and resilience to negotiate the challenges of university life and graduate progression	Develop students' study skills and capacity for academic attainment and graduate progression	Develop students' understanding by contextualizing subject knowledge

Social and academic capital

The impact of family background and cultural traditions on the likelihood of progressing to higher education is significant. The development of social capital is a key element of the framework along with academic capital, the capacity to understand the unspoken rules of the academy. Bourdieu (2003) regarded academic capital as an aspect of cultural capital, but the practice-based interrogation of the theoretical base revealed a close connection between activities that enabled students to develop social capital and those fostering academic capital, resulting in the conjoining of academic and social capital within the framework.

While lack of awareness unsurprisingly remains an issue in communities with little tradition of HE engagement, the concept of low aspiration is more problematic. Archer *et al.* (2012) compared the aspirations of school students based on the concept of 'science capital', which was present when parents possessed: 'science-related qualifications, understanding, knowledge (about science and "how it works"), interest and social contacts (e.g. knowing someone who works in a science-related job)'. By Year 9 (ages 13–14) only 32 per cent of those with low science capital had career aspirations in science, technology, engineering or mathematics (STEM) subjects as compared with 60 per cent of those with high science capital. Burke explores the notion of aspirations in depth, concluding: 'It is crucial to understand that aspirations are not constructed exclusively at the individual level but are tied in with complex structural, cultural and discursive relations, identities and practices' (2012: 119).

Even when students from lower socio-economic groups have 'aspirations' to progress to HE, they are 'less likely to have developed the capacities to realise them' (Reay *et al.*, 2005; Bok, 2010: 176). The process of choosing and applying to an undergraduate degree requires a highly sophisticated understanding of the relationships between school subjects, undergraduate degrees, type of HEI and potential careers, leading Paczuska (2002) to use the term 'Admissions curriculum' to describe the information and activities required to enable students to make a successful application. As schools and colleges with lower rates of progression to HE often do not have the institutional habitus to develop the capacities required to navigate the application and admissions process (Appadurai, 2004), the development of these capacities informs the Progression Curriculum section of the framework and the first two of the framework's overarching aims, to:

1   'Develop students' knowledge and awareness of the benefits of higher education and graduate employment.'
2   'Develop students' capacity to navigate higher education and graduate employment sectors and make informed choices.'

Habitus and identity

The concept of habitus underpins the next strand of the framework, and theoretical insights based on *student identities* have been used to explore how individual change and transformation takes place. The framework recognizes that by engaging with HE, students from underrepresented groups are encountering a culture that is likely to challenge their habitus. Building on Bourdieu's concept of cleft habitus, Ingram and Abrahams (2016: 150) have explored the impact on individuals experiencing habitus interruption when operating in an unfamiliar field. They use the concepts of disjunctive responses, where student identities remain situated in their original habitus, and conjunctive responses, where a degree of accommodation is made with the cultural practices of the new context. In both cases, the individuals experience a process of internalizing an unfamiliar field that is not without emotional cost, and this is acknowledged in the third aim of the framework, to:

3   'Develop students' confidence and resilience to negotiate the challenges of university life and graduate progression.'

WP outreach activities that recognize the potentially alien nature of HE culture can provide a positive foundation for utilizing concepts of 'possible selves', providing a context for challenging the habitus: 'a "new space", a "third space", one where those caught between two worlds are accepted and feel at home' (Ingram and Abrahams, 2016: 155).

Intellectual and skills capitals

In later work, Bourdieu refined the concept of cultural capital, using the term 'intellectual' or scientific capital' to encompass specific subject knowledge and expertise. In order to avoid confusion, the term 'intellectual' capital has been used when referring to subject knowledge within the NERUPI framework. While the concept of intellectual capital was able to encompass existing and potential activities relating to subject knowledge, a separate category of 'skills capital' was created to reflect WP outreach activities specifically designed to develop HE study skills and distinguish them from those related to subject knowledge. The separation of skills development and subject knowledge has been the subject of much debate and in our programmes they are frequently delivered together. Nevertheless, study skills do appear to be less developed in student groups currently underrepresented in higher education and inclusion as a separate category in the framework recognizes this, as well as reflecting practice in outreach and student success activities. The fourth aim in the framework is therefore concerned with skills development and builds on Bourdieu's taxonomy through the notion of Skills Capital, which is acquired and demonstrated through academic practice. It incorporates WP outreach activities that set out to:

4   'Develop students' study skills and capacity for academic attainment and successful graduate progression.'

The final strand of the framework relates to the *knowledge curriculum* and developing students' Intellectual Capital. The objectivity or otherwise of knowledge and the curriculum has been a continuing area of enquiry in the sociology of education over the last 40 years. Arising from the ambition to explore and understand lower academic attainment and disengagement from schooling among certain socio-economic groups, this debate has particular relevance to WP, concerned as it is to minimize differences in progression to HE. As Moore and Young state (2010: 32), there is no question that knowledge is socially constructed and that essentialist theories of knowledge are profoundly flawed. Also, as Bourdieu so powerfully demonstrated, the value assigned to different forms of knowledge is dependent on context, with 'academic' knowledge being validated by the academy. This has led to a number of exclusionary practices within HE, including assumptions about who is deemed worthy of admission. The other danger inherent in this self-referential system is that of curriculum ossification, famously demonstrated by Oxford University's continued attachment to the Classics in the rapidly changing social and economic context of the 19th century, 'as the only effective mind-sharpener', a capacity that, it was believed, could not be developed through study and acquisition of more useful knowledge (Brock and Curthoys, 2000: 13–14).

However, a recognition of the power and subjectivity of 'knowers' does not necessarily mean that the knowledge created is not legitimate. I would argue that exclusionary practices make it more likely that knowledge is partial and flawed but agree that 'knowledge is not merely a reflection of power relations but also comprises more or less epistemologically powerful claims to truth' (Maton, 2010: 37). Certainly without engagement through the school curriculum with what Young (2008) describes as 'powerful knowledge', young people are placed at a serious disadvantage. The competitive nature of admissions to undergraduate degree programmes, particularly at high tariff universities, means that good grades in the 'facilitating subjects' such as maths, sciences, English, history and languages (Russell Group, 2015) related to 'powerful knowledge' and valued by selective universities are critical. Nevertheless, for students without a cultural tradition of HE, these subjects can appear as distant and pointless as they did to Willis's working-class 'lads' 40 years ago (Willis, 1977). Young (2008) argues that relating education purely to students' experience is limiting and that it is good teaching, that is, pedagogy, which enables school students to engage with theoretical concepts outside of their immediate sphere. However, students from privileged backgrounds are more likely to have friends and relatives who have consciously engaged with and utilized these fields of knowledge; they are also more likely to understand that the school curriculum is only one element of a particular field, making the journey towards understanding its relationship to them and their futures shorter and more relevant to their current identities. By providing access to facilities and opportunities to engage with expert academic staff and current students, WP outreach activities can explore how broader fields of knowledge, often cutting across school subject boundaries, relate to the school curriculum and future careers. This leads to the fifth aim, to:

5   'Develop students' understanding by contextualizing subject knowledge.'

Utilizing the NERUPI framework

To recap, the five aims of the NERUPI framework are to:

1 Develop students' knowledge and awareness of the benefits of higher education and graduate employment.
2 Develop students' capacity to navigate higher education and graduate employment sectors and make informed choices.
3 Develop students' confidence and resilience to negotiate the challenge of university life and graduate progression.
4 Develop students' study skills and capacity for academic attainment and successful graduate progression.
5 Develop students' understanding by contextualizing subject knowledge.

Objectives relating to the five overarching aims of the framework were developed in five, loosely age-related levels allowing the programme of activities to be considered by level while providing the flexibility to encompass a wider variety of experience (for example a mature student entering HE), which a strictly age-related structure could not encompass. Level 0 generally corresponds to younger age groups and Level 3 to post-16 students in the last stages of UK compulsory schooling. While the aims are overarching, the objectives are specific to each level. Those associated with the first aim are shown in table 3.2.

Table 3.2: Aim 1 and top-level objectives

Aim 1		Develop students' knowledge and awareness of the benefits of higher education and graduate employment
Level	(Age)	Top-level objectives
		Enable students to:
4	18 +	Increase awareness of study options, social and leisure facilities, and career opportunities for (University of Bath) students
3	16–18	Investigate course and placement options, career progression routes, and social and leisure opportunities at the (University of Bath) and other universities
2	14–16	Explore academic, social, economic and personal benefits of progressing to higher education
1	11–13	Understand how GCSE study relates to higher education and future career opportunities
0	<11	Experience a positive introduction to higher education and the (University of Bath) campus

These top-level objectives have then been further refined to include more detailed objectives couched in the language of learning outcomes, for example in table 3.3.

Table 3.3: Aim 1 and objectives

Aim 1	**Develop students' knowledge and awareness of the benefits of higher education and graduate employment**	
Level 2 (age 14–16)	Top-level objective	Explore academic, social, economic and personal benefits of progressing to higher education
	Objectives or learning outcomes	*Understand economic benefits of higher education and career opportunities for graduates*
		Explore benefits of higher education in terms of personal development and cultural enrichment
		Discover study and research opportunities at the (University of Bath)

The result is a framework summarizing objectives for widening participation outreach activities as a whole that also provides sufficient flexibility to focus on developing an intervention to meet a particular aim and set of objectives. The framework has been trialled through a consortium of universities and a protracted process of testing and revision was envisaged, but it soon became apparent that substantive changes were not necessary. The framework proved sufficiently flexible to encompass a variety of outreach activities in a range of universities working with different age groups and characteristics. The underpinning theoretical base has proved robust and the broad aims and objectives for each age group remained unchanged, providing a foundation for development of specific learning outcomes for individual activities.

Methods and impact

The NERUPI framework approach has a number of significant advantages in comparison with more loosely defined approaches to evaluation. First, by mapping a programme of activities against the framework, a strategic assessment can be made to identify gaps and overlaps in provision, enabling the programme to be adjusted accordingly. The common aims and objectives also provide a clear basis for evaluating the impact of individual activities, as well as a mechanism for comparing their relative effectiveness. In addition, the framework enables the aggregation of qualitative and quantitative data from different activities with the same aims. Furthermore, additional data sources can be used to evaluate the success of an activity in meeting its overarching aims, for example internal admissions data or tracking data from the Higher Education Access Tracker (HEAT). These elements facilitate evaluation of whole institutional programmes and the production of summary reports useful for senior management teams within HEIs, funders and regulators such as OFFA.

Although the framework provides structure, it does not specify the content of activities or evaluation methods, remaining sufficiently flexible to encompass innovative activities and appropriate evaluation methodologies to allow improvement in the process. For example, the appropriate methodology to assess the impact of a low-intensity campus visit for a group of 10-year-old children could be light touch and creative, capturing responses to the overarching aims through pictorial methods. In contrast, if the main aim of an activity is to increase knowledge of a specific topic or subject, a different approach can be used. Data can also be collected from a range of sources, including participants, teachers, parents, student ambassadors, academic staff and WP practitioners. This enables an analysis of multiple accounts from the various actors to reveal correlations and contradictions in their perceptions and the impact of the activity. Whichever method is employed, results can be interrogated in terms of common aims, providing rich, mixed method data to inform and enhance practice.

Given the relatively powerful position of HEIs within the field of higher education progression, there is a significant risk that WP outreach activities might reflect exclusionary practices. Critical pedagogies that encompass an interactive approach to learning and value the experiences participants bring to the learning context are more likely to lead to positive student engagement (Moore, 2012; Burke *et al.*, 2017). This is particularly important in the delivery of WP outreach activities, which actively set out to engage 'contingent choosers' from underrepresented groups in a culturally challenging environment. The negative impact of habitus interruption can be countered through activities that provide challenge, develop agency, build capitals and mobilize the valuable capacities that participants already possess (Clegg, 2011). The active learning terms encompassed in the aims, objectives and learning outcomes of the NERUPI framework are designed to promote this approach.

Case study: 'On Track to Bath'

One of the more complex, intensive programmes on offer at the University of Bath is 'On Track to Bath'. It is designed as a supplementary offer for post-16 students with potential to secure a place at a more selective 'high tariff' university through the A-Level qualification route. It has been chosen as a case study as it sets out to meet all five aims in the NERUPI framework. To a great extent, like the students in Bowers-Brown's (2006) study, 'On Track to Bath' students are already in possession of considerable intellectual and skills capital (although perhaps not quite sufficient to achieve the A-Level grades required for the most selective HEIs), but they have less capacity to 'play the game' in the same way as their middle-class counterparts. Students make regular visits to the university campus over a period of 18 months, joining a subject track supported by a subject-specialist coordinating tutor. The tutor also facilitates the engagement of academic staff in delivering lectures and initiating the project work so critical to the success of this attainment-raising programme, and coordinates the involvement of subject-specialist student ambassadors. Year One consists of expert subject-based sessions, an independent research project and a campus residential. Year Two is mainly concerned with supporting the HE application process. Participant monitoring data are collected, analysed and reported to indicate the number of participants, gender, class, ethnicity, residence in low-participation neighbourhoods and parental education, along with information on participant retention, completion and progression to HE. In addition to this basic monitoring exercise (now standard for most WP outreach activities), the NERUPI framework also enables a summary of performance against top-level aims and objectives, in this case using survey data combined with qualitative data from reflective discussions with participants. Evaluation methods have included pre- and post-activity student surveys, reflective discussions, observation, and feedback from WP practitioners, student ambassadors, teachers and parents. Two examples are provided in tables 3.4 and 3.5 to illustrate how the process operates in practice.

Some elements of 'On Track to Bath' have the capacity to meet several aims and objectives and this is captured through methods such as reflective discussions and interviews. For example:

> The (academic) project really gave an insight into what it would be like to develop a university project, like researching everything ourselves, working in groups where people do separate things. This is the first time I have done anything like this and it felt like a good preparation.

Table 3.4: Social and academic capital: Aim 2

Aim 2		
Develop students' capacity to navigate higher education and graduate employment sectors and make informed choices	**Top-level objective:** Evaluate course, student finance and graduate opportunities and make informed choices that align with personal interests and career aspirations	
	Sub-objective or learning outcome	*Engage effectively with the UCAS process and generate and submit a strong university application*
	Result of survey data	97% thought 'On Track' had improved their ability to submit a strong UCAS application
	Qualitative data	'On Track' has given me the skills, confidence and knowledge I need to be able to make a decision about what course I would like to do at university and what I need to look for to choose one.

Table 3.5: Intellectual capital: Aim 5

Aim 5		
Develop students' understanding by contextualizing subject knowledge	**Top-level objective:** Situate existing knowledge within wider fields of knowledge and apply to other contexts, and situate existing knowledge and interests within the context of university degree programmes and academic disciplines.	
	Sub-objective or learning outcome	*Locate existing knowledge within wider fields of knowledge and other contexts*
	Result of survey data	68% agreed 'On Track' had enabled them to take what I am learning at college/6th form and see how that is developed further at university
	Qualitative data	This has given me a better understanding of the subject and ideas that I can incorporate into my work at college.

The general programme of 'On Track to Bath' has a specific focus on developing intellectual and skills capital but also includes a residential summer school with a focus on the habitus element of the framework (see table 3.6).

Table 3.6: Habitus: Aim 3

Aim 3	Top-level objective: Anticipate challenges they will face in higher education and make a successful transition to university	
Develop students' confidence and resilience to negotiate the challenge of university life and graduate progression	*Sub-objective or learning outcome*	*Interact with other students on programme, student ambassadors and current University of Bath students*
	Qualitative data	I have found the ambassadors really helpful. It has been really good to have people to talk to who have experienced things and are able to answer questions from a student's perspective
		It's been good before when we were in our own tracks, but with this we've had a chance to integrate with everybody. ... It has been really helpful and it kind of represents what it would be like at uni. To have to meet new people and have to get on with them.

Additional perspectives: Parents

Evaluation of 'On Track' also includes data collection from multiple voices, including academic staff, student ambassadors, teachers and parents. The involvement of parents in 'On Track' is a key element of the programme as many of the participants have parents who have not attended HE. Therefore, their familial habitus (Reay *et al.*, 2005: 61) means that they do not possess the same capability to support their children as parents from cultural traditions where HE progression is the norm, and the involvement of parents in 'On Track' sets out to address this. The following report reflects an end-of-course discussion with parents.

Overall, parents were very positive about 'On Track'. One parent said she was really nervous about coming onto campus for the first time at the welcome event but she felt that the information given was very clear and easy to understand, and so if her son needed support she was now able to provide it. In the discussion around Aim 2, many parents said they really appreciated the support with applications and one reported that 'On Track' had really helped her son to choose the right course for him. The discussion then moved to Aim 3 and parents noted increased confidence in their children and the benefits of meeting like-minded people. 'On Track' was perceived as taking away fear factor – especially the residential experience.

Parents felt that students had really grown in maturity. One parent said: 'It gives them a head start – they are familiar with the environment and know what is expected of them.'

Improving practice and increasing understandings

The various elements of 'On Track' are also evaluated, which provides additional insights both to improve activities and to better support students. For example, participants reported mixed feelings about one aspect of the residential focused around a debate and this has been changed for future years. Also, student feedback revealed that the importance of the residential had been underestimated. In planning the programme it was felt that a short residential would be sufficient to achieve the main of aim of 'developing students' confidence and resilience to navigate the challenges of university life', as students were already familiar with the university environment through other aspects of the programme. Although they valued the residential for precisely these features, they asked for it to be extended, a call reinforced by parent feedback. While this is certainly 'process improvement' in the sense that the activity was changed, the feedback also increased our understanding of the challenges that university can present for prospective students without a cultural tradition of HE study. As the process of reflection-action-action-reflection is refined and the circle of reflective actors increases, the institutional habitus within the academy can be interrogated to identify exclusionary culture and practices.

Concluding remarks

The framework has proved an extremely useful tool, allowing all those involved to see at a glance the range of outcomes it embraces and the specific objectives for a particular activity. This offers a common focus for activity and a vocabulary for discussion and developing shared understandings. It also provides a strong foundation for robust, yet reflexive, evaluation, enabling identification of areas that meet the objectives and those that are less successful. Furthermore, it highlights shortcomings in a programme, leading to the adaptation of activities and the creation of new interventions.

The NERUPI framework itself cannot specify how it might be used in a particular context, but the praxis-based approach fundamental to its design promotes the use of a reflexive, action-research approach to evaluation. Within this paradigm, the aim is to make 'a direct contribution to transformative action' (Kemmis, 2010: 425), placing the focus of research and evaluation on improving the effectiveness of activities. An important element of the action-research approach is to promote personal and institutional reflexivity. Opportunities for those involved in delivering an activity to reflect on and learn from the evaluation data not only improve the activity, but can also increase staff awareness about the issues facing students from underrepresented groups and challenge preconceptions (Clegg *et al.*, 2016). Most importantly, they can open up space for dialogue to explore the complex exclusionary forces at play in the field of higher education progression and provide a basis for developing innovative and effective strategies to counter inequalities and truly widen participation.

References

Appadurai, A. (2004) 'The capacity to aspire: Culture and the terms of recognition'. In Rao, V. and Walton, M. (eds) *Culture and Public Action*. Stanford: Stanford University Press, 59–84.

Archer, L., DeWitt, J., Osborne, J., Dillon, J., Willis, B. and Wong, B. (2012) 'Science aspirations, capital, and family habitus: How families shape children's engagement and identification with science'. *American Educational Research Journal*, 49 (5), 881–908.

Archer, L., Hutchings, M. and Ross, A. (eds) (2003) *Higher Education and Social Class: Issues of exclusion and inclusion*. London: RoutledgeFalmer.

Ball, S.J. (2010) 'New class inequalities in education: Why education policy may be looking in the wrong place! Education policy, civil society and social class'. *International Journal of Sociology and Social Policy*, 30 (3–4), 155–66.

Ball, S.J. and Vincent, C. (1998) '"I heard it on the grapevine": "Hot" knowledge and school choice'. *British Journal of Sociology of Education*, 19 (3), 377–400.

Bathmaker, A.-M., Ingram, N. and Waller, R. (2013) 'Higher education, social class and the mobilisation of capitals: Recognising and playing the game'. *British Journal of Sociology of Education*, 34 (5–6), 723–43.

Bhabha, H.K. (2004) *The Location of Culture*. London: Routledge.

BIS (Department for Business, Innovation and Skills) (2014) *National Strategy for Access and Student Success in Higher Education*. London: Department for Business, Innovation and Skills.

Bok, J. (2010) 'The capacity to aspire to higher education: "It's like making them do a play without a script"'. *Critical Studies in Education*, 51 (2), 163–78.

Bourdieu, P. (1984) *Distinction: A social critique of the judgement of taste*. London: Routledge and Kegan Paul.

Bourdieu, P. (1986) 'The forms of capital'. In Richardson, J.G. (ed.) *Handbook of Theory and Research for the Sociology of Education*. New York: Greenwood Press, 241–58.

Bourdieu, P. (1990) *The Logic of Practice*. Trans. Nice, R. Cambridge: Polity Press.

Bourdieu, P. (2003) *Homo Academicus*. Trans. Collier, P. Cambridge: Polity Press.

Bourdieu, P. and Passeron, J.-C. (1979) *The Inheritors: French students and their relation to culture*. Trans. Nice, R. Chicago: University of Chicago Press.

Bourdieu, P. and Wacquant, L.J.D. (1992) *An Invitation to Reflexive Sociology*. Chicago: University of Chicago Press.

Bowers-Brown, T., McCaig, C., Stevens, A. and Harvey, L. (2006) *National Evaluation of Aimhigher: Survey of higher education institutions, further education colleges and work-based learning providers*. Bristol: Higher Education Funding Council for England.

Brock, M.G. and Curthoys, M.C. (eds) (2000) *Nineteenth-Century Oxford, Part 2*. Oxford: Clarendon Press. Vol. 7 of *The History of the University of Oxford*. 8 vols. 1984–94.

Burke, C. (2016) 'Bourdieu's theory of practice: Maintaining the role of capital'. In Thatcher, J., Ingram, N., Burke, C. and Abrahams, J. (eds) *Bourdieu: The next generation*. London: Routledge, 8–24.

Burke, P.J. (2012) *The Right to Higher Education: Beyond widening participation*. London: Routledge.

Burke, P.J., Crozier, G. and Misiaszek, L.I. (2017) *Changing Pedagogical Spaces in Higher Education: Diversity, inequalities and misrecognition*. London: Routledge.

Callender, C. and Scott, P. (eds) (2013) *Browne and Beyond: Modernizing English higher education*. London: Institute of Education Press.

Clegg, S. (2011) 'Cultural capital and agency: Connecting critique and curriculum in higher education'. *British Journal of Sociology of Education*, 32 (1), 93–108.

Clegg, S., Stevenson, J. and Burke, P.-J. (2016) 'Translating close-up research into action: A critical reflection'. *Reflective Practice*, 17 (3), 233–44.

Complete University Guide (2017) https://www.thecompleteuniversityguide.co.uk/ (accessed 8 December 2017).

Crawford, C. (2014) *The Link between Secondary School Characteristics and University Participation and Outcomes* (CAYT Research Report). London: Department for Education.

Freire, P. (1972) *Pedagogy of the Oppressed*. Trans. Ramos, M.B. Harmondsworth: Penguin Books.

Gamarnikow, E. and Green, A. (1999) 'Developing social capital: Dilemmas, possibilities and limitations in education'. In Hayton, A. (ed.) *Tackling Disaffection and Social Exclusion: Education perspectives and policies*. London: Kogan Page, 46–64.

Gartland, C. (2015) 'Student ambassadors: "Role-models", learning practices and identities'. *British Journal of Sociology of Education*, 36 (8), 1192–211.

Gewirtz, S. (2001) 'Cloning the Blairs: New Labour's programme for the re-socialization of working-class parents'. *Journal of Education Policy*, 16 (4), 365–78.

Gorard, S., Smith, E., May, H., Thomas, L., Adnett, N. and Slack, K. (2006) *Review of Widening Participation Research: Addressing the barriers to participation in higher education: A report to HEFCE by the University of York, Higher Education Academy and Institute for Access Studies*. Bristol: Higher Education Funding Council for England.

Hart, C.S. (2013) *Aspirations, Education and Social Justice: Applying Sen and Bourdieu*. London: Bloomsbury.

Hayton, A. (1999) 'Introduction'. In Hayton, A. (ed.) *Tackling Disaffection and Social Exclusion: Education perspectives and policies*. London: Kogan Page.

Hayton, A. and Bengry-Howell, A. (2016) 'Theory, evaluation, and practice in widening participation: A framework approach to assessing impact'. *London Review of Education*, 14 (3), 41–53.

Hayton, A.R., Haste, P. and Jones, A. (2015) 'Promoting diversity in creative art education: The case of fine art at Goldsmiths, University of London'. *British Journal of Sociology of Education*, 36 (8), 1258–76.

Hayton, A. and Paczuska, A. (eds) (2002) *Access, Participation and Higher Education: Policy and practice*. London: Kogan Page.

HEFCE (Higher Education Funding Council for England) (2010) *Trends in Young Participation in Higher Education: Core results for England* (Issues Paper 2010/03). Bristol: Higher Education Funding Council for England. Online. www.hefce.ac.uk/media/hefce/content/pubs/2010/201003/10_03.pdf (accessed 10 December 2017).

HEFCE (Higher Education Funding Council for England) (2013) *Trends in Young Participation in Higher Education* (Issues Paper 2013/28). Bristol: Higher Education Funding Council for England. Online. www.hefce.ac.uk/media/hefce/content/pubs/2013/201328/2013_28.pdf (accessed 10 December 2017).

Ingram, N. and Abrahams, J. (2016) 'Stepping outside of oneself: How a cleft-habitus can lead to greater reflexivity through occupying "the third space"'. In Thatcher, J., Ingram, N., Burke, C. and Abrahams, J. (eds) *Bourdieu: The next generation*. London: Routledge, 140–56.

Kelly, K. and Cook, S. (2007) *Full-Time Young Participation by Socio-Economic Class: A new widening participation measure in higher education* (Research Report RR806). Nottingham: Department for Education and Skills.

Kemmis, S. (2010) 'What is professional practice? Recognising and respecting diversity in understandings of practice'. In Kanes, C. (ed.) *Elaborating Professionalism: Studies in practice and theory*. Dordrecht: Springer, 139–65.

Leathwood, C. and Hayton, A. (2002) 'Educational inequalities in the United Kingdom: A critical analysis of the discourses and policies of New Labour'. *Australian Journal of Education*, 46 (2), 138–53.

Macrae, S. and Maguire, M. (2002) 'Getting in and getting on: Choosing the best'. In Hayton, A. and Paczuska, A. (eds) *Access, Participation and Higher Education: Policy and practice*. London: Kogan Page.

Maton, K. (2010) 'Analysing knowledge claims and practices: Languages of legitimation'. In Maton, K. and Moore, R. (eds) *Social Realism, Knowledge and the Sociology of Education: Coalitions of the mind*. London: Continuum, 35–59.

Millar, F. (2016) '"Tutor-proof" 11-plus professor admits grammar school test doesn't work'. *The Guardian*, 12 September. Online. www.theguardian.com/education/2016/sep/12/tutor-11plus-test-grammar-schools-disadvantaged-pupils (accessed 10 December 2017).

Mills, C. (2008) 'Reproduction and transformation of inequalities in schooling: The transformative potential of the theoretical constructs of Bourdieu'. *British Journal of Sociology of Education*, 29 (1), 79–89.

Moore, A. (2012) *Teaching and Learning: Pedagogy, curriculum and culture*. 2nd ed. London: Routledge.

Moore, R. and Young, M. (2010) 'Reconceptualizing knowledge and the curriculum in the sociology of education'. In Maton, K. and Moore, R. (eds) *Social Realism, Knowledge and the Sociology of Education: Coalitions of the mind*. London: Continuum, 14–34.

OFFA (Office for Fair Access) (2015) *How to Produce an Access Agreement for 2016–17* (OFFA Publication 2015/01). Bristol: Office for Fair Access.

OFFA (Office for Fair Access) (2016) *Strategic Guidance: Developing your 2017–18 access agreement* (OFFA Publication 2016/01). Bristol: Office for Fair Access.

OFFA (Office for Fair Access) (2017a) 'Find an access agreement'. Online. https://www.offa.org.uk/access-agreements/ (accessed 6 December 2017).

OFFA (Office for Fair Access) (2017b) *Strategic Guidance: Developing your 2018–19 access agreement* (OFFA Publication 2017/01). Bristol: Office for Fair Access.

Paczuska, A. (2002) 'The applications process: Developing an admissions curriculum'. In Hayton, A. and Paczuska, A. (eds) *Access, Participation and Higher Education: Policy and practice*. London: Kogan Page.

Reay, D. (2004) '"It's all becoming a habitus": Beyond the habitual use of habitus in educational research'. *British Journal of Sociology of Education*, 25 (4), 431–44.

Reay, D., Crozier, G. and Clayton, J. (2009) '"Strangers in paradise"? Working-class students in elite universities'. *Sociology*, 43 (6), 1103–21.

Reay, D., Crozier, G. and James, D. (2013) *White Middle-Class Identities and Urban Schooling*. Basingstoke: Palgrave Macmillan.

Reay, D., David, M. and Ball, S. (2001) 'Making a difference? Institutional habituses and higher education choice'. *Sociological Research Online*, 5 (4). Online. www.socresonline.org.uk/5/4/reay.html (accessed 10 December 2017).

Reay, D., David, M.E. and Ball, S. (2005) *Degrees of Choice: Class, race, gender and higher education*. Stoke-on-Trent: Trentham Books.

Russell Group (2015) *Informed Choices: A Russell Group guide to making decisions about post-16 education: 2015/16*. 4th ed. London: Russell Group.

Sen, A. (2005) 'Human rights and capabilities'. *Journal of Human Development*, 6 (2), 151–66.

Thatcher, J., Ingram, N., Burke, C. and Abrahams, J. (eds) (2016) *Bourdieu: The next generation*. London: Routledge.

Thornton, A., Pickering, E., Peters, M., Leathwood, C., Hollingworth, S. and Mansaray, A. (2014) *School and college-level strategies to raise aspirations of high-achieving disadvantaged pupils to pursue higher education*. DFE-RR296. London: Department for Education.

UCAS (Universities and Colleges Admission Service) (2016) *End of Cycle Report 2016: UCAS analysis and research*. Cheltenham: Universities and Colleges Admission Service.

Whitty, G., Hayton, A. and Tang, S. (2015) 'Who you know, what you know and knowing the ropes: A review of evidence about access to higher education institutions in England'. *Review of Education*, 3 (1), 27–67.

Wilkins, A. and Burke, P.J. (2015) 'Widening participation in higher education: The role of professional and social class identities and commitments'. *British Journal of Sociology of Education*, 36 (3), 434–52.

Willis, P.E. (1977) *Learning To Labour: How working class kids get working class jobs*. Farnborough: Saxon House.

Young, M.F.D. (2008) *Bringing Knowledge Back In: From social constructivism to social realism in the sociology of education*. London: Routledge.

Chapter 4

Admission to medicine and law at Russell Group universities: The impact of A-level subject choice

Catherine Dilnot and Vikki Boliver

Introduction

In recent years there has been a growing political desire to widen access not just to higher education generally but to the United Kingdom's most academically selective universities in particular (Sutton Trust and BIS, 2009; BIS, 2015; DfES, 2003). There is clear evidence that the type of university attended and the subject studied can make a considerable difference to future earnings (Britton *et al.*, 2016; Chevalier and Conlon, 2003; Hussain *et al.*, 2009; Walker and Zhu, 2011), with subjects related to professional careers, such as medicine and law, commanding particularly high premiums (Britton *et al.*, 2016). Less privileged graduates remain less likely to access professional careers (Macmillan *et al.*, 2015), with particularly large socio-economic gradients observed in medicine and law (Macmillan, 2009; Milburn, 2009; Milburn, 2012) . In the third of top law firms publishing social mobility data, some 40 per cent of graduate entrants come from private schools (Ashley *et al.*, 2015), as do 38 per cent of trainee doctors (Milburn, 2012). For aspiring lawyers, the socio-economic make-up of the profession reflects the universities and degree subjects from which graduates are recruited (Ashley *et al.*, 2015). Although having a law degree is not essential for access to the legal profession, the majority of those becoming solicitors or training for the bar are admitted with a law degree (Bar Standards Board, 2015; Law Society, 2015). For those wishing to become doctors and dentists, the university dental and medical schools themselves act as gatekeepers to the profession.

Although 90 per cent of entrants to universities in England and the wider United Kingdom in 2014/15 previously attended state-funded secondary schools (HESA, 2015), fewer than 70 per cent of English students entering medical and dental school with three A levels in three recent cohorts were from state schools. Excluding those from selective state grammar schools, the proportion falls to just 46 per cent (Steven *et al.*, 2016). The proportion of law students from English state schools at UK universities is very similar to the national average for all subjects, but state school students are underrepresented on law degrees at the highly selective Russell Group universities, where just 78 per cent of law students come from state maintained schools and colleges.

A large part of the reason for this disparity is that state school pupils are less likely than their privately educated peers to achieve the high grades required for entry to selective subjects such as medicine and law, and to high tariff universities such as Russell Group institutions (Sutton Trust and BIS, 2009). But there is also mounting evidence that selective universities are less likely to offer places to applicants from state schools than to private school applicants, even when they have the same A-level grades (Boliver, 2013; Noden *et al.*, 2014; Boliver, 2016). Work to date has examined the significance of grades, but has paid only superficial attention to the A-level subjects taken by applicants. This is a potentially important limitation of prior research because, according to the Director General of the Russell Group, Wendy Piatt:

> Many good students haven't taken the subjects needed for entry and universities need students not only to have good grades but grades in the right subjects for the course they want to apply for. This is precisely why we publish *Informed Choices*, a guide which gives pupils information on choosing the right subjects at school for different degree courses. (Quoted in Ward, 2015)

Similarly, the Russell Group's recent publication *Opening Doors: Understanding and overcoming barriers to university access* reports that:

> Admissions staff in several of the most selective universities report that it is commonplace for able candidates to seek places on degrees for which they are not qualified. The Russell Group's online publication *Informed Choices* seeks to address this problem. (Russell Group, 2015b: 5)

While these statements and others like them seem authoritative, a closer look suggests that they rest on anecdotal evidence – 'Admissions staff in several … universities report that it is commonplace …' (Russell Group, 2015b: 5) – rather than being based on a robust statistical analysis of the data. Where statistical data are cited, they tend to amount to circumstantial evidence – 'We know that independent and selective state school students are much more likely to achieve AAB in two or more facilitating subjects' (Russell Group, 2015b: 28) – rather than evidence directly demonstrating that offer rates are lower for state school applicants *because* they are less likely to have good grades in the subjects required for their chosen course.

The fact that certain degree courses have particular subject prerequisites, and that certain subjects are more generally favoured by universities than others, is evident from the Russell Group's *Informed Choices*, referred to in the earlier quote (Russell Group, 2015a). This guide, which first appeared in 2011, provides prospective university applicants with information about which advanced level subjects are typically considered 'essential' and 'useful' for particular degree courses. *Informed Choices* also identifies eight so-called 'facilitating subjects' that are 'required more often than others' for entry to degree courses at Russell Group universities and so keep 'a much wider range of options open' to applicants still deciding which subject to pursue at university (Russell Group, 2015a: 26, 28). These 'facilitating subjects' are biology, chemistry, English literature, history, geography, languages, mathematics, and physics. The importance of these eight subjects for gaining access to highly selective universities in the UK is underscored by the fact that the Department for Education has introduced a performance indicator for providers of education for 16–19-year-olds that measures the percentage of students obtaining AAB or above at A level, including at least two 'facilitating subjects' (DfE, 2016).

Although it seems clear that certain subjects matter for entry to particular degree courses, no study to date has directly tested the proposition that school type differences in offer rates for applicants with identical grades at A level are substantially diminished once we consider whether those grades were achieved in subjects formally required for their chosen degree programme. A related proposition is that differences in offer rates by school type of competitive degree courses with no specific subject requirements are diminished when subject choice is taken into account, because certain subjects are informally preferred, despite the lack of explicit guidance from universities. In this chapter we set out to test these propositions, by analysing anonymized individual-level data provided by the Universities and Colleges Admissions Service (UCAS) relating to applicants seeking places on degree courses in medicine (as an example of a subject with relatively prescriptive subject requirements) and law (as a subject without specific subject requirements) at Russell Group universities in 2010, 2011 and 2012. As we explain later in the chapter, our ability to provide a definitive answer to our research question is limited by the restricted nature of the data currently available to researchers (Machin, 2015). But insofar as our data will allow, we find that, while the combinations of grades and subject choices at A level do influence an applicant's chances of admission to a Russell Group university, substantial differences in offer rates by school type remain after this is taken into account.

We commence with a review of previous literature regarding school type differences in the take-up of different A-level subjects, and the impact of A-level subject choices on university admission chances. We then discuss the existing evidence in relation to admission to medicine and law degrees in the UK. We then go on to set out our research questions and describe the dataset and analytical strategy we use to answer them. Finally, we present our main results and discuss their implications.

School type and A-level subject choices

We begin by considering the evidence that state school students are less likely than their privately educated peers to take so-called 'facilitating subjects' at A level. According to official statistics for 2013/14, just 8.7 per cent of state school pupils achieved AAB or above at A level in two or more facilitating subjects – currently a school performance metric and social mobility indicator – compared to 22.6 per cent of private school students (Deputy Prime Minister's Office, 2015). Importantly, this large gap is due mainly to school type differences in achieved grades rather than to differences in subject choices. Looking at the percentages who achieved AAB or above at A level in any subjects, the figures were similarly disparate: 17.4 per cent for state school students and 42.6 per cent for private school students. Among those who achieved AAB or better at A level, in contrast, the percentages of state and private school students with at least two facilitating subjects are more similar, 77.6 per cent and 82.9 per cent respectively. So while private school students do indeed tend to study more facilitating subjects than state school students, the difference is modest at the upper end of the achievement spectrum. Among high achievers, family socio-economic background seems to matter more than school type for A-level subject choice. A longitudinal study of 3,000 students followed since age 3 has found that 'bright' students from disadvantaged homes are much less likely to take at least one facilitating A-level subject than their comparably 'bright' but socio-economically more advantaged peers, at 33 per cent compared to 58 per cent (Sammons *et al.*, 2015).

Research focusing on the specific subjects chosen by A-level students has found that private school students are more likely to take maths, biology, chemistry and physics – all facilitating subjects – than state school and college students (Vidal Rodeiro, 2007). The patterns are similar when comparing students from different socio-economic backgrounds. The children of higher managers and lower managers/professionals are significantly less likely to take at least two science subjects than the children of higher professionals, while the children of higher managers are more likely to take (non-facilitating) business-related subjects such as accounting, business and economics, and manual workers' children are significantly less likely to take a (facilitating) foreign language A level (Vidal Rodeiro, 2007). Other studies have shown that students eligible for free school meals are significantly less likely than their more privileged peers to take maths and science at A level (Gorard and See, 2009; Gorard *et al.*, 2008); that the probability of taking A-level physics is lower for pupils living in areas with low car ownership even after controlling for prior attainment (Gill and Bell, 2013); that there is a similar relationship between socio-economic status and the uptake of A-level maths (Cheng *et al.*, 1995); and that the number of facilitating subjects taken by students varies by background measured using the Income Deprivation Affecting Children Index (Gill, 2015a).

School type and socio-economic group differences in subject choice are of course likely to be mediated by differences in prior attainment. Students with high prior attainment in the General Certificate of Secondary Education (GCSE) are more likely to choose maths and science subjects at A level (Gill and Bell, 2013; Vidal Rodeiro, 2007), and conversely the lower their scores at GCSE the more likely students are to choose newer or vocational subjects (Vidal Rodeiro, 2007), which are non-facilitating and often have lower prior attainment requirements for enrolment. Some of the raw difference in uptake of these subjects by school type is therefore likely to be linked to differences in the mean attainment levels of their students (Crawford, 2014). Dilnot (2015) has developed a taxonomy of A levels, categorizing them according to the published preferences of Russell Group universities as facilitating, useful, 'less suitable' and non-counting. Using this taxonomy, she shows that for state school students the gap between the top and bottom quintiles by socio-economic status (SES) in choice of at least two facilitating subjects and in choice of two 'less suitable' subjects is explained by differential prior attainment in scores achieved at GCSE and in differential GCSE subject choices, made at age 14 (Dilnot, 2016).

School type differences in A-level subject choices have also been attributed to poorer advice and guidance in state schools, leading to state school students choosing suboptimal A-level subjects for degree courses they wished to apply for – as the Russell Group's recent report on barriers to university access implies (Russell Group, 2015b). Considerable differences in the amount of general university admissions advice and guidance given by school type were found in a study of high-achieving applicants: students from private schools received more advice than those from grammar schools, followed by state maintained schools, sixth form colleges and finally further education colleges (UCAS, 2012). An ex post survey of students also suggests that almost a quarter of all students were unhappy with the quality of information advice and guidance on A-level subject choice that had been available to them, and that non-traditional applicants were among those most dissatisfied with the quality of advice they received (Student Room, 2014).

A further possible reason for school type differences in A-level subject choices is school type differences in subject availability. Private and selective state grammar schools have been shown to offer fewer 'non-traditional' (and so non-facilitating) subjects than non-selective state schools and colleges (Vidal Rodeiro, 2007). The Sutton Trust suggests that non-selective schools and colleges introduced a disproportionate number of non-facilitating subjects in the 15 years from the mid-1990s in order to appeal to a wider range of pupils (Sutton Trust, 2011), although the balance has subsequently changed (Deputy Prime Minister's Office, 2015). Among facilitating subjects, a recent analysis of A-level provision by school type shows much higher proportions of traditional modern and classical languages offered at independent schools and selective state grammar schools than at comprehensives and academies, although similar proportions offer maths, sciences, history and geography (Gill, 2015b). A review of the literature in the context of uptake of science, technology, engineering and mathematics (STEM) subjects suggests that a range of other school-level characteristics may play a part in the decisions schools make about which subjects to offer at A level, including whether the school is girls only, boys only, or mixed sex; the vision of school leaders and managers; the selectivity of A-level entry policies; and the availability of specialist teachers (Bennett *et al.*, 2013).

A second important question to ask of the existing literature is what impact A-level subjects are known to have on university admission chances and on school type differences therein. One possibility is that having more facilitating subjects increases the chances of admission for applicants with otherwise equivalent A-level grades. This prediction is in line with *Informed Choices*, which suggests taking two facilitating subjects for students who have not yet decided on their degree course in order to keep their options open (Russell Group, 2015a), and with the official school performance metric and social mobility indicator, which also favours two facilitating subjects. Crawford (2014) takes account of the number of facilitating subjects at each grade in her study of secondary school characteristics and university participation outcomes, and concludes that having high grades in facilitating subjects matters, with each facilitating subject at grade A or above increasing the probability of high status university attendance by 1.8 percentage points controlling for other prior attainment at age 11, 16 and 18.

Other studies have explored the effects of having studied individual facilitating subjects on the chances of being offered a place at a highly selective university (Boliver, 2013; Boliver, 2016; Chowdry *et al.*, 2013) and have found positive effects for all but one facilitating subject, the exception being English literature. Importantly, these studies find that school type gaps in admission and participation rates remain after controlling for individual facilitating subjects. However, these studies are limited because they do not investigate the effect of having different combinations of facilitating subjects, or of any interaction between the number of facilitating subjects and grades.

A further limitation of the existing literature is that there has been no consideration of whether having facilitating subjects improves university admission chances because these subjects are required preparation for particular degree courses, rather than because they are esteemed by university admissions tutors as good general preparation for study at degree level. Noden *et al.* (2014) examine A-level subjects in their study of ethnic differences in university offer rates. They find that many subjects are associated with increased chances of receiving an offer for some courses but decreased chances for others, suggesting that the specific preparation mechanism is important. But rather than interacting all subjects with all degree programmes in their models, they use three categories of 'difficulty' of A level, drawing on the work of Coe *et al.* (2008). All but two of the facilitating subjects considered by Coe *et al.* are classified as above average 'difficulty', and five of them (maths, further maths, chemistry, biology and physics) are the most difficult of the 33 subjects examined. The two below average 'difficulty' are English literature and geography. Noden *et al.* (2014) find higher 'difficulty' A levels (in whatever subject) to be positively associated with chances of receiving an offer. This adds weight to the idea that facilitating subjects help applicants achieve offers not only in meeting course requirements, but also through the esteem in which they are held. This hypothesis can be tested by comparing the chances of gaining an offer to specific degree courses with highly prescriptive requirements (in our example, medicine) with those for similarly competitive courses with no course-specific requirements (in our case, law).

Admission to undergraduate medical degrees

The medical profession has for some decades been concerned about equality and diversity (BMA, 2009), particularly in terms of social background – concerns echoed in the report of the Panel on Fair Access to the Professions (Milburn, 2009) – and therefore with the admissions processes of medical schools as gatekeepers (McManus, 1998; Medical Schools Council, 2014; Patterson *et al.*, 2016). The social gradient of recent cohorts of students at medical school is a consequence not just of the pattern of applications, but also the lower odds of admission for less privileged and non-selective state school students compared with their more privileged and private or grammar school educated peers (Mathers *et al.*, 2016; Steven *et al.*, 2016). The use of A levels in selection, known to favour students from more privileged backgrounds (Schwartz, 2004), has been identified as problematic (Patterson *et al.*, 2016). Aptitude tests (UK Clinical Aptitude Test (UKCAT) or BioMedical Admissions Test) are now used by all Russell Group medical schools to inform admissions decisions, in response to concerns about the lack of discriminatory power of A levels at the high end of the attainment distribution (McManus *et al.*, 2008), and preliminary evidence suggests that these may have had a positive effect on widening participation (Tiffin *et al.*, 2012; Wright and Bradley, 2010). A-level grades remain an important tool for selection, although the role of choice of subjects beyond those required, or within those suggested as alternatives, has not been thoroughly examined, with the exception of some older evidence that having a non-science A level to add balance to applications makes no difference to chances of application success (McManus, 1998).

In response to the criticism from the Commission on Social Mobility that the medical profession was doing too little to address the dearth of medical students from lower SES backgrounds, the Medical Schools Council has published recommendations relating to selection practices, and the monitoring of participation by social background (Medical Schools Council, 2014). While it considers there is still too little evidence for a national framework for selection, it suggests that medical schools should select based on academic attainment, performance in aptitude tests and multiple mini interviews (MMIs). The majority of Russell Group medical schools now publish details of the importance of the various elements of their selection process. In the case of academic attainment, the majority (11) of the Russell Group medical schools in our data use A-level predicted grades and subjects only as a threshold in shortlisting for interview, although it should be noted that this is the practice for 2016 entry, and may have changed since the cohorts in this study made their applications. In many cases the threshold A-level scores are slightly reduced to take contextual data into account for students from non-traditional backgrounds or underperforming schools. Two universities include predicted (or actual, if available) A-level scores in ranking applicants for shortlisting for interview. For four universities the way A levels are used is unclear. Only one of the 18 universities in our data does not interview 18-year-old applicants, and uses A-level scores as part of the offer ranking. Attainment at GCSE is more widely used in ranking for selection than A-level grades are, with eight universities using achieved GCSE grades in ranking applicants for shortlisting and six using them as thresholds. (For one university the way GCSE scores are used is unclear.)

Medical schools differ considerably in their use of personal statements in admissions, with their weighting in ranking for shortlisting varying from 80 per cent of all factors taken into account to zero. Patterson *et al,* (2016) cast doubt on their predictive validity and reliability in selection, and suggest their use may bias selection decisions. There is evidence that the quality of personal statements differs by school type (Jones, 2013) that is suggestive of a mechanism through which differential offer rates by school type might arise. In the context of medical admissions, and controlling for examination performance once at medical school, coming from a private or grammar school rather than a non-selective maintained school predicted scores given to personal statements on application, particularly for women, but did not predict scores on the UKCAT (Wright and Bradley, 2010).

For the majority of medical schools, the final decision to admit is made on the basis of interviews, with a move towards MMIs, typically a series of scenario-based short interviews or 'stations', and away from the traditional interview. Criticism of interviews in the medical literature has concentrated on their weak association with future academic and clinical performance (Goho and Blackman, 2006; Wright and Bradley, 2010), their lack of both clarity about what they are trying to measure and reliability, and the better predictive validity of MMIs on performance at medical school (Patterson *et al.,* 2016), rather than any consideration of possible differential performance in interview by applicants from different social backgrounds. This aspect is little researched (Patterson *et al.,* 2016), although Wright and Bradley (2010) note that interview scores are not predicted by school type.

Admission to law degrees

The legal profession has also seen recent research into barriers to entry, with the Legal Services Board identifying the importance of early education both through its effect on ability to gain a training contract and on university attended (Sullivan, 2010). Rolfe and Anderson (2003) found some law firms had stronger links with grammar and private schools than with non-selective maintained schools, and younger partners were as likely to be educated privately in 2004 as in 1998 (Sutton Trust, 2009). Although the Legal Services Board discussed the importance of doing the right A-level subjects and going to a prestigious university in general terms, less research attention has been paid to admission to undergraduate law degrees at such universities, with research into fair access instead concentrating on the next step of successfully getting a pupillage at the bar or employment at a law firm (Ashley *et al.*, 2015; Zimdars, 2010), although these studies note the association of getting such positions with having been at a Russell Group university, and, for the bar, Oxford or Cambridge in particular (Zimdars, 2010). Given that the majority of those entering both branches of the profession have law degrees, and presumably most of those applying to do law at university aim to become lawyers, understanding the barriers to entry to law in particular at university admissions stage is clearly valuable. Like medicine, law is a competitive subject at university with high grades demanded: Russell Group universities standard offers vary from A*AA to ABB. But unlike medicine, specific subjects are not generally required for Russell Group law degrees. A third of Russell Group universities require their applicants to take the Law National Aptitude Test (LNAT), run by the LNAT consortium, which suggests that its use increases the capacity to discriminate between highly qualified applicants, but their analyses are not published. Only Oxford and Cambridge among the Russell Group institutions in our data interview applicants for law.

Research questions, data and methods of analysis

We now turn to assess three key claims: (1) that state school applicants seeking entry to medicine and law at Russell Group universities are less likely than their privately educated peers to have studied the subjects required or preferred for admission, (2) that state school applicants for these courses who have studied the required subjects tend to have poorer grades than their privately educated counterparts, and (3) that offer rates from Russell Group universities for these courses are lower for candidates from state schools because state school candidates are less likely to have 'the right grades in the right subjects'.

These questions are examined by means of a statistical analysis of anonymized individual-level applications and admissions data for the years 2010–12 supplied by the Universities and Colleges Admissions Service. We take as our unit of analysis applications for entry to Russell Group universities submitted by candidates studying for three or more A levels.[1] We focus first on applications to medicine/dentistry,[2] beginning with a basic bivariate analysis to compare the A-level subject and grade profiles of candidates from private, grammar and non-selective state schools. We then run a series of binary logistic regression models that enable us to compare the marginal probabilities of being offered a place on a medicine/dentistry course at a Russell Group university for candidates from different school backgrounds, both before and after controlling statistically for any differences in A-level subject and grade profiles.[3] We then repeat the entire analysis with a focus on applications to law.

Informed Choices advises that students wishing to study medicine or dentistry at a Russell Group university are generally required to have studied chemistry and biology at A level, and that either maths or physics may also be required or considered useful (Russell Group, 2015a: 39, 43). We therefore distinguish between candidates who have studied chemistry and biology and maths or physics at A level, those who have studied chemistry and biology but not maths or physics, and those who have *not* studied one or both of chemistry and biology. We further disaggregate these three A-level subject profiles in relation to achieved grades at A level, distinguishing between those whose best three grades range from three A stars to three B grades or below.

In relation to studying law at a Russell Group university, *Informed Choices* advises that there are no essential A-level subject requirements. It is noted that English (literature) is sometimes required and that history and other facilitating subjects may be considered useful (Russell Group, 2015a: 43). We therefore distinguish between candidates on the basis of how many facilitating subjects they have studied at A level, ranging from 3+ to 0. We further disaggregate these subject profiles in relation to achieved grades at A level, distinguishing between those whose best three grades range from three A stars to three B grades or below. Interestingly, A-level law is not listed as a useful subject when applying for admission to a law degree at a Russell Group university. We suspect that having studied law at A level may in fact put applicants at a disadvantage. We therefore also consider the impact on admissions chances of whether or not law was studied at A level and if so what grade was achieved.

An important caveat is that, in our data, only the A-level grades actually achieved by applicants are available to us. This is important because students typically apply to university in their final school year, with teachers supplying predicted grades to support applications. Predicted grades are known to vary in their accuracy (UCAS, 2013). For the A levels of one board in 2014, forecast grades were correct only 43 per cent of the time, although 88 per cent were correct within one grade. Of the inaccurate grades, around three times as many were optimistic as pessimistic, with over-optimistic predictions more common for those from comprehensive schools and Further Education colleges than for grammar and private schools (Gill and Benton, 2015). It is possible that part of the difference in offer rates between students with equivalent achieved grades by school type is a result of institutions 'discounting' the predicted grades of students from institutions known to be less accurate with their predictions, but where those students do actually achieve their predictions. Without predicted grades in the dataset (which UCAS does not provide), it is not possible to test this hypothesis.

Results

Table 4.1 shows that around two-thirds of applications to medicine/dentistry courses at Russell Group were submitted by candidates studying for A levels in chemistry and biology (both required subjects) and in maths and/or physics (both considered useful subjects). This was the case regardless of whether the applications came from candidates attending private (69.4 per cent), grammar (72.1 per cent) or non-selective state schools (67.4 per cent). Across all school types, around a quarter of applications were submitted by candidates studying for A levels in chemistry and biology but not also maths and/or physics. Only a small minority of applications (about 5 per cent) were submitted by candidates who did not have one or both of the required A-level subjects, chemistry and biology, again with no substantial difference across school types. Interestingly, A-level grade profiles are fairly similar across school types, although candidates from non-selective state schools are slightly less likely to achieve the highest sets of grades.

Table 4.1: Percentages of applications to courses in medicine/dentistry at Russell Group universities with specified A-level subject and grade profiles, by school type (column percentages)

	Private	Selective state grammar	Non-selective state school
A-level physics & biology, plus maths or physics	69.4	72.1	67.4
A*, A*, A*	9.0	10.1	5.0
A*, A*, A	10.0	10.2	5.8
A*, A, A	11.6	15.7	10.2
A, A, A	17.1	16.0	14.3
A*/A, A*/A, B or below	10.6	11.2	11.6
A*/A, B or below, B or below	5.5	5.2	9.1
B or below, B or below, B or below	5.6	3.7	11.4
A-level physics & biology, but not maths/physics	25.9	24.2	26.9
A*, A*, A*	1.8	1.3	0.6
A*, A*, A	1.8	2.0	2.2
A*, A, A	5.3	3.6	4.0
A, A, A	6.8	6.8	5.2
A*/A, A*/A, B or below	4.5	5.3	5.5
A*/A, B or below, B or below	3.2	3.5	4.4
B or below, B or below, B or below	2.3	1.8	4.8
A levels do not include one or both of physics & biology	4.7	3.5	5.7
A*, A*, A*	0.8	0.2	0.1
A*, A*, A	0.1	0.2	0.1
A*, A, A	1.1	0.7	1.0
A, A, A	1.0	0.7	0.9
A*/A, A*/A, B or below	1.7	1.6	3.6
A*/A, B or below, B or below	0.0	0.0	0.0
B or below, B or below, B or below	0.0	0.0	0.0
N	1,684	1,650	3,447

Note: Based on applications submitted via UCAS in 2010–12 by applicants who achieved 3+ A levels.

Table 4.2 reports the results of a binary logistic regression analysis of the probability that an application to study medicine or dentistry at a Russell Group university is met with an offer of a place. Model 1 shows the marginal probability of being offered a place by school type for students with mean other characteristics (A-level profile, year of application and specific institution applied to). The probability of being offered a place is ten percentage points lower for applicants from non-selective state schools and four percentage points lower for applicants from grammar schools compared to applicants from private schools (offer rates of 12 per cent, 18 per cent and 22 per cent, respectively). The difference between the private school rate and the grammar and non-selective state school rates are significant at 5 per cent confidence levels.

Model 2 shows the odds of being offered a place for candidates with different A-level subject and grade profiles. Here it can be seen that candidates with three A* grades including both chemistry and biology have the highest chances of admissions success, regardless of whether they also have maths and/or physics A level (50 per cent offer rate) or not (48 per cent offer rate). The importance of having both chemistry and biology is evident from the fact that the offer rate is considerably lower for those who lack one or both of these A-level subjects even if they have achieved three A* grades in other subjects (13 per cent). Grades as well as subjects are clearly important: among those with chemistry and biology at A level, the offer rate falls considerably as grades decline from A*A*A (50 per cent) to A*A*A (37 per cent) to A*AA (25 per cent) and so on.

Model 3 includes school type and candidates' A-level profiles in the same model. Comparing Model 1 and Model 3, it is clear that school type differences in offer rates are reduced after taking A-level profiles into account, reflecting the fact that state school applicants are less likely to achieve the top grades than their privately educated counterparts. However, offer rates continue to be five percentage points lower for non-selective state school applicants and four percentage points lower for grammar school applicants compared to applicants from private schools with the same A-level profiles (offer rates of 14 per cent, 15 per cent and 19 per cent, respectively).

Table 4.2: Binary logistic regression models predicting the marginal probabilities of being offered a place on a medicine/dentistry degree programme at a Russell Group university (N=6,781)

	Model 1	Model 2	Model 3
School type			
Private school (reference category)	0.22		0.19
Selective state grammar school	0.18*		0.15*
Non-selective state school	0.12*		0.14*
A-level profile			
Chemistry & biology, plus maths or physics: A*, A*, A* (reference category)		0.50	0.50
Chemistry & biology, plus maths or physics: A*, A*, A		0.37*	0.37*
Chemistry & biology, plus maths or physics: A*, A, A		0.25*	0.25*
Chemistry & biology, plus maths or physics: A, A, A		0.17*	0.17*
Chemistry & biology, plus maths or physics: A*/A, A*/A, B or below		0.14*	0.14*
Chemistry & biology, plus maths or physics: A*/A, B or below, B or below		0.05*	0.06*
Chemistry & biology, plus maths or physics: 3 x B or below		0.03*	0.03*
Chemistry & biology, not maths or physics: A*, A*, A*		0.48	0.46
Chemistry & biology, not maths or physics: A*, A*, A		0.33*	0.34*
Chemistry & biology, not maths or physics: A*, A, A		0.28*	0.28*
Chemistry & biology, not maths or physics: A, A, A		0.19*	0.19*
Chemistry & biology, not maths or physics: A*/A, A*/A, B or below		0.10*	0.10*
Chemistry & biology, not maths or physics: A*/A, B or below, B or below		0.05*	0.05*
Chemistry & biology, not maths or physics: 3 x B or below		0.03*	0.03*
Not chemistry and/or biology: A*, A*, A*		0.13*	0.11*
Not chemistry and/or biology: A*, A*, A		0.57	0.43
Not chemistry and/or biology: A*, A, A		0.26*	0.26*

Table 4.2 continued

	Model 1	Model 2	Model 3
Not chemistry and/or biology: A, A, A		0.32[†]	0.32[†]
Not chemistry and/or biology: A*/A, A*/A, B or below		0.02*	0.02*
Chi-square (df)	329 (21)	565 (37)	571 (39)
Log likelihood	–3,401	–3,175	–3,167

Note: Analysis is restricted to applications submitted via UCAS in 2010–12 by applicants who achieved 3+ A levels. All models include controls for year of application and specific institution applied to. Statistically significant differences relative to the reference category are indicated by * (p < 0.05) and [†] (p < 0.10).

Table 4.3 shows that around two-thirds of private school and grammar school applicants to law at Russell Group universities have studied two or three facilitating subjects at A level, and only a very small minority have studied only non-facilitating subjects. Private and grammar school applicants are similar with respect to subject choice and with respect to grades achieved, although grammar school applicants are slightly less likely to have achieved the top grades. In contrast, less than half of all non-selective state school applicants studied two or three facilitating A-level subjects, a third studied just one facilitating subject, and more than a fifth studied only non-facilitating subjects. Moreover, non-selective state school applicants are notably less likely than private and grammar school applicants to have achieved top grades. State school applicants are also much more likely to have studied law at A level (44.6 per cent) than applicants from private (2.0 per cent) and grammar (6.2 per cent) schools.

Table 4.3: Percentages of applications to courses in law at Russell Group universities with specified A-level subject and grade profiles, by school type (column percentages)

	Private school	Selective state grammar school	Non-selective state school
Three facilitating subjects	33.1	33.9	14.0
A*, A*, A*	3.2	2.3	0.4
A*, A*, A	7.1	2.9	1.8
A*, A, A	6.8	5.5	1.5
A, A, A	2.9	7.8	2.0
A*/A, A*/A, B or below	8.1	8.4	3.6
A*/A, B or below, B or below	2.6	3.6	2.1
B or below, B or below, B or below	2.6	2.4	2.6

	Private school	Selective state grammar school	Non-selective state school
Two facilitating subjects	46.0	42.4	29.0
A*, A*, A*	1.7	2.3	0.5
A*, A*, A	5.3	5.2	2.4
A*, A, A	11.4	5.0	4.0
A, A, A	8.2	7.9	3.3
A*/A, A*/A, B or below	11.4	13.4	9.0
A*/A, B or below, B or below	5.3	5.2	4.6
B or below, B or below, B or below	2.7	3.5	5.1
One facilitating subject	16.7	16.6	34.7
A*, A*, A*	0.2	0.0	0.5
A*, A*, A	0.5	0.6	3.1
A*, A, A	1.4	0.5	0.9
A, A, A	3.8	3.5	4.4
A*/A, A*/A, B or below	4.4	5.0	8.9
A*/A, B or below, B or below	4.1	3.2	8.5
B or below, B or below, B or below	2.4	3.8	8.5
No facilitating subjects	4.0	8.2	22.2
A*, A*, A*	0.0	0.6	0.6
A*, A*, A	0.0	1.1	1.0
A*, A, A	1.8	1.1	2.0
A, A, A	0.0	1.5	2.5
A*/A, A*/A, B or below	0.3	2.1	4.4
A*/A, B or below, B or below	0.8	0.6	4.8
B or below, B or below, B or below	1.1	1.2	7.0
Law A level	2.0	6.2	44.6
A*	0.0	2.4	9.5
A	0.6	2.1	19.2
B or below	1.4	1.7	15.8
N/A	98.0	93.8	55.4
N	658	658	2,613

Note: Based on applications submitted via UCAS in 2010–12 by applicants who achieved 3+ A levels.

Model 1 of table 4.4 shows that, while applicants from grammar schools are just as likely as private school applicants to be offered places on law courses at Russell Group universities (offer rates of 86 per cent and 87 per cent, respectively), applicants from non-selective state schools are much less likely to be offered places (a statistically significantly different offer rate of 55 per cent).

Model 2 shows that, among applicants with three facilitating subjects at A level, grades of AAA or better virtually guarantee an offer of a place on a law programme at a Russell Group university (offer rates of 98–9 per cent). Applicants with one or two facilitating subjects are also virtually guaranteed to be offered a place provided they have the highest possible grades of A*A*A* (offer rates of 97–9 per cent). Offer rates are notably lower for those whose three facilitating subjects include at least one B grade (19–90 per cent), and for those with one or two facilitating subjects at anything less than A*A*A* (10–96 per cent). Applicants with no facilitating subjects at A level have the lowest offer rates at all grade levels (6–92 per cent).

Model 3 includes both school type and A-level profile as predictors of admissions chances. The difference in offer rates for those from grammar as compared to private schools remains non-statistically significant (offer rates 78 per cent compared to 80 per cent). The difference in offer rates for those from non-selective state schools as compared to private schools is substantially reduced, but remains large and statistically significant at ten percentage points.

Finally, Model 4 adds law A level to the model. This shows that holding an A level in law yields no advantage whatsoever with respect to admissions chances, with the probability of admission being essentially the same for those without law A level as for those with an A* in that subject (offer rates of 76 per cent and 77 per cent, respectively). In this final model, the difference in offer rates for those from non-selective state schools as compared to private schools reduces slightly to seven percentage points and is now statistically significant at only the 0.10 level (offer rates of 71 per cent and 78 per cent, respectively). Taken together, these findings indicate that a significant proportion of law degree applicants from non-selective state schools may be wasting an A level by studying A-level law from the point of view of Russell Group law degree admission, and those achieving lower than a B in law A level are actually at a disadvantage, compared with similar students without law at all (62 per cent offer rate compared with 76 per cent)

Table 4.4: Binary logistic regression models predicting the marginal probabilities of being offered a place on a law degree programme at a Russell Group university (N=3,929)

	Model 1	Model 2	Model 3	Model 4
School type				
Private school (reference category)	0.87		0.80	0.78
Selective state grammar school	0.86		0.78	0.77
Non-selective state school	0.55*		0.70*	0.71[†]
A-level profile				
Three facilitating subjects: A*A*A*		0.99	0.99	0.99
Three facilitating subjects: A*, A*, A		0.99	0.99	0.99
Three facilitating subjects: A*, A, A		0.98	0.98	0.97
Three facilitating subjects: A, A, A		0.98	0.98	0.98
Three facilitating subjects: A*/A, A*/A, B or below		0,90*	0.89*	0.88*
Three facilitating subjects: A*/A, B or below, B or below		0.73*	0.72*	0.69*
Three facilitating subjects: B or below, B or below, B or below		0.19*	0.20*	0.19*
Two facilitating subjects: A*, A*, A*		0.99	0.99	0.99
Two facilitating subjects: A*, A*, A		0.96*	0.96[†]	0.95[†]
Two facilitating subjects: A*, A, A		0.94*	0.94*	0.93*
Two facilitating subjects: A, A, A		0.91*	0.90*	0.90*
Two facilitating subjects: A*/A, A*/A, B or below		0.82*	0.82*	0.81*
Two facilitating subjects: A*/A, B or below, B or below		0.70*	0.69*	0.68*
Two facilitating subjects: B or below, B or below, B or below		0.14*	0.14*	0.14*
One facilitating subject: A*, A*, A*		0.97	0.97	0.97
One facilitating subject: A*, A*, A		0.89*	0.90*	0.89*
One facilitating subject: A*, A, A		0.96[†]	0.96	0.95
One facilitating subject: A, A, A		0.85*	0.86*	0.86*
One facilitating subject: A*/A, A/A, B or below		0.71*	0.72*	0.73*
One facilitating subject: A*/A, B or below, B or below		0.36*	0.37*	0.39*
One facilitating subject: B or below, B or below, B or below		0.10*	0.11*	0.11*

Table 4.4 continued

	Model 1	Model 2	Model 3	Model 4
No facilitating subjects: A*, A*, A*		0.92†	0.92†	0.90†
No facilitating subjects: A*, A*, A		0.83*	0.84*	0.85*
No facilitating subjects: A*, A, A		0.83*	0.83*	0.83*
No facilitating subjects: A, A, A		0.60*	0.63*	0.67*
No facilitating subjects: A*/A, A*/A, B or below		0.64*	0.66*	0.71*
No facilitating subjects: A*/A, B or below, B or below		0.28*	0.30*	0.35*
No facilitating subjects: B or below, B or below, B or below		0.06*	0.07*	0.09*
Law A level				
Law A-level: A* (reference category)				0.77
Law A level: A				0.66
Law A level: B or below				0.62*
No law A level				0.76
Chi-square (df)	339 (22)	410(47)	413(49)	414(52)
Log likelihood	−1,891	−1,582	−1,578	−1,572

Note: Analysis is restricted to applications submitted via UCAS in 2010–12 by applicants who achieved 3+ A levels. All models include controls for year of application and specific institution applied to. Statistically significant differences relative to the reference category are indicated by * ($p < 0.05$) and † ($p < 0.10$).

Discussion and conclusion

We first address the question of whether part of the admissions gap by school background is accounted for by students applying for courses without the appropriate subjects at A level. We find little evidence for this for those applying for medicine and dentistry. Very similar proportions of those applying from private, grammar and non-selective state schools have at least chemistry and biology A levels, which would fulfil the A-level criteria of all of the Russell Group medical schools. This evidence for medicine and dentistry cannot be generalized to other subjects with prescriptive course requirements: arguably those applying for medicine are likely to be highly aware of subject requirements as part of the long list of elements in their selection. Compared with many other subjects, applying for medicine and dentistry requires considerable forward planning (for example, because of the work experience requirement and the early UCAS deadline). A-level students applying for courses where forward planning might be thought less important but with essential subject requirements may realize late that their

A-level subject choices are inappropriate, but might think it worth applying anyway. This may conceivably vary by school type (perhaps because of differentials in the quality of information, advice and guidance on A-level subject choice), but this question remains to be answered for courses with prescriptive A levels outside medicine and dentistry.

The patterns in application success for medicine and dentistry by A-level subject and grade observed are interesting. Although for current applicants, the standard offer at Russell Group universities varies from AAA to A*A*A* (and if anything has increased since the cohorts in these data), dropping even one A* for the cohorts in this data significantly reduces the chances of admission. It seems that although standard offers are generally AAA and above, in practice those shortlisted for interview and progressing through the selection process are likely to exceed the minimum offer. The highest grades at A level are likely to be highly correlated with other measures of attainment (aptitude tests and GCSEs), which, as discussed earlier, are often scored and used in shortlisting students for interview. Having a third science subject (maths or physics) in addition to biology and chemistry slightly increases the chances of admission if one A* grade is dropped, but overall the choice of a third A-level subject seems unimportant, in contrast with the advice that a third science is useful in *Informed Choices*. (This is with the exception of Cambridge, which publishes favourable admission rates for those with at least three rather than only two science A-levels.)

Although entry to read law at Russell Group universities is considered very competitive, offer rates are considerably higher than for medicine/ dentistry. Despite the fact that in contrast with medicine, law degrees require no essential subjects, facilitating A levels do indeed seem to be facilitating of entry, although their importance varies somewhat with the grade pattern. The chances of successful application drop off generally once any A level is held at grade B, but less so for students with more facilitating subjects. The patterns suggest that holding facilitating subjects can compensate for lower grades. It could be that admissions tutors in law consider the skills acquired in the study of subjects such as history and English mean that someone with a lower grade may be a more successful undergraduate than someone with other subjects that they believe do not confer such skills. But the majority of facilitating subjects taken by English school students are in maths and science, which suggests there might be other reasons for this favourable view. Previous evidence on subject difficulty, which has shown that most facilitating subjects are more difficult than most other subjects, may plausibly account for this compensation.

But what of A levels whose subject content might be considered particularly useful for university study? Russell Group law faculties either remain silent on the desirability or otherwise of having law A level, or describe themselves as neutral on admissions web pages. For students achieving at least an A, law A level is no more or less helpful than the same grade in any other subject. For those with B or below, law A level is associated with considerably lower offer rates than for a similar student without law (62 per cent rather than 76 per cent). These findings may explain some of the difference in the composition of the law student body between Russell Group and other universities as law is disproportionately offered by applicants from non-selective state schools and colleges (Dilnot, 2015). In the study of subject difficulty by Coe *et al.* (2008), law is ranked immediately below the two 'easiest' facilitating subjects, English literature and geography, and some way below languages and STEM subjects. It ranks just below average subject difficulty for all subjects, and is similar to or more difficult than most non-facilitating subjects, which suggests its difficulty is not the reason applications with it meet with less success. Perhaps a clue to the apparent unattractiveness of A-level law at lower grades can be found in research commissioned by the Office of Qualifications and Examinations Regulation (Ofqual) in preparation for the reform of A levels. Some tutors interviewed at highly selective universities felt subjects like law, psychology and computer science were undesirable as preparation for the related degree course as they resulted in students with the 'wrong type of understanding' and 'complacency' (Higton *et al.*, 2012: 38). Given the premium in offer rates relating to having facilitating A-level subjects, applicants to Russell Group law faculties might do well to take an extra facilitating subject, rather than law.

Finally, we consider the role of school type in being offered a place to read a competitive, vocational subject at a Russell Group university. Given that only A-level subjects, grades achieved and school type are in the model, the school type coefficients will effectively capture all the unobserved characteristics of students that vary on average by school type and are related to chances of being made an offer. For medicine and dentistry, A levels provide only one piece of evidence used by universities in making their decisions from a wide variety of assessments of both cognitive and non-cognitive skills. These skills are measured and scored by universities through attainment tests, GCSE scores, predicted (rather than achieved) A-level grades and subjects, personal statements, teacher references and interviews, but only data on achieved A levels and subjects are made available by UCAS. There is evidence that at least some of these unobserved characteristics vary by school type: research on admission to highly selective universities outside medicine and dentistry suggests that once a rich set of attainment measures at GCSE are controlled for, the difference in participation between independent and grammar schools and non-selective local authority controlled schools disappears (Crawford, 2014). We know that much higher proportions of private school students gain at least five A*–C grades than non-selective local authority controlled school students (91 per cent rather than 39 per cent) (Crawford, 2014), so given the importance of GCSEs in scoring applications for medicine and dentistry, it would not be surprising if this omitted variable accounted for some of the difference by school type.

We know, too, that there is some differential in the accuracy of A-level grade prediction by school type, but it seems unlikely to be an important factor in explaining the gap given the relative unimportance of grades in the selection process, other than as a threshold. It is difficult to see how universities might screen out more students from non-selective state schools on this basis, given that if anything their predicted grades tend to be more optimistic, and should result in more students from state schools being shortlisted for interview.

It is more plausible to think that the quality of personal statements and teacher references may be a way in which private school students are at a particular advantage. Medical and dental schools are looking for particular non-cognitive skills. There is considerable information on their websites about these skills and the evidence that applicants might provide in their personal statements and teacher references to demonstrate them. It is time-consuming to check and see what is important for a particular course at a particular university. Private schools are likely to have considerably more resources to allocate to this. One of the ways students demonstrate non-cognitive skills in their personal statements is through the discussion of their work experience, and presumably the longer and more interesting the work experience, the better the personal statement can be. Better work experience opportunities may be available to more privileged students with wider social networks.

For law, A-level attainment is a more important in the selection of students by Russell Group departments than it is for medicine and dentistry. Once patterns of A-level attainment are taken into account in our models, the gap in offer rates between private school and non-selective state school pupils is barely significant at conventional levels. Previous work on university admission generally suggests that differentials in GCSE performance by school type (even if predicted A levels are the same) might account for the remaining gap. The use of LNAT by a minority of Russell Group universities in these data may already be somewhat reducing the gap, but without access to the data it is not possible to judge.

Our analysis shows that having more facilitating subjects at higher grades is indeed associated with having a higher chance of admission to Russell Group universities to study medicine/dentistry and law, as the Russell Group argues, but that the mean differences in number and grades of facilitating subjects do not account for the admissions gap that is still observed between those applying for medicine and dentistry from private and both selective and non-selective state schools, nor fully for the smaller gap for law applicants from private and non-selective state schools. We have argued that this is not surprising for medicine and dentistry, given the large number of other pieces of evidence that are taken into account in evaluating applicants, and because for all applicants it is not possible to control for the achieved measures of prior attainment seen by university admission officers. We look forward to the provision of linkable UCAS data from 2017 onwards that will not only allow an analysis of applications and acceptances but will also allow measures of prior attainment, in particular GCSE scores, to be taken into account in assessing the fairness of admissions.

In the meantime, the findings presented in this chapter raise a number of points for consideration by government, by universities admissions policymakers and outreach coordinators, and by schools and colleges helping students prepare to apply to university. First, government policymakers should consider whether it is appropriate and fair to use of the percentage of students obtaining AAB or above at A level in two or more 'facilitating subjects' as a key performance indicator for schools and colleges. While it is the case that studying 'facilitating subjects' at A level leaves more degree course options open to students who are undecided about their disciplinary specialism at university, and while studying 'facilitating subjects' does appear to boost applicants' chances of university admission all other things being equal, 'facilitating subjects' cannot be uncritically championed as the 'best' subjects for all to pursue. Schools and colleges should be encouraged to signpost students to A-level subjects that they enjoy, are good at, and are likely to need (formally or informally) for the subjects they are considering studying at degree level. In many individual instances, the best three A-level subject choices for a given student may include only one 'facilitating subject' and possibly none at all. Moreover, in some schools and colleges, particularly those serving deprived communities, certain 'facilitating subjects' are simply not available as A-level options. As such, a more appropriate and fairer key performance indicator might be the percentage of students studying subjects relevant to their intended degree subject area, whether these are 'facilitating subjects' or not. An alternative, halfway solution might be to change the key performance indicator from two 'facilitating subjects' to just one.

Related to this, although universities now typically declare on their websites and in prospectuses that A-level subjects are required or preferred for admission to particular degree courses, universities could do more to publicize the importance of A-level subject prerequisites, including through their outreach work with schools and colleges. Universities also need to do more to justify why certain A-level subjects are required or preferred for certain degree courses, noting that current reforms to all A levels are motivated, at least in part, by the aim that A-level subject content should meet the needs of students planning progression to a UK university 'particularly (but not only) in the same subject area' (Ofqual, 2014: 8). For 'preferred' A-level subjects, in particular, universities need to provide a clear rationale for their preferred status, based on empirical evidence confirming any claims made as to, for example, the better preparation such A levels provide for the degree course concerned. If an A level in a particular subject area, such as law, is not considered by universities to be good degree preparation in that subject, it should be made very clear on admissions pages. When making decisions about which A-level subjects are preferred and why, universities should also recognize that some A-level subjects are less readily available to students from disadvantaged backgrounds, and should consider widening the range of preferred subjects accordingly.

Finally, schools and colleges need to do more early on to ensure that their students choose A-level subjects that best serve their personal higher education ambitions. This is likely to be more challenging for stand-alone sixth form colleges and further education colleges than for sixth forms attached to secondary schools, where there is greater opportunity during the final year of GCSE study to offer detailed individual advice and guidance to students about the fit between A-level subject options and longer-term educational and career goals. The National Careers Service launched in 2012, and what remains of the Connexions advice and guidance service for young people, could help bridge this gap for young people attending schools without sixth form provision. In any case, schools, colleges, universities and advice and guidance services offered through the public and third sectors need to work together to ensure that prospective university students get the information and support they need. This is standard practice in independent schools, which are typically staffed by alumni of Russell Group universities.

Notes

[1] Our data include the 20 institutions that were members of the Russell Group during the admissions cycles 2010–12: Birmingham, Bristol, Cambridge, Cardiff, Edinburgh, Glasgow, Imperial, King's, Leeds, Liverpool, London School of Economics, Manchester, Newcastle, Nottingham, Oxford, Queen's Belfast, Sheffield, Southampton, University College London, and Warwick. Four more members joined in mid-2012: Durham, Exeter, Queen Mary, and York.

[2] In this study, applications to medicine and dentistry jointly are considered, because of the level of aggregation of data provided by UCAS. The admissions processes and required A-level subjects are very similar for the 11 Russell Group dental schools and for the medical schools in the data.

[3] We use the xtlogit command in Stata to take into account the fact that individual applicants make multiple applications, and the margins command to calculate marginal predicted probabilities of being offered a university place. All models control for year of application and particular institution applied to.

References

Ashley, L., Duberley, J., Sommerlad, H. and Scholarios, D. (2015) *A Qualitative Evaluation of Non-Educational Barriers to the Elite Professions*. London: Social Mobility and Child Poverty Commission.

Bar Standards Board (2015) *BPTC Key Statistics 2011–2014: An analysis of students over three academic years*. London: Bar Standards Board.

Bennett, J., Braund, M. and Sharpe, R. (2013) *Student Attitudes, Engagement and Participation in STEM Subjects*. London: Royal Society and Department of Education, University of York.

BIS (Department for Business, Innovation and Skills) (2015) *Widening Participation in Higher Education*. London: Department for Business, Innovation and Skills.

BMA (British Medical Association) (2009) *Equality and Diversity in UK Medical Schools*. London: British Medical Association.

Boliver, V. (2013) 'How fair is access to more prestigious UK universities?'. *British Journal of Sociology*, 64 (2), 344–64.

Boliver, V. (2016) 'Exploring ethnic inequalities in admission to Russell Group universities'. *Sociology*, 50 (2), 247–66.

Britton, J., Dearden, L., Shephard, N. and Vignoles, A. (2016) *How English Domiciled Graduate Earnings Vary with Gender, Institution Attended, Subject and Socio-Economic Background* (IFS Working Paper W16/06). London: Institute for Fiscal Studies.

Cheng, Y., Payne, J. and Witherspoon, S. (1995) *Science and Mathematics in Full-Time Education after 16*. London: Department for Education and Employment.

Chevalier, A. and Conlon, G. (2003) *Does It Pay To Attend a Prestigious University?* London: Centre for the Economics of Education.

Chowdry, H., Crawford, C., Dearden, L., Goodman, A. and Vignoles, A. (2013) 'Widening participation in higher education: Analysis using linked administrative data'. *Journal of the Royal Statistical Society: Series A (Statistics in Society)*, 176 (2), 431–57.

Coe, R., Searle, J., Barmby, P., Jones, K. and Higgins, S. (2008) *Relative Difficulty of Examinations in Different Subjects*. Durham: Centre for Evaluation and Monitoring.

Crawford, C. (2014) *The Link between Secondary School Characteristics and University Participation and Outcomes* (CAYT Research Report). London: Department for Education.

Deputy Prime Minister's Office (2015) 'Social mobility indicators'. Online. www. gov.uk/government/publications/social-mobility-indicators/social-mobility-indicators (accessed 10 December 2017).

DfE (Department for Education) (2016) 'Find and compare schools in England'. Online. www.compare-school-performance.service.gov.uk (accessed 20 July 2016).

DfES (Department for Education and Skills) (2003) *The Future of Higher Education*. Norwich: The Stationery Office.

Dilnot, C. (2015) *A Taxonomy of A-Level Subjects According to the Expressed Preferences of Russell Group Universities: Who does what?* (DoQSS Working Paper 15-12). London: UCL Institute of Education. Online. http://repec.ioe. ac.uk/REPEc/pdf/qsswp1512.pdf (accessed 14 January 2016).

Dilnot, C. (2016) 'How does the choice of A-level subjects vary with students' socio-economic status in English state schools?'. *British Educational Research Journal*, 42 (6), 1081–106.

Gill, T. (2015a) *Uptake of GCE A Level Subjects 2014* (Statistics Report 82). Cambridge: Cambridge Assessment.

Gill, T. (2015b) *Provision of GCE A Level Subjects 2014* (Statistics Report 83). Cambridge: Cambridge Assessment.

Gill, T. and Bell, J.F. (2013) 'What factors determine the uptake of A-level physics?'. *International Journal of Science Education*, 35 (5), 753–72.

Gill, T. and Benton, T. (2015) *The Accuracy of Forecast Grades for OCR A Levels in June 2014* (Statistics Report 90). Cambridge: Cambridge Assessment.

Goho, J. and Blackman, A. (2006) 'The effectiveness of academic admission interviews: An exploratory meta-analysis'. *Medical Teacher*, 28 (4), 335–40.

Gorard, S. and See, B.H. (2009) 'The impact of socio-economic status on participation and attainment in science'. *Studies in Science Education*, 45 (1), 93–129.

Gorard, S., See, B.H. and Smith, E. (2008) 'The impact of SES on participation and attainment in science: An analysis of available data'. In Royal Society *Exploring the Relationship between Socioeconomic Status and Participation and Attainment in Science Education* (SES and Science Education Report). London: Royal Society, 10–21.

HESA (Higher Education Statistics Agency) (2015) 'Table T1b: Participation of under-represented groups in higher education: UK domiciled young full-time undergraduate entrants 2013/14'. Online. www.hesa.ac.uk/data-and-analysis/ performance-indicators/releases/2013-14-widening-participation (accessed 10 December 2017).

Higton, J., Noble, J., Pope, S., Boal, N., Ginnis, S., Donaldson, R. and Greevy, H. (2012) *Fit for Purpose? The view of the higher education sector, teachers and employers on the suitability of A levels*. Coventry: Office of Qualifications and Examinations Regulation.

Hussain, I., McNally, S. and Telhaj, S. (2009) *University Quality and Graduate Wages in the UK* (CEE Discussion Paper 99). London: Centre for the Economics of Education. Online. http://eprints.lse.ac.uk/25486/1/University_quality_and_graduate_wages_in_the_UK.pdf (accessed 10 December 2017).

Jones, S. (2013) '"Ensure that you stand out from the crowd": A corpus-based analysis of personal statements according to applicants' school type'. *Comparative Education Review*, 57 (3), 397–423.

Law Society (2015) *Trends in the Solicitors' Profession: Annual statistics report 2014*. London: Law Society.

Machin, D. (2015) *Data and Public Policy: Trying to make social progress blindfolded*. London: Social Mobility and Child Poverty Commission.

Macmillan, L. (2009) 'Social mobility and the professions'. Report for submission to the Panel on Fair Access to the Professions. Centre for Market and Public Organisation, University of Bristol.

Macmillan, L., Tyler, C. and Vignoles, A. (2015) 'Who gets the top jobs? The role of family background and networks in recent graduates' access to high-status professions'. *Journal of Social Policy*, 44 (3), 487–515.

Mathers, J., Sitch, A. and Parry, J. (2016) 'Population-based longitudinal analyses of offer likelihood in UK medical schools: 1996–2012'. *Medical Education*, 50 (6), 612–23.

McManus, I.C. (1998) 'Factors affecting likelihood of applicants being offered a place in medical schools in the United Kingdom in 1996 and 1997: Retrospective study'. *BMJ*, 317 (7166), 1111–16.

McManus, C., Woolf, K. and Dacre, J.E. (2008) 'Even one star at A level could be "too little, too late" for medical student selection'. *BMC Medical Education*, 8, Article 16, 1–4.

Medical Schools Council (2014) *Selecting for Excellence: Final report*. London: Medical Schools Council.

Milburn, A. (2009) *Unleashing Aspiration: The final report of the Panel on Fair Access to the Professions*. London: Cabinet Office.

Milburn, A. (2012) *Fair Access to Professional Careers: A progress report by the Independent Reviewer on Social Mobility and Child Poverty*. London: Cabinet Office.

Noden, P., Shiner, M. and Modood, T. (2014) 'University offer rates for candidates from different ethnic categories'. *Oxford Review of Education*, 40 (3), 349–69.

Ofqual (Office of Qualifications and Examinations Regulation) (2014) *An Update on the Reforms Being Made to AS Qualifications and A Levels*. Coventry: Office of Qualifications and Examinations Regulation.

Patterson, F., Knight, A., Dowell, J., Nicholson, S., Cousans, F. and Cleland, J. (2016) 'How effective are selection methods in medical education? A systematic review'. *Medical Education*, 50 (1), 36–60.

Rolfe, H. and Anderson, T. (2003) 'A firm choice: Law firms' preferences in the recruitment of trainee solicitors'. *International Journal of the Legal Profession*, 10 (3), 315–34.

Russell Group (2015a) *Informed Choices: A Russell Group guide to making decisions about post-16 education: 2015/16*. 4th ed. London: Russell Group.

Russell Group (2015b) *Opening Doors: Understanding and overcoming the barriers to university access.* London: Russell Group.

Sammons, P., Toth, K. and Sylva, K. (2015) *Subject to Background: What promotes better achievement for bright but disadvantaged students?* London: Sutton Trust.

Schwartz, S. (2004) *Fair Admissions to Higher Education: Recommendations for good practice.* Nottingham: Department for Education and Skills.

Steven, K., Dowell, J., Jackson, C. and Guthrie, B. (2016) 'Fair access to medicine? Retrospective analysis of UK medical schools application data 2009–2012 using three measures of socioeconomic status'. *BMC Medical Education*, 16, Article 11, 1–10.

The Student Room (2014) *Options 2014.* Brighton: The Student Room Group. Online. www.thestudentroom.co.uk/images/feature/options2014.pdf (accessed 10 December 2017).

Sullivan, R. (2010) *Barriers to the Legal Profession.* London: Legal Services Board.

Sutton Trust (2009) *The Educational Backgrounds of Leading Lawyers, Journalists, Vice Chancellors, Politicians, Medics and Chief Executives: The Sutton Trust submission to the Milburn Commission on access to the professions.* London: Sutton Trust.

Sutton Trust (2011) *Degrees of Success: University chances by individual school.* London: Sutton Trust.

Sutton Trust and BIS (Department for Business, Innovation and Skills) (2009) *Applications, Offers and Admissions to Research Led Universities* (BIS Research Paper 5). London: Department for Business, Innovation and Skills.

Tiffin, P.A., Dowell, J.S. and McLachlan, J.C. (2012) 'Widening access to UK medical education for under-represented socioeconomic groups: Modelling the impact of the UKCAT in the 2009 cohort'. *BMJ*, 344, Article e1805, 1–27.

UCAS (Universities and Colleges Admissions Service) (2012) *Tracking the Decision-Making of High Achieving Higher Education Applicants* (BIS Research Paper 86). London: Department for Business, Innovation and Skills.

UCAS (Universities and Colleges Admissions Service) (2013) *Investigating the Accuracy of Predicted A Level Grades as Part of the 2010 UCAS Admission Process* (BIS Research Paper 120). London: Department for Business, Innovation and Skills.

Vidal Rodeiro, C.L. (2007) *A Level Subject Choice in England: Patterns of uptake and factors affecting subject preferences.* Cambridge: Cambridge Assessment.

Walker, I. and Zhu, Y. (2011) 'Differences by degree: Evidence of the net financial rates of return to undergraduate study for England and Wales'. *Economics of Education Review*, 30 (6), 1177–86.

Ward, H. (2015) 'Black and ethnic minority students miss out on university, finds report'. *Times Education Supplement*, 2 February. Online. www.tes.com/news/school-news/breaking-news/black-and-ethnic-minority-students-miss-out-university-finds-report (accessed 2 February 2015).

Wright, S.R. and Bradley, P.M. (2010) 'Has the UK Clinical Aptitude Test improved medical student selection?'. *Medical Education*, 44 (11), 1069–76.

Zimdars, A. (2010) 'The profile of pupil barristers at the Bar of England and Wales 2004–2008'. *International Journal of the Legal Profession*, 17 (2), 117–34.

Chapter 5

Student mothers in higher education: Tackling widening participation and child poverty

Claire Callender

Introduction

The Conservative government, like others since the late 1980s, has a stated desire to widen participation in higher education (HE). This has led to a burgeoning literature on widening HE access and participation, examining the experiences of 'non-traditional' undergraduate students and policies aimed at tackling their underrepresentation (Leathwood and Read, 2009; Archer *et al.*, 2003; Tett, 2000; OFFA and HEFCE, 2014). The category of 'non-traditional' student has changed over time but is often ill-defined. Largely missing from this literature and policy initiatives are those concentrating exclusively on students with dependent children, despite the fact that in England, about 7 per cent of all full-time undergraduates and 45 per cent of all part-time undergraduates are parents (Pollard *et al.*, 2013) (although not all are socio-economically disadvantaged). In the US, a third of low-income and first-generation undergraduates are parents (Nelson *et al.*, 2013).

Underpinning the case for wider participation is research on the relationship between HE participation, parental education and children's educational attainment. Studies in the United Kingdom and the United States and by the Organisation for Economic Co-operation and Development demonstrate that parental characteristics, especially education levels and socio-economic status, are key determinants of HE participation (Blanden and Gregg, 2004; Blanden and Machin, 2004; Carneiro and Heckman, 2002). Other UK and international research shows that socio-economic gaps in children's attainment emerge very early, before they start school, and grow over time, and that a child's family background has a substantial influence on their educational development (Cunha and Heckman, 2007;

Feinstein, 2003; Demack *et al.*, 2000). Consequently, by the time these children reach university age they do not have the academic qualifications required for HE entry. This suggests that policies need to be targeted at improving poorer children's early educational attainment (Vignoles, 2013), which is assumed to lie outside the remit of HE (OFFA and HEFCE, 2014).

In parallel to widening participation initiatives aimed at school-aged children, a raft of policies aimed at reducing child poverty and the socio-economic gaps in children's attainment have emerged. The flagship UK policy is the Sure Start Children's Centres. Sure Start was part of the New Labour government's strategy to prevent social exclusion and to reduce child poverty. Its initial objective in 1999 was 'To work with parents and children to promote the physical, intellectual and social development of pre-school children – particularly those who are disadvantaged – to ensure they are ready to thrive when they get to school' (Eisenstadt, 2011: 32). Its core services were designed to improve parenting skills and mothers' self-esteem. A later expansion brought the programme under local authorities' control, with a greater emphasis on helping mothers into work. By 2006, there were 2,500 Sure Start Children's Centres offering a wide range of services, covering the 30 per cent most deprived communities and including 70 per cent of children in poverty.

New Labour sought to tackle the 'social problems of disadvantage by inculcating [white] middle-class values at the level of the family' (Gillies, 2005: 838). Child-rearing moved from being a private concern to a public one, while good parenting was to compensate for social disadvantage:

> Upskilling parents, it was claimed, could reduce crime, antisocial behaviour and poverty whilst increasing the social mobility and life chances of poor children. Following this reasoning the state has a responsibility to regulate and enforce good parenting for the sake of the nation and its vulnerable children. (Gillies, 2014: 209)

New policies and guidelines on early intervention began to emerge, all emphasizing parenting skills.

From 2010, the core purpose of Sure Start Children's Centres changed, emphasizing targeted interventions 'to improve outcomes for young children and their families and reduce inequalities between families in greatest need and their peers in: child development and school readiness; parenting aspirations and parenting skills; and child and family health and life chances' (DfE, 2013: 7).

The 2010–15 Coalition government pitted parenting against poverty, and conceptually and ideologically sidelined poverty, severing it from its root causes, while the complex relationship between parenting, poverty and outcomes for children elided. This special status attributed to parenting in overcoming material and social disadvantage is a new development and continued to guide the 2015 Conservative government's thinking and policies.

This chapter seeks to help fill some of the gaps in the limited existing research on parent students. More ambitiously, it attempts to link two, usually separate but interconnected, sets of policies: one on widening participation, the other on tackling child poverty and inequality.

Research and conceptual context

There is relatively little research concentrating on parent students in HE, and what exists is limited in scope (Brooks, 2012). Recent studies both in the UK and the United States analyse parents' experiences at individual, institutional and national levels (Lynch, 2008; Hinton-Smith, 2012; NUS, 2009; Marandet and Wainwright, 2009; Moreau and Kerner, 2012; Brooks, 2012; Brooks, 2013).

According to this literature, the challenges to parents' participation and success in HE include lacking confidence and motivation; finding appropriate courses; finding affordable childcare; negotiating the complex system of financial support; juggling their studies around family and work responsibilities, with implications for course organization and attendance; and being unfamiliar with the educational culture and context, which has implications for retention, course design and pedagogic approach. Thus student parents often struggle within HE institutions, which take little note of their gendered and classed positions (Reay, 2003; Jackson, 2003), or of the demands of mothering. For example, the scheduling of classes ignores school hours, and there is a severe lack of crèche and other facilities (Moreau and Kerner, 2012). Such findings informed the design and delivery of the courses examined here.

However, this research has limitations. First, it focuses on parents in mainstream HE provision, usually on full-time undergraduate courses, rather than part-time undergraduate courses targeted at parents. Second, it is often more concerned about increasing HE participation rather than with widening participation (e.g. Moreau and Kerner, 2012; Brooks, 2012; Brooks, 2013). While rightly promoting greater gender equality in HE, few studies focus exclusively on mothers from low socio-economic groups. Third, most research has stopped at the door of the HE institution, concentrating on what happens to parents while studying. Often missing is an exploration of both the benefits and outcomes of study, and their impact on the domestic sphere.

When families and children are discussed, the research frequently, explicitly or implicitly, portrays them negatively as part of a wider 'narrative of disadvantage' (Woodfield, 2011: 410). Families are often depicted as a burden, a financial strain, generating guilt and constraining students' ability to study, engage in university life and develop a social life (Hinton-Smith, 2012; Marandet and Wainwright, 2009; Brine and Waller, 2004).

Much has been written about the role, purpose and function of HE, although not specifically in relation to parents in HE. This chapter calls upon Watson's (2014) overview as a conceptual lens for analysing the outcomes of study for the course participants. The advantage of his approach for the present study is his focus on individual outcomes rather than institutions acting collectively as moral actors. Taking a historical perspective, Watson explores the moral, social and political underpinnings of the HE sector. He identifies ten claims about the 'purpose' of university for individuals: religious; personal development, such as self-realization; social, such as the way individuals improve their relationships with the wider world, culturally, economically and politically; technical know-how; professional acculturation; networking; maturation; protected time; love of the subject; mental gymnastics. These claims about what HE does for students encapsulate its potentially transformational nature. Put together, they also include claims about the role of HE 'in existential terms (how students come to be); in epistemological terms (how they think and appraise information); in behavioural terms (how they learn to conduct themselves); and in positional terms (both through competition and collaboration)' (Watson, 2014: 20). Above all, Watson questions whether the claims combine to create a moral compass – a form of personal responsibility, to take part in what Sen (2009) calls 'public reasoning'.

The study and methodological approach

The study described in this chapter, funded by the Nuffield Foundation, assessed part-time undergraduate courses targeted at low-income student parents delivered in Sure Start Children's Centres and run by two pre-1992 universities between 2007/08 and 2011/12. One university (henceforth called University 1) is based in London and focuses on part-time study, while the other (University 2) only provides courses via distance learning. The study explored the setting up of these courses and their organization, and the courses' perceived effects on the lives of the course participants, their families and their children, from the perspective of the course participants;

staff responsible for managing and teaching the courses; and the Sure Start Children's Centre staff. Here, we focus on the outcomes of studying for the participants and their children, exclusively from the mothers' perspective.

These universities' collaboration with the Children's Centres in areas of London with exceptionally low HE participation aimed to make HE learning available to parents who were unlikely to access more traditional routes offered by HE providers. The Children's Centres, by design, were in neighbourhoods with high-density social housing, making them easy to reach for the parents, avoiding the use of costly public transport. In addition, at the time of the study, all the Children's Centres had free on-site childcare facilities that course participants could use while attending their course or support sessions. Another significant advantage of these Children's Centres was that the learning environment was familiar and supportive, in contrast to the often alienating and isolating nature of many HE institutions (Archer *et al.*, 2003; Reay, et al., 2009).

When this study was undertaken and up to 2012/13, both courses studied were free. The vast majority of students were eligible for government tuition fee and course grants available to part-time undergraduate students and/or institutional bursaries. (In 2012/13 government tuition fee and course grants were abolished for new students and replaced with student loans, see Callender, 2013.) At University 1 students were taught face to face, with one three-hour session per week over the academic year. They were aiming for a Certificate of Higher Education, requiring 120 credit points and usually consisting of four modules, two of which they could take at the Children's Centre, and the remainder at the university's main campus. The courses were during school hours so students could fit them around other commitments. In contrast, University 2 students' Openings course required 15 credit points and was distance learning. All the learning materials were provided to the student in advance and they could study at their own pace. Students were given telephone support from a module tutor, and offered five study skills sessions and weekly peer- and tutor-supported face-to-face sessions at the Children's Centre.

Both courses aimed to prepare students for HE and further study. They were created for those with no or limited exposure to HE and its culture and conventions. The inclusive pedagogic approaches to learning and teaching adopted called upon the liberal, emancipatory theory of HE and ideas based on self-discovery that aimed to help learners achieve an independent point of view and a personal voice (Watson, 2014).

Both courses were explicitly designed to help overcome some of the impediments to accessing HE (Gorard *et al.*, 2006) faced by student parents. In policy terms, they incorporated features promoted for widening participation and greater equality of opportunity by the government (OFFA and HEFCE, 2014), including outreach activities, cross-sector and intersector partnerships, and flexible and part-time provision.

The study included all the courses run by University 1 at nine London Children's Centres between 2007/08 and 2011/12, and University 2 courses between 2008/09 and 2011/12 at two Children's Centres, one in London and another in the north of England. The findings reported here are based on a survey of course participants conducted in autumn 2012 and follow-up, in-depth interviews in early 2013 with 30 female survey respondents, selected using a grid to ensure we interviewed a representative group. (The study also included in-depth interviews with staff at the Children's Centres and the universities' staff responsible for managing and teaching the courses.)

There were numerous advantages to this mixed methods approach and the multiple stages of data collection (Johnson and Onwuegbuzie, 2004). The survey allowed us to collect the same data from all participants, while the interviews provided opportunities to gain a more nuanced understanding and explanation of the survey results. The different data collection approaches helped validate the findings from a range of perspectives. In combination, this provided a better understanding of the outcomes of study for the participants than would have been possible from either research approach alone.

The intention was to survey all University 1's students enrolled in courses at Children's Centres since 2007/08 (N = 145), and all University 2's students who had studied via the two Children's Centres since 2008 (N = 103), a total of 248 people. However, inaccurate student contact details gave an effective survey population of 220. Of these 220, 115 responded to the survey, an overall response rate of 52 per cent. Students completed the questionnaire online or over the telephone.

The characteristics of the survey respondents (table 5.1) show that the majority were women (90 per cent), aged over 30 (59 per cent), lone parents (56 per cent), who had left school under the age of 18 (58 per cent), and started their course with low-level entry qualifications (67 per cent). Most respondents were not employed before starting their course (73 per cent) and were living in low-income households – living just above the poverty line (65 per cent) (in 2011/12, median household income was £23,200 (ONS, 2013); 60 per cent of the median household income is the most common measure of poverty). Most did not have another family member who had studied for a HE qualification (53 per cent). Just under half came from an ethnic minority (49 per cent) and had a child under the age of 5 when they started the course (47 per cent).

Table 5.1: Characteristics of course participants by institution attended

Characteristic	University 1 %	University 2 %	All %
Gender			
Female	96	92	90
Male	4	8	5
Age at start of course			
30 and under	38	50	41
Over 30	62	50	59
Ethnicity			
White	33	61	37
Non-White	66	39	49
Family type			
Lone-parent family	49	69	56
Two-parent family	51	31	34
Age of youngest child when started course			
Under 5	48	44	47
5 and over	52	56	53
Economic status when started course			
In paid employment	32	17	27
Not in paid employment	68	83	73
Gross annual household income			
Under £14,999	59	82	65
£15,000 and over	41	18	35
Age left full-time education			
Under 18	55	63	58
18 and over	45	37	42
Highest qualification on entry			
Level 2 or below	56	86	67
Level 3 or above	34	11	33
Family member studied for HE qualification			
Yes	45	53	47
No	55	47	53
Number of respondents	**79**	**36**	**115**

Source: Survey of course participants, 2012.

Although respondents' characteristics were broadly similar, University 1 students were significantly more likely than their University 2 peers to come from an ethnic minority, to be living with a partner or spouse, and to have started their course with a Level 3 or higher qualification. All these socio-economic characteristics are typically associated with 'widening participation' and 'non-traditional' students. It is clear, therefore, that these courses, in line with their mission, attracted students who were financially, socially and educationally disadvantaged, especially when compared with the part-time undergraduate population nationally (Oxford Economics, 2014).

Course participants' views on the effects of their learning

To assess course participants' perceptions of the impact of their courses on their family and children, survey respondents were asked whether their views about their children's education had changed as a direct result of their course. Over four out of five believed that as a result of their course, they had higher educational aspirations for their children; a half that their children were more interested in learning; and nearly a half that their relationship with their children had improved (figure 5.1). These outcomes exceeded respondents' initial motivations for studying as under two in five claimed to have started their course to be a 'role model' for their children, and under a quarter to help their children with their education.

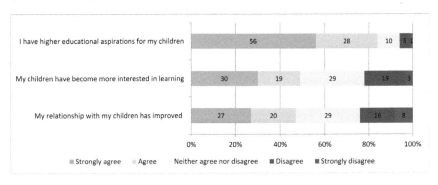

Figure 5.1: Course participants' views on outcomes of the courses for their children (all survey respondents, N=115)
Source: Survey of course participants, 2012.

These outcomes broadly support the overall mission underpinning Children's Centres, in terms of raising the parents' aspirations. However, the interviews revealed that the mothers strongly associated their reported changed attitudes with other learning benefits. The survey gives some indication of how many course participants thought they had profited from these wider benefits of learning (figure 5.2). The high proportion of respondents realizing they could get a higher education qualification is noteworthy, fulfilling the courses' overall aim – to increase confidence in participants' capability to take a degree. Important too were the private, non-market benefits (McMahon, 2009; Brennan *et al.*, 2013), especially intangible assets such as improved self-confidence, attitudes to learning, and optimism, which Jamieson et al. classify as identity capital (2009: 10). Enhanced generic skills (human capital) were also significant for mothers in this study, especially in their engagement with their children's learning. Even so, in the interviews, the mothers repeatedly referred to their improved self-confidence, a finding echoed in other studies, especially of adult learners (Dolan *et al.*, 2012; Callender *et al.*, 2010). Taking a broader view, these findings resonate with Watson's (2014) claims about the purpose of HE, especially in terms of personal development, and the elaboration of 'character' as formed through 'liberal' HE.

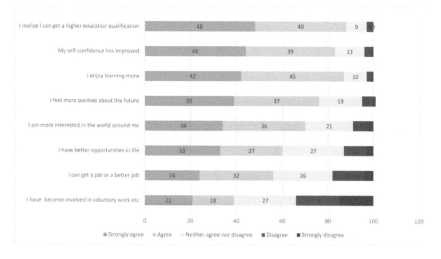

Figure 5.2: Course participants' views on some of the wider benefits of learning (all survey respondents, N=115)
Source: Survey of course participants, 2012.

Another linked recurrent theme in the women's narrative was the transformational nature of their HE learning experiences, in the sense used by Mezirow and Associates (2000) of irreversibly changing the way they understand the world. This transformation could be characterized as a more critical understanding of the world, through the academic study of social sciences, and endorsement of foundational values of HE such as respect for diverse opinions and ways of debating them. These changes were far broader in scope and reach than the narrow focus on parenting skills that preoccupies the work of Children's Centres and other government-sponsored parenting interventions. Indeed, the majority (70 per cent) of course participants surveyed claimed that as a direct result of their course they were more interested in the world around them (figure 5.2).

The mothers' interviews showed that central to this was the way the courses changed how they saw their worlds, their children and themselves, including, for some, an understanding of their classed and gendered position. Sarmeen (all names are pseudonyms) is a 35-year-old married woman with three sons aged under 10, and her experiences are indicative of such changes, including a greater political awareness:

> It's opened my mind up a *lot* ... It does change you. I mean, before I was in this other little world, taking my children to school, coming home, doing the housework and I really didn't know that much about the world out there. I'm not aware of everything that's going on around me or the decisions that are being made in political life and things like that, I didn't really take note of what's going on but really, when you hear things and there's things that you've looked at on your course and you think, 'Oh, okay, so I understand what they mean.' ... so when there's things on the news, when there's things in the papers, it sort of makes me take note and think ... 'Oh, hold on, this is what's going on around me, this is what the government are doing – how do I feel about it?' ... It *has* enlightened me and it *has* made me want to, almost want to learn a lot more.

Kaylee, 34 years old, disabled, married with a 9-year-old daughter and 6-year-old son, like other mothers, claimed her course had changed her life in terms of personal development and social and political engagement:

> Best decision of my life, next to having my two children! [Laughter] ... Really. It's changed my life immensely. ... the things I'm interested in these days, be it on TV or in the media, be it the people I follow on Twitter, it's all changed. I don't follow Victoria Beckham, I'm following Owen Jones! ... The news, you know, before I didn't care but now I'm always watching *Question Time* and I don't miss what's going on. ... Even the *books* I read these days. ... It's understanding things, the social world. It's like before I didn't see the point of volunteering but now I do that, I started two years ago, but I didn't see the point of demonstration and marches and all this, or petitioning for something, I didn't understand the point of it.

Amna, 23 years old, separated from her husband with three sons aged 9, 5 and 3, talked about how her learning experiences changed her, including her relationship with her husband:

> I definitely feel so much more liberated! Yes, I do feel a lot more free within myself and a lot more ... I don't know how to put it, but you know when you just feel intelligent? [Laughter] ... as I got more and more educated I felt more liberated and for that reason I'd talk more and ask more questions and was more curious, and some people don't like changes, some people don't like challenges, and I didn't know that my husband was one of those people.

Moreover, her liberating experience altered her ambitions for her children and what she wanted for them:

> I would like them [children] to go on and do further education and maybe get degrees and stuff, but I don't think it is necessary. ... It's their choice completely, something that I didn't get, I had no choices and I don't want that for my children. They can do whatever they want ... I just want them to be good human beings. ... now, since I've got my education all I want for them is to feel as liberated as I do.

These claims echo Watson's notion of the social purpose of HE in the way that individuals improve their relationship with a 'wider world: culturally, economically, politically' (Watson, 2014: 19). It can also be a form of education for citizenship in its broadest sense of obligations to civil society, the state and wider international interests. Here Watson is concerned about 'soft citizenship' and:

> not just self-awareness, but also awareness of others, and of deeper senses of sympathy and connection than civic conformity will ever bring about. In so far as institutions succeed in stimulating and nurturing it, they contribute to the more individual sense of personal responsibility and capacity for 'public reasoning'. (Watson, 2014: 59)

Course participants' views on their involvement in their children's learning

This small-scale study cannot claim a statistically robust causal link between the course participants' learning and changes in their behaviour and that of their children. However, our findings do feed into other large-scale longitudinal quantitative research that shows the strong relationship between poverty, parenting and intergenerational effects. They contribute to a qualitative understanding of some of the dynamics underpinning such studies. And they illustrate how exposing poor mothers to HE, not just parenting skills, might affect their ability to engage in their children's education in ways that potentially can enhance their children's educational trajectories.

Goodman and Gregg (2010), drawing on the Millennium Cohort Study, found that the socio-economic gap in attainment widens as children enter and move through the schooling system, especially during primary school years. Other research questions some of these findings and whether parents' involvement in home learning, parental warmth, and discipline explain the significant variance in teacher-rated attainment outcomes (Hartas, 2015).

Carter-Wall and Whitfield conclude it is 'not possible to establish a clear causal relationship between AAB [attitudes, aspirations, and behaviour] and children's educational outcomes' (2012: 1). Positive parent–child relationships may be a consequence rather than a cause of high-performing children (Dermott, 2012: 5). However, the review by Gorard *et al.* (2012) of over 1,000 studies on the impact of attitudes, aspirations, and behaviour on children's attainment and participation confirmed a causal link between parental involvement in their children's education, school readiness and subsequent attainment. Parenting and home environment are important contributors to income-related gaps in cognitive development (Waldfogel and Washbrook, 2010), and parenting consistently emerges as the single most important factor in gaps in school readiness. However, poverty matters too. Underpinning the achievement gaps at school entry is both parenting and poverty.

Thus there is promising evidence that interventions to improve parental involvement in their children's education, especially their early education, could be effective in improving children's attainment. The research evidence (Carter-Wall and Whitfield, 2012) suggests this would demand improving at-home parenting; involving parents in school; engaging parents in their children's learning and in their own learning; and aligning school–home expectations.

Improving at-home parenting

Many mothers in the interviews talked about how they believed their learning experiences had improved their ability to parent their children.

Particularly significant was that the women's courses frequently covered child development and psychology, which the mothers claimed increased their knowledge and understanding of their children and how they parented them.

Kaylee recounted how what she learned about children through her studies led her to consciously break with what she described as the traditional cultural practice of using physical punishment for children. Reading about the ineffectiveness of punishment had made her observe other parents who did use physical punishment, and that their children were no better behaved, so she decided to test what she learned in practice. Her husband also became part of her experiment and would call her at work for parenting advice. She reflected that her course had given her new parenting strategies:

> Yes, because I think if it was before I did this course, I would have been, 'I've told you THREE times!!!' but then I realize that when I think about it, try another technique. If you've told someone twice and they cannot learn that way, then maybe try another way.

Other mothers talked about how the way they thought they communicated with their children had changed; Callie, 24 years old, married with two sons aged 5 and 1, and a 2-year-old daughter:

> I learned a lot about children, looking after children. ... Before, I don't think about it. I just think, 'I have to ask the child to do this. You have to do it.' But now I've realized that while you are telling the child to do it, you have to explain to the child the reason you want him to do it ... so that he will understand and he won't say, 'Mummy hates me.' He will see that mummy loves, him, they attach. I really learned a lot.

Makayla, aged 34, lone parent with a 5-year-old daughter and 2-year-old son similarly felt she was better able to cope with her children.

> Before, I didn't know how to handle my daughter. ... The way we were learning it is to apply it to our daily lives, so if you apply it, and reflect to your daily life, then I have learnt a lot, it's changed a lot. I approach things differently and I look at things differently. ... I've learnt that I can calm down and approach it in a calm and different way, so I don't scream anymore.

None of these mothers had been taught parenting skills *per se* on their courses, but their broader academic HE studies had given them invaluable insights into parenting. It was this wider context and deeper understanding that were essential to the transformational nature of their learning. The courses called on their experiences, and applied ideas within sociology and psychology to the women's lives, starting from their existing knowledge and endorsing the centrality given to critically reflective learning that helped students to situate their feelings about, and experiences of, learning in a broader context.

Involving parents in school

There were numerous women who during or after their course became more involved in their children's school, especially as volunteer teaching assistants or as members of the Sure Start Children Centre's parents' board. For instance, for Shanara, a 31-year-old married woman with a daughter aged 10 and a son aged 4, her course increased her confidence, allowing her to get involved in her son's school:

> I wasn't involved in my daughter's school activities but this [course] boosted my confidence to be with the other parents and the teachers. ... I've been volunteering [at son's school], but last year my son was not in full-time education so I couldn't be there for a long time so I used to go for two hours a day, but now I am going for full time actually, doing volunteering.

As a result of Shanara's course, she felt she understood her children better and this helped her in the school voluntary work and in dealing with children there. It aided her knowledge about 'how children learn to read and how to blend sounds and I can understand how much they can understand and then I need to stop'. Shanara hopes to get a paid teaching assistant post.

Amna also enthused how her course had changed her life, and prompted an interest in education and involvement in her children's schooling. Following her course, she had started a BA in Education and Special Educational Needs at a local further education college.

> There's no words I have to describe how it's made so much difference to the children's lives ... how much happiness it gives me as well, to be able to know what my children are doing at school, and understanding it and then question it if something isn't right. ... I was not good at Maths at all but I went out and bought ... this Maths dictionary, it's called the *Oxford Maths*

Dictionary for Children, and it's brilliant and it teaches me! But before, I wouldn't have had the confidence to see what I need to buy for my children, what would help them, and I'm doing Education [at further education college] so I know what's happening with the current curricula and what they're expecting from children and also I know how to find things out now.

Engaging parents in their children's learning and in their own learning

Around two out of five survey respondents continued studying after they had finished their modules at the Children's Centre, while over three-quarters reported that they intended to take another course within the next three years.

The vast majority of survey respondents also claimed that as a direct result of their courses, their skills had improved 'a lot' (figure 5.3). These skills and approaches to learning had been integrated into their courses. Most were wide-ranging generic skills that parents could apply to their lives beyond their studies. The mothers' interviews confirmed that these skills, alongside their learning and improved self-confidence, made them feel better equipped to support their children in school tasks. This ability and willingness were probably aided by the finding that the vast majority of survey respondents realized they could get a HE qualification (88 per cent) and enjoyed learning more (87 per cent) (figure 5.2). They felt they had the competences, capacity, and confidence to assist their children.

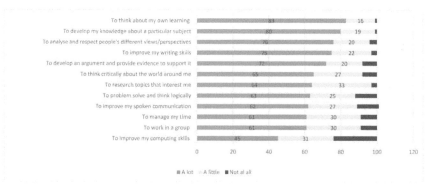

Figure 5.3: Course participants' views on learning outcomes (all survey respondents, N=115)

Source: Survey of course participants, 2012.

The mothers' interviews revealed how their engagement with their younger children's learning often took the form of reading to them and teaching them how to read, while with older children it often involved helping with homework. More generally, mothers reported an increased confidence in their ability to search for information and to write academically, enabling them to assist with many different aspects of their children's schoolwork, often enriching the experience.

Lesia, aged 24, lone parent to a 4-year-old son, believed that without the skills learnt on her course, she most probably would have avoided helping her son with his reading.

> So getting on to the course and having to do assignments and essays and stuff, having him now in Reception where he comes home with a book every day, it helps me because I could actually deal with him. If I didn't get on to that course, maybe I would say, 'Oh, later, mum will do it later.' And later never comes. ... So it's helped us quite a lot.

For Sarmeen and other mothers such as Grace, it was the combination of technical competence in knowing how to study, seeking out information, research topics, and reflecting upon them, along with their new-found confidence and improved writing skills, that allowed them to engage in their children's learning. Some felt more empowered as mothers.

> I've used the skills that I've been taught on how to study, how to look up different sources of information, 'Oh, you don't just need to go on the internet, let's go to the library', 'Why don't we go on a trip and look at this?'. So those sort of areas really. And also like reading newspapers like the *Guardian* and taking a bit more ... [Laughter] ... you know, you can't get away with the *Daily Mail*! (Sarmeen)

> It impacted my children's lives as well because now I can, I help them with their work ... Now I look and support him [son], give him advice and guidance around each of these assignments, things like that. With my younger son we sit and do the homework together, I support him ... It's amazing! That's the greatest thing for me, that I can support my children with their education now. (Grace, aged 46, lone parent with two sons aged 17 and 9)

There were also examples of mothers with teenage children where the engagement was a two-way process – the mothers engaged with their teenagers' studies and the teenagers engaged with their mothers'. An example is Alvita, a 36-year-old lone parent with a 10-year-old son and two daughters aged 12 and 16. Her eldest daughter is studying Health and Social Care.

> One of the things that she does quite a lot, with studying Health and Social Care, is all these psychological things that she learns, she said, 'Oh, do you know this yet?' so she kept on coming to me before and saying, 'Oh, this and this', so now I am going as well to her and saying, 'Oh, did you know this?' and then she says, 'Yes, and …', we could exchange our ideas.

Once again, it was the academic nature of the women's courses that gave them the skills to help their children. Such educational skills went well beyond those associated with 'parenting'. Taking a broader perspective, these findings resonate with Watson's (2014) technical know-how purpose of HE and its role in imbuing competences and capabilities.

Aligning school–home expectations

Amna's experiences illustrate the potential for the alignment of home and school experiences, primarily because of the degree in Education she was taking as a result of her earlier course:

> Even at nursery, the amount of things I could have done with Rayan, I didn't do because I just didn't know, I was just so ignorant, but with Mikhail, he's at nursery now and I know … the language programmes they do at schools, the groups they have, the phonics, everything that's going on, so I know exactly how to interact with my children, how to talk to them, and they won't be confused because that's how they are being taught at school; I think it makes a difference.

For other mothers, the alignment between school and home expectations arose more because they acted as a role model for their children. However, the notion of role models is problematic. Their absence is often used to explain, for instance, underachievement in boys, despite the lack of evidence and the misplaced assumptions upon which such a discourse is based (Moreau, 2011).

Yet the women interviewed for this study believed that setting a good example for their children was influential in their children's academic attainment. For instance, Janet, a 39-year-old widow with a 12-year-old girl and 7-year-old boy, was convinced: 'My children are doing fantastic at school, because they see me studying, they now are doing their homework and are studying harder and their grades have gone up at school as well.'

Some used their studies as a way to discipline their children to ensure they went to school, such as Ruth, aged 34, a single parent with a 4-year-old son:

> This morning my little boy said he didn't want to go to school and I said, 'Well you've got to because mummy's got to go to school today.' And it's nice for him to know that I'm learning and studying and it encourages him to want to go. He knows mummy's got to do it.

Other parents exhorted their children to work hard at school, using themselves as a warning of the consequences of failure to study when young, and the difficulties of returning to study as an adult and a parent. This could be deployed alongside the parent as a present role model. Some parents, such as Evelyn, aged 48, married with three sons aged 6, 12 and over 18, presented themselves as a cautionary tale: 'it gives you more *push* to help them and so let them realize that they can accomplish things, they don't have to wait until they get older.'

Conclusions and implications for widening participation policies: Two for the price of one

Policies targeted at widening HE participation largely have been divorced from those aimed at reducing child poverty and inequality such as Sure Start Children's Centres. This study, and the courses run in Children's Centres, brings together these policies and the thinking underpinning them. In a sense, the courses acted as a bridge between these two interconnected, but often separate, policy domains.

This study was based on the experiences of low-income parents taking part in initiatives conceived and designed to challenge the educational, social, and economic inequalities such disadvantaged parents frequently encounter. It explored the perceived benefits of study within the domestic sphere, moving away from a narrative of disadvantage. Specifically, it examined mothers' views on the impact of the courses on their lives, and especially on their children's educational trajectories.

The mothers reported that as a result of their course, they had become more involved in their children's education. They claimed their parenting skills had improved; they had become more active in their children's nursery and school; they were more engaged in their children's learning and their own learning; and there was a greater alignment between school and home expectations. All these recounted changes are, according to extant literature, likely to influence children's school readiness and subsequent attainment.

These outcomes were inextricably linked to the HE nature of the parents' courses, and especially their transformational and liberating character, and the broader ideas about the role and purpose of HE, as proposed by Watson (2014). The mothers maintained that the courses altered the way they saw the world, how they thought and appraised information, and how they behaved in general and in relation to their children. They insisted the courses enabled and encouraged their involvement in, and engagement with, their children's learning. Such outcomes are not new, nor are they unique to these courses, but they remind us of the power of HE's potential to transform. They reflect Watson's claim 'that HE's purposes come together in terms of self-creating and the authentic life, the habit of thinking deeply, and the capacity to connect with others empathetically' (2014: 107).

These transformations were facilitated by a pedagogical approach reflecting an emancipatory theory of HE. This stance and these courses' broader conceptualization were not based on an individualistic deficit model – where the victim is blamed for their poverty, for not participating in HE, for being a 'bad' parent, for lacking certain skills, values, and aspirations – an ideology underpinning many widening participation initiatives (Burke, 2012) and those aimed at tackling child poverty through improved parenting skills (Dermott, 2012). They went well beyond a focus on narrowly defined parenting skills, characteristic of policy initiatives aimed at tackling child poverty, underscoring Hartas's argument that:

> Educational inequalities cannot (and should not) be approached as the product of values and attitudes that parents hold but as outcomes of structure, exacerbated by different access to resources and possibilities for social advancement, and the gradual diminishing of the welfare state. (2015: 33)

The HE courses in this study recognized that 'widening access to and participation in HE is primarily a project of social justice, which must attend in detail to complex issues of inequality, exclusion and mis-recognition' (Burke, 2012: 117). On a small scale, they attempted to address structural inequalities. They provided low-income mothers with educational opportunities and the prospect of social advancement. The provision, tailored to parents' needs, was of at least equal potential value for future generations of children from low-income families as widening participation projects aimed at raising the aspirations of high-achieving primary and secondary schoolchildren. The courses, according to the mothers, changed their lives, and in doing so, their involvement in their children's education, which potentially could contribute to improvements in their children's educational attainment – two possible achievements for the price of one. This raises issues about the purpose of HE. It brings into question the widely asserted assumption that universities have a limited role to play in tackling socio-economic gaps in children's underachievement.

Note
This chapters draws on a research project funded by the Nuffield Foundation, but the views expressed are those of the author and not necessarily those of the Foundation.

References

Archer, L., Hutchings, M. and Ross, A. (eds) (2003) *Higher Education and Social Class: Issues of exclusion and inclusion.* London: RoutledgeFalmer.

Blanden, J. and Gregg, P. (2004) 'Family income and educational attainment: A review of approaches and evidence for Britain'. *Oxford Review of Economic Policy,* 20 (2), 245–63.

Blanden, J. and Machin, S. (2004) 'Educational inequality and the expansion of UK higher education'. *Scottish Journal of Political Economy,* 51 (2), 230–49.

Brennan, J., Niccolo, D. and Tanguy, S. (2013) *Things We Know and Don't Know about the Wider Benefits of Higher Education: A review of the recent literature* (BIS Research Paper 133). London: Department for Business, Innovation and Skills.

Brine, J. and Waller, R. (2004) 'Working-class women on an Access course: Risk, opportunity and (re)constructing identities'. *Gender and Education,* 16 (1), 97–113.

Brooks, R. (2012) 'Student-parents and higher education: A cross-national comparison'. *Journal of Education Policy,* 27 (3), 423–39.

Brooks, R. (2013) 'Negotiating time and space for study: Student-parents and familial relationships'. *Sociology,* 47 (3), 443–59.

Burke, P.J. (2012) *The Right to Higher Education: Beyond widening participation.* London: Routledge.

Callender, C. (2013) 'Part-time undergraduate student funding and financial support'. In Callender, C. and Scott, P. (eds) *Browne and Beyond: Modernizing English higher education.* London: Institute of Education Press, 130–58.

Callender, C., Hopkin, R. and Wilkinson D. (2010) *Futuretrack: Part-time students: Career decision-making and career development of part-time higher education students.* Manchester: Higher Education Careers Services Unit.

Carneiro, P. and Heckman, J.J. (2002) 'The evidence on credit constraints in post-secondary schooling'. *Economic Journal,* 112 (482), 705–34.

Carter-Wall, C. and Whitfield, G. (2012) *The Role of Aspirations, Attitudes and Behaviour in Closing the Educational Attainment Gap.* York: Joseph Rowntree Foundation. Online. www.jrf.org.uk/sites/files/jrf/education-achievement-poverty-summary.pdf (accessed 23 July 2013).

Cunha, F. and Heckman, J. (2007) 'The technology of skill formation'. *American Economic Review*, 97 (2), 31–47.

Demack, S., Drew, D. and Grimsley, M. (2000) 'Minding the gap: Ethnic, gender and social class differences in attainment at 16, 1988–95'. *Race Ethnicity and Education*, 3 (2), 117–43.

Dermott, E. (2012) '"Poverty" versus "parenting": An emergent dichotomy'. *Studies in the Maternal*, 4 (2), 1–13. Online. www.mamsie.bbk.ac.uk/articles/10.16995/sim.37/galley/34/download/ (accessed 10 December 2017).

DfE (Department for Education) (2013) *Sure Start Children's Centres Statutory Guidance: For local authorities, commissioners of local health services and Jobcentre Plus*. London: Department for Education. Online. www.gov.uk/government/publications/sure-start-childrens-centres (accessed 5 December 2013).

Dolan, P., Fujiwara, D. and Metcalfe, R. (2012) *Review and Update of Research into the Wider Benefits of Adult Learning* (BIS Research Paper 90). London: Department for Business, Innovation and Skills.

Eisenstadt, N. (2011) *Providing a Sure Start: How government discovered early childhood*. Bristol: Policy Press.

Feinstein, L. (2003) 'Inequality in the early cognitive development of British children in the 1970 cohort'. *Economica*, 70 (277), 73–97.

Gillies, V. (2005) 'Raising the "meritocracy": Parenting and the individualization of social class'. *Sociology*, 39 (5), 835–53.

Gillies, V. (2014) 'Troubling families: Parenting and the politics of early intervention'. In Wagg, S. and Pilcher, J. (eds) *Thatcher's Grandchildren? Politics and childhood in the twenty-first century*. Basingstoke: Palgrave Macmillan, 204–24.

Goodman, A. and Gregg, P. (eds) (2010) *Poorer Children's Educational Attainment: How important are attitudes and behaviour?* York: Joseph Rowntree Foundation.

Gorard, S., See, B.H. and Davies, P. (2012) *The Impact of Attitudes and Aspirations on Educational Attainment and Participation*. York: Joseph Rowntree Foundation.

Gorard, S., Smith, E., May, H., Thomas, L., Adnett, N. and Slack, K. (2006) *Review of Widening Participation Research: Addressing the barriers to participation in higher education: A report to HEFCE by the University of York, Higher Education Academy and Institute for Access Studies*. Bristol: Higher Education Funding Council for England.

Hartas, D. (2015) 'Parenting for social mobility? Home learning, parental warmth, class and educational outcomes'. *Journal of Education Policy*, 30 (1), 21–38.

Hinton-Smith, T. (2012) *Lone Parents' Experiences as Higher Education Students: Learning to juggle*. Leicester: National Institute of Adult Continuing Education.

Jackson, S. (2003) 'Lifelong earning: Working-class women and lifelong learning'. *Gender and Education*, 15 (4), 365–76.

Jamieson, A., Sabates, R., Woodley, A. and Feinstein, L. (2009) 'The benefits of higher education study for part-time students'. *Studies in Higher Education*, 34 (3), 245–62.

Johnson, R.B. and Onwuegbuzie, A.J. (2004) 'Mixed methods research: A research paradigm whose time has come'. *Educational Researcher*, 33 (7), 14–26.

Leathwood, C. and Read, B. (2009) *Gender and the Changing Face of Higher Education: A feminized future?* Maidenhead: Open University Press.

Lynch, K.D. (2008) 'Gender roles and the American academe: A case study of graduate student mothers'. *Gender and Education*, 20 (6), 585–605.

Marandet, E. and Wainwright, E. (2009) 'Discourses of integration and exclusion: Equal opportunities for university students with dependent children?'. *Space and Polity*, 13 (2), 109–25.

McMahon, W.W. (2009) *Higher Learning, Greater Good: The private and social benefits of higher education.* Baltimore: Johns Hopkins University Press.

Mezirow, J. and Associates (2000) *Learning as Transformation: Critical perspectives on a theory in progress.* San Francisco: Jossey-Bass.

Moreau, M.-P. (2011) 'The societal construction of "boys' underachievement" in educational policies: A cross-national comparison'. *Journal of Education Policy*, 26 (2), 161–80.

Moreau, M.-P. and Kerner, C. (2012) *Supporting Student Parents in Higher Education: A policy analysis.* London: Nuffield Foundation.

Nelson, B., Froehner, M. and Gault, B. (2013) *College Students with Children Are Common and Face Many Challenges in Completing Higher Education* (IWPR Briefing Paper). Washington, DC: Institute for Women's Policy Research.

NUS (National Union of Students) (2009) *Meet the Parents: The experience of students with children in further and higher education.* London: National Union of Students.

OFFA (Office for Fair Access) and HEFCE (Higher Education Funding Council for England) (2014) *National strategy for access and student success in higher education.* London: Department for Business, Innovation and Skills.

ONS (Office for National Statistics) (2013) 'Median household income in the UK, 1977–2011/12.' Online. www.ons.gov.uk/ons/rel/household-income/middle-income-households/1977---2011-12/sty-middle-income-households.html.

Oxford Economics (2014) *Macroeconomic Influences on the Demand for Part-Time Higher Education in the UK.* Bristol: Higher Education Funding Council for England. Online. www.hefce.ac.uk/pubs/rereports/year/2014/ptdemand/ (accessed 6 June 2014).

Pollard, E., Hunt, W., Hillage, J., Drever, E., Chanfreau, J., Coutinho, S. and Poole, E. (2013) *Student Income and Expenditure Survey 2011/12* (BIS Research Paper 115). London: Department for Business, Innovation and Skills.

Reay, D. (2003) 'A risky business? Mature working-class women students and access to higher education'. *Gender and Education*, 15 (3), 301–17.

Reay, D., Crozier, G. and Clayton, J. (2009) '"Strangers in paradise"? Working-class students in elite universities'. *Sociology*, 43 (6), 1103–21.

Sen, A. (2009) *The Idea of Justice.* Cambridge, MA: Harvard University Press.

Tett, L. (2000) '"I'm working class and proud of it": Gendered experiences of non-traditional participants in higher education'. *Gender and Education*, 12 (2), 183–94.

Vignoles, A. (2013) 'Widening participation and social mobility'. In Callender, C. and Scott, P. (eds) *Browne and Beyond: Modernizing English higher education.* London: Institute of Education Press, 112–29.

Waldfogel, J. and Washbrook, E. (2010) *Low Income and Early Cognitive Development in the UK.* London: Sutton Trust.

Watson, D. (2014) *The Question of Conscience: Higher education and personal responsibility*. London: Institute of Education Press.

Woodfield, R. (2011) 'Age and first destination employment from UK universities: Are mature students disadvantaged?'. *Studies in Higher Education*, 36 (4), 409–25.

Chapter 6

Respecting difference: Researching the intersectionality of gender, race, faith and culture in higher education

Heidi Safia Mirza

Introduction: Situating gender, race, faith and culture in research

The challenge for me in this chapter is to explore the ways in which gender, race, faith and cultural identity play out in the 'affective' learning landscapes, or 'eduscapes' of our seemingly cosmopolitan but inherently white elitist universities (Caluya *et al.*, 2011). As a woman of colour and a black feminist academic, I have found the need to constantly ask questions about what shapes the worlds of profound difference that I witness daily for racialized staff and students in the 'hideously white' places where I teach and work (Bhopal and Jackson, 2013). The task of being an 'embodied raced and gendered researcher' is not easy and the notion of 'embodied intersectionality' (Mirza, 2009; Mirza, 2013) that I draw on in this chapter is a powerful concept I have developed to enable me to excavate the 'affective' processes of exclusion and marginality that I have encountered on my journeys in and through academia (Mirza, 2013; Mirza, 2017). By focusing on the racialized institutional 'flashpoints' of recruitment, retention and progression that black and minority ethnic students encounter on a teacher education course, I take a situated 'embodied' journey into the micro-institutional practices that feed the systemic institutional structures that maintain endemic patterns of racist exclusion in higher education. Ultimately I argue that widening participation practitioners and researchers in the field of higher education must invoke intersectionally reflexive strategies of investigation if they are to remain focused on the invisible roots of racism *still* lodged deep within our institutional walls.

The research study I discuss here investigates the everyday barriers to recruitment, retention and progression for black and minority ethnic students on a Postgraduate Certificate of Education (PGCE) teacher education course. Over 85 per cent of undergraduate and postgraduate initial teacher education courses are to be found in higher education institutions (HEIs). However less than 12 per cent of student teachers on these courses are from black and minority ethnic backgrounds and they are twice as likely to drop out or not to qualify as teachers as their white counterparts (Mirza and Meetoo, 2012). In the wake of this 'hidden crisis' in the teaching profession (Wilshaw, 2016), the research investigated the professional practice of teacher educators on a PGCE course in a university situated in a large multicultural city in England. The narratives of the mainly white tutors' personal strategies and professional 'good practice' revealed the contradictory and multiple challenges they faced within the emotive (affective) space of the higher education classroom. In contrast, the narratives gathered of students from different ethnic, religious, gender, disability, class and cultural backgrounds expressed their hopes and desires for an equitable education, and explored how the intended and unintended discrimination they faced on their courses had real consequences for their access and progression.

Evaluating gender, race, faith and culture: An embodied approach

The study's main aim was to identify and share the good practice of PGCE tutors when engaging with black and minority ethnic students. Two main research questions informed the study: First, 'Do white tutors, trainers and mentors working with black and minority ethnic students understand the nature of their specific learning and life experiences?' Second, 'Do professionals have the practice and skills to deal with issues as they arise for black and minority ethnic students on their courses?' The research was carried out 2007–8 in a higher education institution that provides initial teacher training. Though the student body was ethnically diverse (27 per cent of all students in the HEI were black and minority ethnic), all of the tutors interviewed, except one, were white. The white tutors engaged with the process of data collection and openly shared their experiences and 'best' practices, describing what they see as crucial cultural and learning issues for black and minority ethnic students. Black and minority ethnic students, in contrast, focused on their academic well-being, making links between how effectively racism was dealt with, tutors' respect for their race, faith and culture, and their ability to progress and stay the course.

The first phase of the project consisted of 14 face-to-face interviews with male and female tutors from the primary, secondary and post-compulsory branches of the PGCE. An outcome of phase one was a best practice booklet that we developed from the findings and which was disseminated to all the tutors on the PCGE. The second phase was a follow-up and consisted of a grounded evaluation of the good practice guidance developed from phase one. To achieve this we consulted widely, holding three focus groups with a total of 23 primary, secondary and post-compulsory PGCE tutors. We also conducted four semi-structured interviews with secondary and post-compulsory tutors and received 20 written feedback evaluations on the best practice guidance from tutors. Additionally in phase two we also held one focus group with a mix of 15 black and minority ethnic and white secondary male and female BTs (beginning teachers) to gain a student perspective. It was vital to understand their experiences on the PGCE. Student experiences were fundamental for framing the study's findings, particularly in respect of racist incidents and the dynamics of institutional racism.

The three case studies that frame this chapter are intended to highlight some of the specific ways in which tutors approached issues of visible race, faith and cultural difference when supporting black and minority ethnic students on their PGCE course. The 'best practice' case studies on recruitment, retention and progression are drawn from collated representative accounts reflecting real professional experiences of the tutors. Due to the sensitive nature of 'race' research, we drew on a Critical Race Theory perspective that advocates storytelling and the use of composite characters to conceal and protect the participants' identity (Gillborn, 2008; Solórzano and Yosso, 2002). Thus, while each case is complex and located in specific circumstances narrated by the tutors, in its reconstruction the narrative does not represent any single tutor or student or event. Similarly, names of the tutors as well as courses have been changed to maintain anonymity. The interviews are also anonymized in the same way, but are still direct quotations from the tutors and students who participated in the research.

The two researchers on the project, Veena Meetoo and myself, were women of colour. This will, of course, have implications for the interaction between the researcher and the researched. In post-race times when race is always an 'absent present' (Nayak, 2006; Lentin, 2014; Kapoor *et al.*, 2013; Bhambra, 2016) what will be revealed in interviews to a white researcher will be different than to a person of colour. In the case studies, white tutors often told us 'happy' and successful stories of overcoming racism (Ahmed, 2012). While such narrative exchanges may seemingly reflect the respondent's interpretation of the racial and gendered dynamics of their social world as they see it, we were always aware that their retelling was embedded in the embodied discursive practices that shape their social world – such as structural white privilege or gendered racialized marginality (Applebaum, 2008). As black feminist researchers, situated as 'outsiders within' academia (Collins, 2000), in the tutors' narrative accounts we recognized an 'affective link 'between structural institutional process (i.e. access and progression) and the 'identity affects' (of how a subject 'feels' in the world). The concept of 'embodied intersectionality' (Mirza, 2009; Mirza, 2013) provided the tools to excavate the 'affective' processes of exclusion and marginality that were emerging in the data. We were able to gain an insight into the work equality discourses 'do' by looking more deeply into how differently situated raced, classed and gendered subjects make sense of the 'self' in relation to the language and practices that give current equality discourses meaning and so make them 'real'.

As an analytic framework, embodied intersectionality draws on the concept of intersectionality, a term developed by Kimberlé Crenshaw (1989; 1991). It rearticulated the foundational scholarship of black feminists such as the Combahee River Collective, Angela Davis, Audre Lorde and Patricia Hill Collins, who were concerned with understanding the 'matrix of domination in which cultural patterns of oppression are not only interrelated, but are bound together and influenced by the intersectional systems of society' (Collins, 2000: 42). Intersectionality provides a standpoint epistemology of 'really useful knowledge' that has been used to systematically reveal the everyday lives of black and postcolonial ethnicized women who are simultaneously positioned in multiple structures of dominance and power as gendered, raced, classed, colonized, sexualized others. It offers a way into understanding how particular identities (i.e. black and female) are tied to particular inequalities (i.e. violence against women) in different historical times and geographic places (McKittrick, 2006). Moreover, intersectionality enables us to see that different dimensions of social life cannot be separated out into discrete and pure strands. As Brah and Phoenix write, 'We regard the concept of intersectionality as signifying the complex, irreducible, varied, and variable effects that ensue when multiple axes of differentiation – economic, political, cultural, psychic, subjective and experiential – intersect in historically specific contexts' (2004: 76).

The original concept of intersectionality is a powerful tool for analysis because it can knit together the macro-economic, political and social discourses that structure inequities with an array of individuated subjectivities that are written on and lived within the body. As a black feminist critical theory of gendered racialization, the notion of embodied intersectionality uses the malleability of the concept of intersectionality and takes it a stage further (Mirza, 2009; Mirza, 2013). In this study, it provides a way to methodologically operationalize intersectionality by mapping the 'affect' of equality discourses as lived in and through the raced and gendered embodied subjectivities of the tutors and the students they teach. That is, it looks at how the external materiality of the black and minority ethnic student's situatedness (i.e. in the political, economic and social structures that produce inequality) is constituted, reconfigured and lived through their corporeal representation as seen by the white tutors (i.e. as 'undeserving', or needy, or 'oppressed' racialized others). In this way it illuminates how intersectional 'othering' that arises at unique historical moments (i.e. when the category 'black and minority ethnic' is invested with a particular affective and linguistic meaning) is then organized into systematic social relations and practices. It is at the intersection of the material external world and the embodied interior world that the identity of the racialized sexualized marginal subject comes into being. As Butler (1993) argues, it is through the repetition of norms on the surface of bodies that the boundaries and fixity of our social worlds materialize.

'It is way too out of my league': Recruitment, admissions and getting in the door

The research investigated the micro-institutional everyday practices that reproduce racism by identifying the 'flashpoints' in an organization that lead to discriminatory practices for black and minority ethnic teacher trainees. As Philomena Essed explains, racism is not only an ideology and a structure but also *a process* because 'structures and ideologies do not exist outside the everyday practices through which they are created and confirmed' (1991: 44). Routine and repetitive practices help to maintain existing social structures and relations and are reflective of and reconstitute the deeper roots or causes of racism. One such everyday institutional 'flashpoint' resides in the recruitment and admissions process. The first hurdle for the students is often the exclusionary effects of a highly cultivated image and reified reputation of a university. Students were often discouraged by advisers or would not apply to certain institutions if they were seen as 'privileged white spaces'. If they did, then admission processes were often influenced by well-meaning 'gatekeepers' who expressed 'commonsense' but prejudicial assumptions about the quality, ability and potential of black and minority ethnic students. As Keith in the following case study was told, 'Don't bother to apply, African Caribbean students have difficulty in getting in.'

Case study: Keith

Keith, a 22-year-old biology student from an undergraduate programme in south London, was advised by one of his university tutors not to apply to the HEI to do his PGCE. He was told that African Caribbean students usually had difficulty getting in because it was very competitive and they usually lacked the minimum degree requirements. However, by chance, a tutor from the HEI came to his college to recruit students to the PGCE. During the session, Keith mentioned the advice he had been given. The tutor reinforced that standards were 'high', but put him in touch with another student who shared his experience with Keith and recommended that he apply. Keith then requested an application and in the pack he found a notice for a pre-admissions workshop to help candidates through the application and admissions process. In the workshop, Keith discussed his interests and experiences and the tutor told him what he should emphasize in his application and personal statement for it to stand out, and how to approach the interview process. He warned Keith that in an attempt to be honest and reflective many black and minority students overemphasize their weaknesses and underemphasize their strengths. Keith submitted his application and was granted an interview. The interview brought out more than just Keith's academic history and enabled him to present a much broader picture of himself and the kind of teacher he would be. Eventually he was successful and was accepted on the course.

This is a not unfamiliar tale of 'embodied lacking', 'personal happenchance' and 'assimilated redemption' that unfolds for many black and minority ethnic students. First, Keith was 'protectively' warned not to apply as he was seen – like *all* other African Caribbean students – to inherently 'lack' the cultural and academic capital to enter the competitive academic spaces of elite whiteness. Many students may fall at this first hurdle where institutional gatekeepers police the boundaries of what is an 'acceptable or unacceptable' body and which 'type' of body has the right racial credentials to be allowed to enter the hallowed doors of white privilege. Many of the black and minority ethnic students in our study said they did not feel they would stand much of a chance of getting into elite universities, with comments including 'it is way too out of my league'. Their decisions tended to be moulded by an embodied sense of who they are and their expected 'place' in relation to how their race, class and gender would be perceived. Many saw the 'old' pre-1992 sandstone and redbrick universities as more traditional and strict, catering to more middle-class white students and therefore less accessible to those from non-traditional educational backgrounds. They often commented on how their familiarity with an HEI influenced their decision, especially if friends and family had gone before. Research shows black and minority ethnic students tend to stick to what they know is achievable and culturally comfortable, and in the light of the rising tuition fees, black and minority ethnic working-class students reduce their costs by not leaving home (Reay *et al.*, 2005; Smith, 2007).

Nirmal Puwar explains how cultures of exclusion operate within the contested social space of higher education. She suggests that black bodies 'out of place' in elite white institutions are perceived as 'space invaders' when they do not represent the 'racial somatic norm' within white institutions. She writes:

> Social spaces are not blank and open for any body to occupy. Over time, through processes of historical sedimentation, certain types of bodies are designated as being the 'natural' occupants of specific spaces ... Some bodies have the right to belong in certain locations, while others are marked out as trespassers who are in accordance with how both spaces and bodies are imagined, politically, historically and conceptually circumscribed as being 'out of place'. (Puwar, 2004: 51)

Such 'somatic' processes of exclusion in higher education are difficult to unpack as they are underscored by the embodied intersectional dynamics of race, class and gender. Diane Reay, Miriam David, and Stephen Ball shed light on these processes of exclusion, suggesting that young working-class and minority ethnic people can engage in 'self-exclusion' when making university choices, saying, 'what's a person like me doing in a place like that' (2005: 161). Processes of exclusion work through having 'a sense of one's place which leads one to exclude oneself from places from which one is excluded' (Reay *et al.*, 2005: 91). For black and minority ethnic students it is a painful journey of what they must 'give up' of themselves in order to belong. Reay *et al.* (2009) show how black and working-class survivors in elite universities learnt to navigate the hostilities of higher education through reflexively incorporating dominant white middle-class academic dispositions into their own working-class habitus. By taking part in the workshop. Keith gained the cultural and academic capital necessary to 'pass' into 'the heart of whiteness'. Kathleen Casey describes how black students' innocent expectations and eager quest for knowledge can take them on an unexpected journey 'to another place' where they are transformed by the consuming, monolithic power of whiteness:

> These young black women set off into the white world carrying expectations of mythic proportions; their odysseys, they believe, ... will transform not only their lives, but also those of other black people. But separated from their families, from their cultural communities, from their system of signification, from their existing black identities, these young women's passages turn out to be isolated, individual journeys 'into the heart of whiteness'.
> (Casey, 1993: 132)

Ultimately, in the tutor's best practice narrative Keith was redeemed through his 'assimilation' into a white HEI, facilitated by his 'white saviour' (the tutor). To be 'acculturated', lose your cultural markers, to learn to 'act white' (Fordham, 1996) and 'fit in' is important for black and minority ethnic students, as 'standing out' can invoke deep feelings of need, rejection and anxiety within the 'white other'. Sara Ahmed (2012) explains that black and minority ethnic students can be exotically different but not too racially, sexually and religiously different as such radical difference is taken as a rejection of the institutional 'host's society's gift of the multicultural embrace'. Thus to be unassimilated or 'stand out' in an institution invites a certain type of surveillance that appears benign but can be deeply distressing for black and ethnicized students. For example, Patricia Hill Collins shows how middle-class African American women in higher education are 'watched' to ensure they remain 'unraced' and assimilated when they enter desegregated institutional spaces of whiteness in the increasingly devalued public sphere from which they were hitherto barred (1998: 38). As the black feminist Patricia Williams explains (1991: 74), you can so easily 'lose a piece of yourself' when navigating the traumatic everyday incursions into your selfhood as a black person on the journey 'into the heart of whiteness'.

'That's so unfair!': Positive action, retention and staying the course

Whether their views were radical or conservative most of the tutors outwardly expressed a social justice ethos and wanted to be more effective in supporting their black and minority ethnic students through their programmes of learning. However, many demonstrated a reluctance to take explicit 'positive action' to support a struggling black or minority ethnic student. They often felt this amounted to unfair 'special pleading' on the grounds of 'racial disadvantage' that would ultimately lead to a 'dilution of quality' and 'lowering standards' on the course. It was common for white tutors to talk about 'merit' and 'ability' as an objective, value-free 'antiracist' arbiter of true equality, without any regard for the caste, class and white privilege that structure access to such opportunities. Such a 'colour-blind' approach to equalities in which everyone is 'treated the same' whatever their background was evident in the case of Sam, a Nigerian engineer. Though bringing a wealth of 'non-traditional experience' to the teaching profession, Sam was given no extra support when he was struggling to complete the course.

Case study Sam

Sam, a 42-year-old black British African student applied to the primary PGCE. He had been educated in Nigeria and had been living for many years in Britain. He had a third class degree in engineering from a British 'new' university, but he had not managed to get a good job since graduating. He ended up in a series of casual jobs for several years. He was now a volunteer youth and community worker on an after-school project on a large and troubled council estate and enjoyed the challenges of teaching the young people very much. He had recently had two children and was committed to becoming a primary teacher in maths and science to help him explore their development and understand them better. Dave and Linda, the two white middle-class tutors, had initially disagreed about his admission onto the course. Dave said, though he believed in positive action, it would be unfair to give Sam the extra time and support he needed to bring him up to the level expected on the course. He argued that though there was a national drive to recruit more men, especially black and minority ethnic men, into primary teaching, and Sam could make a good teacher and role model for black pupils, he did not think he would survive the course. Linda, however, stressed that the different routes that ethnic minority students come through enrich the course and the different understandings of education and culture that Sam brought with him are just as important. Linda 'won' and Sam was finally admitted to the course. However he was treated 'the same' as all the other students with no extra help with his assignments. He also experienced unfair treatment and discrimination in his school placement, which he was left to deal with alone. When it reached crisis point and Sam was about to drop out, a mentor was found to support him. He took a lot longer to get through, but finally he graduated but not in the same year as his class.

Sam's story is a tale of the racialized consequences of liberal equity policies and a student's resilience to overcome the structural systemic racism it engenders. Sam was caught up in the complex web of disadvantage inherent in the liberal approach to equal opportunities. On the one hand, it recognizes the need to 'level up the playing field' of opportunities to ensure people from excluded or disadvantaged ethnic minority or other protected groups can compete on equal terms with more privileged groups. On the other hand, certain policies like 'positive action' that are intended to either prevent discrimination or make up for the accumulated effects of past discrimination do not tackle the underlying structural causes of racism (Bhavnani *et al.*, 2005; Essed, 1991). Thus, while numerical targets and policies can be set if there is evidence of underrepresentation of minority ethnic groups within various levels of an organization, professional interventions based on such race equality initiatives are imbued with contradictions inherent in their racialized development. For example, while Linda celebrated and embraced Sam's 'difference' as a positive attribute to facilitate his access, David interpreted equity as treating everyone the same in a colour-blind way. Sam fell into the gap between the two interpretations of equity (of access) and equality (of outcome) that circulate in our policies in HE institutions.

Sara Ahmed (2012) argues that equality policies and diversity documents alone cannot remove racism from the institution. These documents constitute 'non-performative' institutional 'speech acts'. Thus a university making a public commitment to diversity, or declaration that they are non-racist and 'for equality', becomes a 'speech act' that works precisely by *not* bringing about the effects it intends. She explains having a 'good' race equality policy gets translated into an institution *being good at race equality*, 'as if saying is doing'. For example, newer universities that are seen as 'diversity led' (as they have many students from ethnic minorities and lower socio-economic backgrounds) present themselves as 'being diverse' without having to do anything. Simply 'being diverse' means new universities need not commit to 'doing diversity'. The significant disparity between universities' policy commitments and the experiences of black and minority ethnic students such as Sam suggests deep ongoing institutional barriers and discriminatory practices in the higher education sector.

There are many costs to 'just being there' for black and minority ethnic students in higher education and Sam's 'price' was high. Black and minority ethnic students are more likely to leave university before completing their course than any other group and least likely to get a good degree (Universities UK, 2016; Richardson, 2015). The most influential reasons for leaving are unmet expectations about higher education. While financial and family difficulties, institutional factors (such as poor teaching) and wrong subject choice also feature, ethnic minority students additionally reported the feeling of isolation or hostility in academic culture (Connor *et al.*, 2004; Reay, 2017). These are worrying findings, as they signal the fact that many black students do not feel they 'belong'. Bodies that are visually recognized as raced and gendered clearly carry unequal value depending on their position in space and place (Skeggs, 1997). Sam's embodied experience as a black African man 'out of place' is articulated in Frantz Fanon's classic analysis of the colonial racialization of the black body, which he poignantly argues is 'sealed in to the crushing object hood of the skin'. As Fanon writes:

> Not only must the black man be black, he must be black in relation to the white man. ... The black man among his own in the twentieth century does not know at what moment his inferiority comes into being through the other. ... In the white world the man of color encounters difficulties in the development of his bodily schema. ... A slow composition of me as a body in the middle of a spatial and temporal world – such seems to be the schema. It does not impose itself on me; it is rather a definitive structuring of the self and of the world – definitive because it creates a real dialectic between my body and the world. (Fanon, 2008: 82–3)

There appear to be two antagonistic forces at play in higher education that frame Sam's intersectional raced, gendered and classed embodied experience. One moves unconsciously and haphazardly towards what Stuart Hall (2000) has called 'multicultural drift', with its eclectic 'grab bag' of solutions for achieving equality through the end goal of 'assimilated difference' (Lentin, 2016). The other remains the 'sheer weight of whiteness', which in HE institutions is overt and impenetrable (Back, 2004; Alexander and Arday, 2015). Gillborn (2008) argues whiteness is a position that involves the maintenance of white interests and white privilege. It does so by excluding non-whites and denying that white people are racialized. By asserting that white supremacy is only claimed by extremists groups, whiteness assumes the 'business-as-usual' silent domination that sustains the symbolic violence of everyday racism. This whiteness is evident in the 'soft', unchallenging, antiracist/multicultural position taken up by white student teachers and tutors (Lander, 2011). For example, Wilkins and Lall (2010) found that racist comments aimed at black and minority ethnic student teachers were perceived as 'unwitting prejudice' rather than racist. A comment such as 'Did you have an arranged marriage?' was normalized rather than seen as racist because of its assumed 'unintentionality'. Solomon *et al.* (2005) found student teachers rejected notions of white privilege, as did Aveling's (2006) study, in which the examination of whiteness led to student hostility, defence and denial.

The white tutors were united in wanting more open dialogue in their institutions about tackling issues of racism that went beyond simple compliance with the law. However, they found little time to do so. They expressed a desire to challenge their professional practice by developing an inclusive classroom pedagogy underpinned by culturally relevant curricula, and desired a 'safe' space for open and frank dialogue about tackling issues of racism at a personal and professional level. However, decolonizing taken-for-granted knowledges and entrenched 'ways of being' inherent within our institutional walls requires deep self-reflection, and an intellectual and institutional 'safe' space to develop critical consciousness is not easy to achieve. As Gaine (2001) asserts, 'If it's not hurting it's not working', alluding to the cognitive conflict associated with race awareness training without which there will be no true shift in understanding the privileges of whiteness. However, in the latest incarnation of bureaucratic antiracist training, concerns about institutional racism in the 1990s have given way to lessons in 'unconscious bias' (ECU, 2013). Such workshops are never 'safe spaces' for people of colour who are so often invited to 'tell their story'. In an inherently violent colonial racial order, race dialogue in white privileged frameworks means that, in reality, 'blacks disappear to give way to educating whites' (Leonardo and Porter, 2010).

'I'll teach you a lesson': Progression, support and navigating gender, race and faith

The experience of racism was not uncommon during the students' placements and tutors reported having to deal directly with incidents around gendered faith-based ethnic and cultural differences. Teacher educators often posed the question, 'How do we tackle cultural, faith-based and familial tensions without being racist or patronising?' Generally, and somewhat surprisingly for a university with a 'diverse' student make-up, tutors were not confident and received very little training and support on issues to do with multiculturalism, bilingualism, and inclusive pedagogy and practice. Topics such as talking about Islam and ethnic and religious difference were consciously avoided in classroom discussions. While supporting black and minority ethnic students through their teaching practice was a core concern of tutors, many felt 'multiculturalism', with its inclusive emphasis on accommodating different cultures and religions, can conflict with their 'neutral' professional aim of supporting *all* students to achieve their potential. As the following case study of Kusbah illustrates, this was particularly so for Muslim female students, who were often stereotyped as either 'passive or oppressed'. The story of Kusbah illuminates how the intersectional complexities of gender, race and religion are lived in, on and through the Muslim female body and have real consequences for how she is perceived and the opportunities to progress that are therefore open to her.

Case study: Kusbah

Cate, a white tutor on the PGCE primary course, received an email from Kusbah, a Muslim student in her tutor group, saying that she felt her school-based mentor was treating her more harshly than the other BTs (beginning teachers) in her placement school. The mentor, Paul, had made comments about Muslim 'girls' [sic] being 'too passive and acquiescent to teach effectively'. She was convinced that this was a case of religious racism and sexism. Cate asked Kusbah to detail her experience in writing so that she could take it up with the school and offered to arrange for Kusbah to finish her placement at another school. Cate arranged to meet with Paul to discuss the matter. He said that it had been his experience that all Muslim women made poor teachers because they were too passive with the pupils and they 'let them walk all over them'. He said that if he was harder on Kusbah, this was the reason. Cate explained that his views represented a racist stereotype and had no place in teacher education. He disagreed and insisted they were merely an accurate assessment of all the Muslim women teachers he had encountered. He was reprimanded and the course leader wrote to the head saying that the situation violated the HEI's and the school's legal duty to promote racial equality, and that the decision had been made to deselect the school until the school had taken steps to prevent this situation arising in the future.

Kusbah's story is one of embodied racialized religious 'threat' and the racist gendered, physical and psychological containment it invokes. Visible Muslim women wearing the veil, such as Kusbah, openly face hostile reactions in a climate of state-sanctioned gendered Islamophobic discrimination (EHRC, 2016). The scholarly interventions of postcolonial critical race feminists shows how the Muslim female body has become a symbolic battlefield in the war against Islam and the perceived Muslim enemy 'within' (Razack, 2008; Razack *et al.*, 2010). Sara Ahmed argues that the discourses of fear and anxiety that have circulated since the September 11th attacks in America work by securing what is the 'truth' about 'the other'. She states that 'fear operates as an affective economy of truth: fear slides between signs and sticks to bodies by constituting them as its objects ... fear sticks to some bodies and not others' (2003: 377). For example the judgement that someone 'could be' a terrorist draws on past and affective associations that stick various signs (such as Muslim, fundamentalist, terrorist) together. In the West's ideological 'War against Terror' the ubiquitous 'Muslim woman' has come to symbolize the 'barbaric Muslim other' in our midst. The visibility of patriarchal community and group cultural practices such as forced marriage and honour crimes conveniently contribute to the Western 'Orientalist' construction of the racialized Muslim other's barbaric customs and cultures (Said, 1985). This is articulated through Muslim women being pathologized as voiceless victims of their 'backward' communities who are in need of 'saving' by the enlightened 'West' (Abu-Lughod, 2002).

Paul was exceptionally hard on Kusbah as a Muslim woman student because he believed *all* Muslim women make poor teachers. She needed 'saving' from herself and to be given a dose of tough love so she could make 'the grade'. Paul believed he had a legitimate right – authority even – to comment and judge Kusbah as a weak and acquiescent 'Muslim woman'. Research shows Muslim young women in schools are often subject to white Western teachers' essentialized expectations about what it means to be a 'true' and 'good' Muslim young woman (Mirza and Meetoo, 2017). Their lives in the classroom were structured by both openly expressed gendered religious racism, as well as by the more subtle forms of covert bodily regulation of their sexuality through the policing of their behaviour and dress. The teachers' perceptions of the young women wearing the veil were bounded by popular concerns about their agency and what they perceived to be their cultural and familial disempowerment and restricted scope for choice. The hypersurveillance Kusbah was subjected to by Paul in the cultural and social space of the school amounted to a form of 'infantilization' of her agency and ability (Puwar, 2004). Here not only was Kusbah pigeonholed as being Muslim and female but she was also seen as less capable of being in authority – with 'pupils walking all over her'. She was viewed suspiciously and had to work harder for recognition outside of the confines of stereotypical expectations. The constant doubt about her skills and the disciplinary measures she was disproportionately subjected to affected her career progression as she was being failed by Paul in her teaching practice.

Paul saw Kusbah's Islamic practices and beliefs through the Western normative assumptions about Muslim female docility and complicity with patriarchal conservative cultural values. However, a Muslim woman's agency and acts of faith are rarely seen within the broader political and social environment. As Sara Ahmed explains (2004), the figure of the veiled Muslim woman challenges the values that are crucial to the multicultural nation, such freedom and the 'British way of life' making her a symbol of what the nation must 'give up' to be itself. Muslim women are conscious of the 'disjunction' between how they see themselves and how they are racially constructed as a 'female Muslim other' in Britain (Khan, 2016). The embodied experience of being a British Muslim woman 'out of place' is articulated by the postcolonial feminist writer Lata Mani. She writes, 'The disjunctions between how I saw myself and the kind of knowledge about me that I kept bumping into in the West opened up new questions for social and political inquiry' (1989: 11). For Kusbah, being a Muslim woman was a crucial aspect of her sense of self and ethnic belonging. It was through her religious disposition that she expressed her embodied gendered religious agency. For many Muslim women the headscarf (hijab) is not a symbol of oppression but experienced as a 'second skin' (Mirza, 2013). Personal embodied acts of piety such as wearing the hijab are an 'identity affect' that enables them to move beyond the simplistic cultural constructions of Muslim women in the media that negate Muslim female agency (Haw, 2009). In contrast to the more outwardly collective masculine expressions of Muslimness, in which Islam has been mobilized as a political and nationalistic power resource in civil society, Muslim women like Kusbah express their faith as a private transcendental spiritual space from which they derive an inner strength. Saba Mahmood (2005) seeks to explain this form of embodied gendered religious agency through the understanding of acts of piety or taqwa. She argues that Muslim women's religious disposition, such as obedience to God, brings spiritual rewards in and of itself to the women. She suggests that in order to understand Islamic female forms of moral subjectivity and embodied spiritual interiority, we must move beyond Western imperialist notions of liberatory emancipation and the deterministic binaries of resistance/subordination by which Muslim female subjectivity and agency are so often judged.

Conclusion: Evaluating widening participation intersectionally through gender, race, faith and culture

In this chapter I take a black feminist embodied approach to evaluating the intersectionality of gender, race, faith and culture as it manifests itself in our overwhelmingly dominant white places of teaching and learning. By interrogating the micro-institutional practices that maintain endemic patterns of racist exclusion in higher education, the three cases studies that frame this chapter, in recruitment, retention and progression, illuminate what I call racialized institutional 'flashpoints'. These are moments when black and minority ethnic students on a teacher education course come up against systemic institutional gendered and racialized disadvantage. 'Embodied intersectionality' (Mirza, 2009; Mirza, 2013) as a concept gave me the theoretical tools to help me make sense of the PGCE tutors' narratives and unpack the ways in which race, class, gender, and other social divisions were simultaneously experienced as lived realities on and through the black male and Muslim female bodies of Keith, Sam and Kusbah. All three students were constructed as 'bodies out of place' in the 'best practice' equality narratives of the tutors. In each case, the students' embodied raced and gendered human agency framed their struggle for life chances and academic well-being on the course.

Evaluating patterns of exclusion in the recruitment and admissions process revealed the ways in which certain black bodies, such as African Caribbean young men, were perceived as 'space invaders' when they did not represent the 'racial somatic norm' within elite white institutions (Puwar, 2004). When Keith does break through the admissions barrier there is the price of 'assimilation' and what he must give up of himself to belong and so successfully 'pass' into 'the heart of whiteness'. The black feminist bell hooks recounts her own story of leaving home and going to university and becoming a successful academic:

> When I left that concrete space on the margins, I kept alive in my heart ways of knowing reality ... [I was] sustained by remembrance of the past, which includes recollections of broken tongues that decolonize our minds, our very beings. (hooks, 1991: 150)

Equal opportunities are not always about equality in white institutions, and evaluating Sam's case demonstrates the contradictions of policies aimed at creating an equitable 'level playing field' for students of colour. On the one hand, Sam suffered from the racialized misrecognition of the African black male 'other' (Fanon, 2008). On the other, his hypervisibility engendered a conscious colour-blind approach among his tutors that cut him adrift in a hostile learning environment. Sam's complex, multilayered habitus as an African man – that is, his ways of standing, speaking, walking, feeling, and thinking – situates his body *in* the social world but his identity and sense of self is how the social world is *in* his body (Bourdieu, 1990). Thus Sam's personalized embodied experience is not only deeply racialized but also gendered. Felly Simmonds, the black feminist writer, explains how racialized gendered racism is simultaneously experienced as a 'weight on the body':

> As a black woman, I know myself inside and outside myself. My relation to this knowledge is conditioned by the social reality of my habitus. But my socialized subjectivity is that of a black

woman and it is at odds with the social world of which I am a product, for this social world is a white world ... in this white world I am a fresh water fish that swims in sea water. I feel the weight of the water on my body. (1997, 226–7)

The overt racism that Kusbah experienced as a veiled Muslim woman illuminated the multiple ways macro-geopolitical discourses of anti-Islamic hostility in Britain and its production of the raced and gendered Muslim female body operate through institutional structures in HE to 'affectively' reproduce racialized gendered divisions that inhibit academic progression. Paul, the white tutor, believed he was 'saving' Kusbah from her culture and religion, which he 'knew'. To be 'known better than you know yourself' is a powerful colonial strategy that renders the 'known' as voiceless – that is 'mute visible objects' without agency or self-determination (Mohanty, 2003). Parallels can be drawn to colonial times when women's bodies were central to the imperial civilizing mission in which the 'heroic' white male colonists claimed to be 'saving brown women from brown men' (Spivak, 1988).

As researchers and practitioners, if we are serious about evaluating the political project of widening participation, we need to ask ourselves, 'What are our principles of antiracist professional and academic engagement, and how do we arrive at them?' If we are to achieve *real* equality of outcome for black and minority ethnic people *in* our places of higher learning, the challenge for widening participation in 'post-race' times is to move the discourse beyond targeting the bodies of raced and gendered others to 'get them in the door'. A more diverse and equitable higher education system is more than just 'good business sense'. It is a moral and legal imperative that fundamentally changes our pedagogy and practice and shifts the way we teach and learn. In post-race times, where 'race' is off the political agenda, new patterns of insidious racism and deep inequalities are evolving. There is a much-needed dialogue on race, faith and culture that goes beyond the performativity of race equality in our institutions. The task is not easy, and as history shows, movements for racial justice are wrought with messy and hard-fought struggles between the powerful and those who are deemed less than human. The sustainability and success of such movements are predicated on a capacity for forgiveness and a commitment to a steep and honest learning curve for all those involved.

References

Abu-Lughod, L. (2002) 'Do Muslim women really need saving? Anthropological reflections on cultural relativism and its others'. *American Anthropologist*, 104 (3), 783–90.

Ahmed, S. (2003) 'The politics of fear in the making of worlds'. *International Journal of Qualitative Studies in Education*, 16 (3), 377–98.

Ahmed, S. (2004) *The Cultural Politics of Emotion*. Edinburgh: Edinburgh University Press.

Ahmed, S. (2012) *On Being Included: Racism and diversity in institutional life*. Durham, NC: Duke University Press.

Alexander, C. and Arday, J. (eds) (2015) *Aiming Higher: Race, inequality and diversity in the academy*. London: Runnymede Trust.

Applebaum, B. (2008) '"Doesn't my experience count?": White students, the authority of experience and social justice pedagogy'. *Race Ethnicity and Education*, 11 (4), 405–14.

Aveling, N. (2006) '"Hacking at our very roots": Rearticulating white racial identity within the context of teacher education'. *Race Ethnicity and Education*, 9 (3), 261–74.

Back, L. (2004) 'Ivory towers? The academy and racism'. In Law, I., Phillips, D. and Turney, L. (eds) *Institutional Racism in Higher Education*. Stoke-on-Trent: Trentham Books, 1–6.

Bhambra, G.K. (2016) 'Class analysis in the age of Trump (and Brexit): The pernicious new politics of identity'. *Sociological Review*, 22 November. Online. www.thesociologicalreview.com/blog/class-analysis-in-the-age-of-trump-and-brexit-the-pernicious-new-politics-of-identity.html (accessed 10 December 2017).

Bhavnani, R., Mirza, H.S. and Meetoo, V. (2005) *Tackling the Roots of Racism: Lessons for success*. Bristol: Policy Press.

Bhopal, K. and Jackson, J. (2013) *The Experiences of Black and Minority Ethnic Academics: Multiple identities and career progression*. Southampton: University of Southampton.

Bourdieu, P. (1990). *In Other Words: Essays toward a reflexive sociology*. Cambridge: Polity Press.

Brah, A. and Phoenix, A. (2004) 'Ain't I a woman? Revisiting intersectionality'. *Journal of International Women's Studies*, 5 (3), Article 8, 75–86.

Butler, J. (1993) *Bodies That Matter: On the discursive limits of 'sex'*. New York: Routledge.

Caluya, G., Probyn, E. and Vyas, S. (2011) '"Affective eduscapes": The case of Indian students within Australian international higher education'. *Cambridge Journal of Education*, 41 (1), 85–99.

Casey, K. (1993) *I Answer with My Life: Life histories of women teachers working for social change*. New York: Routledge.

Collins, P.H. (1998) *Fighting Words: Black women and the search for justice*. Minneapolis: University of Minnesota Press.

Collins, P.H. (2000) *Black Feminist Thought: Knowledge, consciousness, and the politics of empowerment*. 2nd ed. New York: Routledge.

Connor, H., Tyers, C., Modood, T. and Hillage, J. (2004) *Why the Difference? A closer look at higher education minority ethnic students and graduates* (Research Report RR552). Nottingham: Department for Education and Skills.

Crenshaw, K. (1989) 'Demarginalizing the intersection of race and sex: A black feminist critique of antidiscrimination doctrine, feminist theory and antiracist politics'. *University of Chicago Legal Forum*, 139–67.

Crenshaw, K. (1991) 'Mapping the margins: Intersectionality, identity politics, and violence against women of color'. *Stanford Law Review*, 43 (6), 1241–99.

ECU (Equality Challenge Unit) (2013) *Unconscious Bias and Higher Education*. London: Equality Challenge Unit.

EHRC (Equality and Human Rights Commission) (2016) *Healing a Divided Britain: The need for a comprehensive race equality strategy*. London: Equality and Human Rights Commission.

Essed, P. (1991) *Understanding Everyday Racism: An interdisciplinary theory*. Newbury Park, CA: Sage.

Fanon, F. (2008) *Black Skin, White Masks*. Trans. Markmann, C.L. London: Pluto Press.

Fordham, S. (1996) *Blacked Out: Dilemmas of race, identity, and success at Capital High*. Chicago: University of Chicago Press.

Gaine, C. (2001) '"If it's not hurting it's not working": Teaching teachers about "race"'. *Research Papers in Education*, 16 (1), 93–113.

Gillborn, D. (2008) *Racism and Education: Coincidence or conspiracy?* London: Routledge.

Hall, S. (2000) 'Conclusion: The multi-cultural question'. In Hesse, B. (ed.) *Un/Settled Multiculturalisms: Diasporas, entanglements, 'transruptions'*. London: Zed Books, 209–41.

Haw, K. (2009) 'From hijab to jilbab and the "myth" of British identity: Being Muslim in contemporary Britain a half-generation on'. *Race Ethnicity and Education*, 12 (3), 363–78.

hooks, b. (1991) *Yearning: Race, gender, and cultural politics*. London: Turnaround Books.

Kapoor, N., Kalra, V.S. and Rhodes, J. (eds) (2013) *The State of Race*. Basingstoke: Palgrave Macmillan.

Khan, A. (2016) 'Sorry, Louise Casey, but Muslim women are held back by discrimination'. *The Guardian*, 6 December. Online. www.theguardian.com/commentisfree/2016/dec/06/louise-casey-discrimination-muslim-women-bradford (accessed 10 December 2017).

Lander, V. (2011) 'Race, culture and all that: An exploration of the perspectives of white secondary student teachers about race equality issues in their initial teacher education'. *Race Ethnicity and Education*, 14 (3), 351–64.

Lentin, A. (2014) 'Post-race, post politics: The paradoxical rise of culture after multiculturalism'. *Ethnic and Racial Studies*, 37 (8), 1268–85.

Lentin, A. (2016) 'The "crisis of multiculturalism" and the global politics of Trumpism'. *Sociological Review*, 4 December. Online. www.thesociologicalreview.com/blog/the-crisis-of-multiculturalism-and-the-global-politics-of-trumpism.html (accessed 10 December 2017).

Leonardo, Z. and Porter, R.K. (2010) 'Pedagogy of fear: Toward a Fanonian theory of "safety" in race dialogue'. *Race Ethnicity and Education*, 13 (2), 139–57.

Mahmood, S. (2005) *Politics of Piety: The Islamic revival and the feminist subject*. Princeton: Princeton University Press.

Mani, L. (1989) 'Multiple mediations: Feminist scholarship in the age of multinational reception.' *Inscriptions*, 5, 1–23.

McKittrick, K. (2006) *Demonic Grounds: Black women and the cartographies of struggle*. Minneapolis: University of Minnesota Press.

Mirza, H.S. (2009) *Race, Gender and Educational Desire: Why black women succeed and fail*. London: Routledge.

Mirza, H.S. (2013) '"A second skin": Embodied intersectionality, transnationalism and narratives of identity and belonging among Muslim women in Britain'. *Women's Studies International Forum*, 36, 5–15.

Mirza, H.S. (2017) '"One in a million": A journey of a post-colonial woman of colour in the white academy'. In Gabriel, D. and Tate, S. (eds) *Inside the Ivory Tower: Narratives of women of colour surviving and thriving in British academia*. Stoke-on-Trent: Trentham Books.

Mirza, H.S. and Meetoo, V. (2012) *Respecting Difference: Race, faith and culture for teacher educators*. London: Institute of Education.

Mirza, H.S. and Meetoo, V. (2017) 'Empowering Muslim girls? Post-feminism, multiculturalism and the production of the "model" Muslim female student in British schools'. *British Journal of Sociology of Education*. doi:10.1080/014256 92.2017.1406336

Mohanty, C.T. (2003) *Feminism without Borders: Decolonizing theory, practicing solidarity*. Durham, NC: Duke University Press.

Nayak, A. (2006) 'After race: Ethnography, race and post-race theory'. *Ethnic and Racial Studies*, 29 (3), 411–30.

Puwar, N. (2004) 'Fish in or out of water: A theoretical framework for race and the space of academia'. In Law, I., Phillips, D. and Turney, L. (eds) *Institutional Racism in Higher Education*. Stoke-on-Trent: Trentham Books, 49–70.

Razack, S.H. (2008) *Casting Out: The eviction of Muslims from Western law and politics*. Toronto: University of Toronto Press.

Razack, S., Smith, M. and Thobani, S. (eds) (2010) *States of Race: Critical race feminism for the 21st century*. Toronto: Between the Lines.

Reay, D. (2017) *Miseducation: Inequality education and the working classes*. Bristol: Policy Press.

Reay, D., Crozier, G. and Clayton, J. (2009) '"Strangers in paradise"? Working-class students in elite universities'. *Sociology*, 43 (6), 1103–21.

Reay, D., David, M.E. and Ball, S. (2005) *Degrees of Choice: Class, race, gender and higher education*. Stoke-on-Trent: Trentham Books.

Richardson, J.T.E. (2015) 'The under-attainment of ethnic minority students in UK higher education: What we know and what we don't know'. *Journal of Further and Higher Education*, 39 (2), 278–91.

Said, E.W. (1985) *Orientalism*. Harmondsworth: Penguin Books.

Skeggs, B. (1997) *Formations of Class and Gender: Becoming respectable*. London: Sage.

Simmonds, F.N. (1997) 'My body, myself: How does a black woman do sociology?'. In Mirza, H.S. (ed.) *Black British Feminism: A reader*. London: Routledge, 226–39.

Smith, H. (2007) 'Playing a different game: The contextualised decision-making processes of minority ethnic students in choosing a higher education institution'. *Race Ethnicity and Education*, 10 (4), 415–37.

Solomon, R.P., Portelli, J.P., Daniel, B.-J. and Campbell, A. (2005) 'The discourse of denial: How white teacher candidates construct race, racism and "white privilege"'. *Race Ethnicity and Education*, 8 (2), 147–69.

Solórzano, D.G. and Yosso, T.J. (2002) 'Critical race methodology: Counter-storytelling as an analytical framework of education research'. *Qualitative Inquiry*, 8 (1), 23–44.

Spivak, G.C. (1988) 'Can the subaltern speak?'. In Nelson, C. and Grossberg, L. (eds) *Marxism and the Interpretation of Culture*. Basingstoke: Macmillan, 271–313.

Universities UK (2016) *Working in Partnership: Enabling social mobility in higher education: The final report of the Social Mobility Advisory Group*. London: Universities UK.

Wilkins, C. and Lall, R. (2010) 'Getting by or getting on? Black student teachers' experiences of teacher education'. *Race Equality Teaching*, 28 (2), 19–26.

Williams, P.J. (1991) *The Alchemy of Race and Rights: Diary of a law professor*. Cambridge, MA: Harvard University Press.

Wilshaw, M. (2016) *The Annual Report of Her Majesty's Chief Inspector of Education, Children's Services and Skills 2015/16* (HC821). London: Ofsted. Online. www.gov.uk/government/publications/ofsted-annual-report-201516-education-early-years-and-skills (accessed 10 December 2017).

Chapter 7

When class trumps university status: Narratives of Zoe and Francesca from the Paired Peers project

Nicola Ingram, Jessica Abrahams and Ann-Marie Bathmaker

Introduction

Graduates in the UK are now facing precarious employment markets with a high demand for limited jobs. The number of graduates flooding these markets has steadily increased over the last decade, altering the supply and demand ratio and increasing the competition for graduate-level employment. Partially in response to this, as well as to shifts in university policy, competition and funding, higher education institutions have been developing an increasing focus on 'employability' as part of their overall educational remit. It is under these socio-economic circumstances that the Paired Peers project has tracked a cohort of young people who entered higher education (HE) in 2010, through their degree programmes and into their early post-graduation destinations (90 over the duration of the first phase of the project; 55 in the second phase). This chapter presents some of the early findings of the second phase of this project, which is focused on graduate transitions. It considers the impact of social class on two young people's attempts to forge their way into elite employment. The research followed a qualitative approach (pairing up students from different class backgrounds) with the aim of providing a rich, textured picture of the ways in which social inequalities can play out in graduates' experiences of employment, contributing to an understanding of what lies beneath statistics that show unequal graduate outcomes by class.

The expansion and diversification of higher education systems, particularly in industrialized and postindustrial countries, mean that more young people, including those from disadvantaged backgrounds, gain access to university. While access remains an important issue, increasingly attention has become focused on employability and employment futures. In a marketized environment predicated on competition and competitiveness, graduate employment, and the return to individuals as a result of completing a degree, are seen as key incentives for participation in HE. However, HE is also implicated in the reproduction of elites, as discussed in the work of Dorling (2014) and the report of the Panel on Fair Access to the Professions (Milburn, 2009), among others. Brown and colleagues (2011) have found that certain global companies only recruit from a small number of top universities worldwide. As their research suggests, while participation in HE in general is perceived to provide access to a wealth of opportunities, the type of university attended can also affect the graduate opportunities available. Moreover, working-class students may remain disadvantaged because they are unable to mobilize and exploit different forms of capital in the same ways as their highly resourced middle-class counterparts, both during their undergraduate studies, and in making the transition to graduate labour markets (Bathmaker *et al.*, 2016; Bathmaker *et al.*, 2013; Brown *et al.*, 2011; Devine, 2004). So while HE has the potential to be game-changing for working-class students, they may need greater resilience and resourcefulness than the average student in order to make HE work for them (Archer *et al.*, 2003; Reay *et al.*, 2009, Reay *et al.*, 2010; Reay *et al.*, 2005).

In this chapter, we address the following questions:

- How do young people from privileged and from disadvantaged backgrounds experience their trajectories through higher education and into work, including the process of finding graduate employment?
- In what ways can social class background affect pathways and opportunities in the transition into labour markets after attaining a degree qualification?
- What are the policy implications for issues of social mobility and social class inequality?

We consider these questions through an in-depth analysis of semi-structured interviews with two recent graduates from Bristol's two universities (University of Bristol and University of the West of England), both of whom studied law. The interview data are from a study funded by the Leverhulme Trust (the Paired Peers project), a longitudinal, qualitative research project that has followed a cohort of students through the first three years of undergraduate study (2010–13) and for three more years (2014–17) as they make transitions beyond undergraduate education. Students were interviewed twice every year during their undergraduate study, and once a year after graduation, enabling us to compare the fortunes of middle-class and working-class students during and beyond university study. In this way the project has aimed to explore the potential of HE as a vehicle for social mobility. The findings from the first phase of the project appear in our published book *Higher Education, Social Class and Social Mobility: The degree generation* (Bathmaker *et al.*, 2016).

Although much HE policy on access and widening participation (WP) does not explicitly name social class as the issue at stake (and instead uses proxies for class such as living in a low-participation neighbourhood or attending a low-performing school), we argue for the importance of retaining class as a unit of analysis when considering issues of equity and mobility. The Paired Peers study selected students on the basis of their social-class background, and named social class as the central focus for analysis. Without considering social class directly, the picture of class inequality can readily be obscured in data, while widening participation strategies can capture, and advantage, those who are already privileged. For example, using neighbourhood participation rates and school performance measures can allow middle-class young people from poorly performing schools or neighbourhoods to be considered as WP students.

Measuring or assessing social class is not an easy task and in order to do this we carried out a survey of all undergraduates in the 11 subject areas that were common to both institutions, and from which we drew participants for the study. Using the information gathered we assigned social class to participants on the basis of a combination of the following: parental occupation, parental participation in higher education, school type, self-reflection on proportion of school friends who moved to HE, self-definition of class, neighbourhood participation, and whether they received a grant or bursary. For some students their class position was clear from this information, so, for example, we were comfortable assigning a student with a professor mother and a general practitioner father as middle-class. But for others this was less clear-cut, for example we were not certain where to position a student whose mother was a nurse and whose father was a builder. The majority of our participants were recruited from the groups we had assigned with certainty. For those we recruited from the less certain groups, we further evaluated our assignment of class after we had conducted the first biographical interview. A more detailed explanation of the complexities of this process and a more thorough discussion of social class can be found in Bathmaker *et al.* (2016).

Our analysis uses the work of Pierre Bourdieu, in particular his concept of capital, and its exploitation in particular fields in accordance with a habitus oriented to appropriating the stakes of that field (Bourdieu, 1986). We work here, as in other analyses from the Paired Peers team (Bathmaker *et al.*, 2016; Bathmaker *et al.*, 2013), with the analogy of 'playing the game' in order to consider graduates' hopes, expectations, outcomes and future orientations. The notion of habitus encapsulates the idea that a person's way of thinking and acting in the world is structured by the accumulation of the history of their interactive experiences in different social fields, and governed by tacit rules. The field acts as a structuring force on the habitus to create individual schemes of perception and action. For Bourdieu, the habitus directs a person's way of being and allows them to know how to play the game in the fields in which it has developed. Bourdieu explains: 'Habitus is that presence of the past in the present which makes possible the presence in the present of the forthcoming' (2000: 210). Habitus shapes what is thinkable and what can be expected, and orients aspiration towards what is probable. In this way the whole history of a person's experiences lives with them through the present and guides their conceptualization of the future.

The connection between habitus and field is an important one, and in education much research has highlighted the significance of the alignment of habitus and field for the emotional well-being and achievement of young people (Reay, 2005; Ingram, 2009; Ingram, 2011; Abrahams and Ingram, 2013). When both habitus and field align, then the way to act and 'knowing what to do' becomes 'naturalized' and taken for granted. Bourdieu argues that one's sense of 'what to do' is defined by 'the structure of the hopes or expectations constitutive of a habitus and the structures of probabilities which is constitutive of a social space' (2000: 211), and this confers a feel for the game, allowing a person to anticipate what is coming and to develop strategies for optimum performance.

Using Bourdieu's tools, we have examined how middle-class students may be able to maintain their advantages through and beyond higher education, through the acquisition, maintenance, development and mobilization of cultural, social and economic resources, building on the cultivation of capitals that occurred through the family (Lareau, 2011).

Graduate employment and inequalities

It is not just participation in HE, but the employment destinations of graduates from HE that is an increasingly important concern in the United Kingdom and other countries in pursuit of competitive advantage in 'knowledge economies' (see, for example, Badriotti and Pappadà, 2011; Ciriaci and Muscio, 2014; Coates and Edwards, 2011; Jacob *et al.*, 2015;

Klein, 2016; Núñez and Livanos, 2010; Puhakka *et al.*, 2010; Schomburg and Teichler, 2006). The Destination of Leavers from Higher Education (DLHE) survey is used to evaluate transitions into the labour market, with data gathered six months after graduation and then three years later. These data are used in university league tables, and also used by institutions as part of their marketing strategies. While reports on destinations of graduates in 2015 suggested a turnaround in progression following undergraduate study, and a positive and upward trend in successful transition to employment, other research has investigated the unequal access to different graduate opportunities that lie behind these headline findings.

In a report to government in 2012, which followed on from an initial report in 2009, the conclusions of the social mobility 'tsar' Alan Milburn on progress towards greater equality in access to a number of key professions (law, medicine, media and journalism, the civil service, and government) was as follows:

> Across the professions as a whole, the glass ceiling has been scratched but not broken. The professions still lag way behind the social curve. If anything, the evidence suggests that since 2009, taken as a whole, the professions – despite some pockets of considerable progress – have done too little to catch up. The general picture seems to be of mainly minor changes in the social composition of the professions. At the top especially, the professions remain dominated by a social elite. (Milburn, 2012: 3)

As Milburn's report indicates, higher education does not automatically level the playing field between students of differing socio-economic backgrounds, and similar conclusions are reached in research by Macmillan *et al.* (2015). They investigated who gets the top jobs among UK graduates, using data from the DLHE survey for those who graduated in 2006/07, and focusing on the data collected 3.5 years after graduation. They found that graduates who had attended private schools were a third more likely to enter high-status occupations, particularly higher managerial, business, medical and law professions, than state-educated graduates from similarly affluent families and neighbourhoods. This was largely due to differences in educational attainment, and choice of university. They also found that social capital in the form of networks (informal channels of job search, employee referrals and social connections) provided an additional advantage.

Other research has focused on recruitment to newer industries. A study by Clark *et al.* (2011) looked at graduates entering information technology professions, based on a longitudinal study that investigated the process of finding and adjusting to employment from the perspective of recent graduates. They used Bourdieu's tools of field, habitus and capital to examine graduates' experience of entering this newer field of employment and to develop an understanding of what is needed to be a player in that field. A different study, by Browne (2010) has examined recruitment practices in the financial services industries, based on case studies of two multinational organizations in England in 2007. Browne looked at possible social and cultural bias in these practices, particularly in relation to recruitment from elite universities, value given to academic credentials from differently positioned institutions, and identification of potential elite professionals.

The findings of these different studies all concur with Macmillan *et al.*'s conclusions that 'among recent UK graduates, socio-economic background remains a significant factor in explaining why some students secure top jobs' and that 'a student's family background has a major influence on their job and life chances' (2015: 508). Macmillan *et al.* suggest a number of possible reasons for their findings:

> More socio-economically advantaged graduates may have other forms of capital that are important for accessing top jobs. These could include non-cognitive skills, including confidence and self-esteem, that help individuals in interviews. Alternatively, these graduates could have greater cultural capital that enables them to exhibit desirable behaviours and conversations in the interview setting. They may have access to greater financial capital that enables them to increase the period of their job search or take unpaid internships and hence increase their likelihood of accessing a top job. Lastly, it may be the case that more advantaged graduates have different preferences and motivations, opting into higher status occupations. (2015: 507)

However, Macmillan *et al.* also note that it is not possible to establish which of these explanations is most important based on the research they have done.

Clark *et al.*'s (2011) approach, which is similar to that of the Paired Peers project, using longitudinal qualitative methods, makes it possible to consider in greater depth the processes involved in gaining and maintaining advantage in relation to graduate recruitment markets, and how the different factors identified by Macmillan and colleagues may play out in practice. In this chapter we begin to unpack these factors through a close look at one of our project's sets of pairs, two female students from different social class backgrounds who both studied law, one at the elite University of Bristol (Zoe, working-class) and one at the 'modern' University of the West of England (UWE) (Francesca, middle-class). Our aim is to provide a more in-depth analysis of the classed processes that orient aspiration and expectation while simultaneously shaping possibilities and opportunities to open and shut down pathways to high-status graduate employment. We provide narrative accounts of two lives for the purpose of illustrating the ways in which class background can, and does, create a legacy of advantage and disadvantage. We make no claims to generalizability but instead provide insights into the mechanisms at play in ensuring the persistence of inequalities even when high-level educational credentials are equally achieved. The following section presents the narratives of Zoe and Francesca, who in our study were 'Paired Peers'.

Narratives of classed experience: Zoe

Zoe is a white working-class law graduate who studied at the University of Bristol. Originally from South Wales, Zoe grew up with her mother, who works for the local authority, and her father, who works as a manual labourer. No one in Zoe's family has a traditional experience of higher education, although her mother was studying for a master's degree when Zoe embarked on her undergraduate studies. Her father left school at 15 with no qualifications and Zoe was unsure of her mother's educational background. Because she had two working parents at home Zoe did not qualify for any government financial support. In her first interview she tells us that she feels guilty, as her situation put pressure on the family, who were unable to provide funds to support her maintenance. In order to be independent and to relieve pressure on her family Zoe worked throughout her degree to support herself, often working 20 hours per week during term-time. This immediate need to generate economic capital prevented Zoe from accumulating vital forms of cultural and social capital through extracurricular activities or work experience, which, as has been demonstrated by previous research, is likely to have a major impact on a young person's chances of securing graduate work (Purcell *et al.*, 2012). Zoe reflected on this during her final interview as a student, telling us that she feels she has gained immensely valuable skill sets from working in the service sector, including understanding people and coping with the pressures of 'real work':

> Having so much experience in the working world, I think that's set me up more than an experience day or work experience would, because I have experienced work and it gives you a much

broader awareness of the real world. The vast majority – sorry to typecast – of people in this university have never work-worked, but they've had work experience because someone's arranged it and they've run vacation schemes. It's all great, but they don't know what 'work' is yet. But I already know what work is, so I think that any employer that I talk to would appreciate and value that as much, or even more, than saying 'oh I have this work experience' blah, blah. I think that's probably more of a beneficial thing to have – well I hope anyway.

However, while Zoe was confident that she had clearly benefited personally from her experiences and arguably developed valuable skills and useful forms of capital, these are not necessarily symbolically recognized by employers and thus lack exchange value on the graduate labour market. As we will go on to demonstrate, when Zoe attempts to secure graduate work she finds her experiences are devalued, because the companies she worked in, and the type of work she was able to find, were not in keeping with the traditional internship model, where symbolic value is derived from connection to company status rather than skills acquired. In a similar vein to her experiences of work, Zoe places a lot of trust in the value of her law degree, and believes that a 2:1 from the elite University of Bristol will provide her with a ticket into the professional world:

I think the law degree from Bristol University (hopefully) – and a 2:1 – it really shows that you've managed to achieve something and it shows that you have a certain level of academic skill and that you've worked really hard. So I think regardless of whatever I try to do, that will always stand as like a really big thing. Having a law degree is one of those things, you know, 'you've got a law degree'.

Throughout her interview she repeats this sentiment, feeling that a law degree would send a strong signal to the world about her, and that this would compensate for the reading of lower intelligence that she thought was attributed to her working-class femininity. Alongside her interest in law, she had a passion for drama and performance and she compared herself to the lead character from the film *Legally Blonde*, who is simultaneously hyper-feminine and incredibly intelligent. Zoe's habitus was developed within a working-class, dominated field, outside of which she finds her classed and gendered tastes, practices and dispositions to be arbitrarily denigrated and devalued. For Zoe, this is a combination of both her class and gender, as she feels that she is perceived by others to be 'just a pretty face' (she is 'hyper-feminine', petite, blonde), and she feels that getting a law degree will enable her to overcome this and be read in terms outside of this restricting framework:

> I think that no matter what I go into in life, having that law degree will always ... there'll always be that sort of 'oh she's got a law degree, she's not just a 4 foot 11 sort of bundle of energy walking around going la-la-la, she's actually got some sort of something about her that's extra'.

The law degree therefore acted for Zoe as a signifier of her value in a context where her working-class femininity was pathologized (Skeggs, 2004). This (over)reliance on the degree as the route to a middle-class job was something that came up during interviews with other working-class students, who were similarly investing immense efforts in the degree rather than developing a curriculum vitae (CV) that packaged their credentials 'in a way which highlighted their added-value attributes and "selling points"' (Tomlinson, 2007: 291). Bourdieu argues that the 'dominated class' are less attuned to the shifts in the qualification marketplace. He writes: 'through a typical effect of *allodoxia* ('misapprehension'), they bestow a value on their devalued diplomas which is not objectively acknowledged' (2010: 138). Thus, in a period of diploma inflation, when more and more young people from all backgrounds begin to secure degrees, the game of distinction shifts and a 'good degree' is no longer enough (Bathmaker *et al.*, 2016). Working-class young people, having less of a 'feel for the game', are likely to continue to rely on the degree. The rules have shifted but they rely on previously successful ways of playing the game because they have had to explicitly learn its rules rather than finding themselves attuned to subtle changes as the game progresses. Arguably this is also because they have no alternative, something Bourdieu acknowledges when he discusses how the dominant class, in comparison, are able to draw upon other forms of capital (such as their 'connections') to help them to 'maximize' the value of their qualifications (2010: 143). In our study we found that those from working-class backgrounds had a sense of discomfort when faced with the possibility of using their connections to seek to rig the game in their favour (Abrahams, 2017).

Reality check: Not understanding the rules of the game

When Zoe graduated, she had to return to her parental home in Wales as she was unable to support herself financially. In her first interview post-graduation, she appears to have experienced a deeply problematic and difficult transition. She applied for endless jobs of all kinds from graduate level to office jobs but was unsuccessful. At one point she was forced to claim jobseeker's allowance and describes the system as being unable to cope with people in her situation. She was in fact over- rather than underqualified for the majority of jobs available. Zoe began to become disillusioned as her search for work was not leading to the fruitful ends she felt she had been promised due to her perception of the high status of a 2:1 law degree from the University of Bristol. She explains:

> I think you get this perception, if you've got a good degree from a good uni you'll come out and people are going to be crawling all over you and it's just the absolute opposite ... It was more like no one cared. And I just thought 'I will apply for all these jobs and someone is going to see you've got this, this and this' and that I've worked through uni the whole time, supported myself and I've got all this like work experience in different kinds of sectors that's like really translatable, and I've done extra things outside of uni, and I've got all these interests and ... it's just almost as if they just don't ...

Zoe's painful realization that 'no-one cared' provides a stark contrast to her pre-graduation optimism. She describes feeling as though she is stuck between a rock and a hard place. Her locality and inability to be geographically mobile played a large role in the problems she encountered. She told us that all the opportunities for graduate work were in London yet she was unable to migrate to the city as she did not have the economic capital to do so. While some of the other Paired Peers graduates were able to access opportunities in London because their family home was there, or they had family financial support to do so, Zoe did not have any relatives in the city with whom she could stay. She says:

> Recruitment consultants would ring me up and say 'do you want to do this sales job in London', so it's not like I couldn't have got that. Because they see the CV and they know Bristol, 2:1, Law – tick – you know it's that kind of thing, they want you, but then obviously I didn't have the money to move to London in the first place to go and chase a job like that to then find another job in something that I wanted to do. It's really, really static in Wales.

It is evident here that a degree alone does not provide access to social mobility; rather social mobility relies on the capacity to be mobile, and to mobilize multiple forms of capital in addition to the degree qualification.

Beginning to understand the game

After a long period of worklessness, Zoe managed to secure a job in a conveyancing firm in Wales as a trainee remortgage case handler earning £14,500 per year. She was not interested in property law at all but accepted the position as she needed some form of income. Arguably for Zoe this job was 'a stop gap', a temporary position to enable her to continue searching for something better. At this point Zoe had decided she wanted to attempt to get into law; she felt that the case handler job would help her to secure a training contract because she was finally getting some symbolically valued law-related experience for her CV. She says:

> I'm going to apply for training contracts because I now know that I've got that proper full-time industry … it's not just work experience it's proper full-time industry experience, handling a massive caseload. And I can also say now, I am enjoying what I'm doing, I want to see the Law in practice in other areas, I'm really eager to start and do this.

That year Zoe applied for various training contracts but was not successful. In the following interview we asked her about it and she said:

> I didn't get any [training contracts] I didn't get an interview for any! 2:1, high 2:1 in Law from Bristol … working in an actual work experience, [having] work experience from when I was 16, like anything I can physically do, and not even one response from the training contract.

We did not probe Zoe further around the sensitive issue during the interview, but in prior correspondence with Zoe when she first received the rejection letters she was asked if she was given any feedback, to which she replied: 'No feedback with the rejections [due to] "too many applications". It's just so disheartening as I have no idea what I'm doing wrong.' At this point, even though Zoe was faced with no better option for work, she decided to leave the conveyancing firm. She said that the job offered no progression route, describing it as 'a literal dead end'. She felt that the longer she stayed there, the more she was liable to become trapped. She reasoned that at this point she was still living at home with no outgoings so this was her best opportunity to leave. A few months later, Zoe got what she describes as a 'London job' that she was able to do from home in Wales. It was a temporary six-month position updating a law database, but it paid extremely well compared with her previous employment (£28,000 per annum compared with £14,500). Meanwhile, aware that this job was due to end soon, Zoe decided to apply to return to university to study for a master's in Acting. Sadly she was not offered a place on the course, which she described as 'extremely competitive'. Following this, she toyed with the idea of reapplying for training contracts, as she felt her current work would add positively to her CV. However, she remained torn between the idea of what she deemed to be a safe, secure, well-paid profession and that of her true passion, which was acting. This moment of insecurity in regard to the future was where we left Zoe, in her last interview, as she continues to attempt to pave a way towards the 'respectable', secure and well-paid graduate-level job that she saw as the promise of HE participation.

Zoe's story is one full of struggle and uncertainty. She is continually unable to capitalize upon her degree due to her inability to supplement it with other forms of institutionally valued capitals. Her attempts to build a graduate career in law or a career in acting are repeatedly blocked and she has experienced multiple rejections and disappointments. Next we turn to Francesca, Zoe's 'Paired Peer', a middle-class law graduate who attended UWE Bristol, to explore the ways in which class can 'trump' institution to enable a transition that is filled with diverse options and freedoms to make 'choices'.

Narratives of classed experience: Francesca

Francesca is a middle-class young woman who graduated with a first class law degree from the University of the West of England. She grew up in a southern English city and attended her local comprehensive. Her parents are both highly educated professionals – her father is a university professor and her mother a social worker. She had expected and been on track to achieve highly in her A-level exams, and then progress to an elite university. In reality she performed less well. She did not gain a place at one of her chosen universities and so went into the UK clearing system, which allocates remaining HE places after students have received their A-level results. She was offered a place at the University of the West of England, a modern, post-1992 university, rather than at an elite university. On advice from her father, she reluctantly accepted. She entered UWE with a lot of apprehension and spent her first year questioning whether she should be there, at one point considering moving to another university:

I really didn't want to come back this summer. I don't know what it was but over the summer I just … even though I had fine grades, friends here and stuff, I was just determined on trying to swap uni so I did [apply for] a transfer, a second year transfer … I'm fine now that I'm back [from the summer break] but I really wasn't happy in the first week, I didn't want to be here – again. I think I just have reoccurring – I'll always be like that – every so often I'll just feel like I don't want to be here any more but yeah it's fine. I'll stick it out for three years, definitely, well I think it's pointless not to carry on.

Francesca here demonstrates a sense of discomfort in being identified with a post-1992 institution. As she describes, she went as far as applying for a transfer to another institution but in the end she decided to remain at UWE. We have written elsewhere (Bathmaker *et al.*, 2016) about her being a 'fish out of water' in a non-elite setting and how her anxieties contributed to a 'hypermobilization of capital' (Ingram and Bathmaker, 2013). Her approach to university and her future career involved intensive work and commitment to increasing her volumes of social and cultural capital.

Work hard, play hard: Being part of a cosmopolitan elite

Francesca's experience of education oriented her towards a future of elite cosmopolitanism. From an early age she engaged in activities building high cultural capital that could be traded on the education and then employment markets through both university and job applications. This was supplemented by other CV-building activities such as internships that were organized through her school (which had a significant number of middle-class students with high expectations and prospects) and through her family's extensive and significant social capital. She was afforded many opportunities to gain experience in the legal sector to which she aspired, including experience at a global non-governmental organization and a prestigious internship at an international company located outside Europe, which was unpaid and funded by her parents. Her extracurricular activities while at university displayed her high cultural status and included proficiency in playing a musical instrument, playing in an orchestra, and taking an active role in the management of a student sporting society. She had extensive experience of travelling, was open to the idea of geographical mobility, and planned to seek work in London.

Stop gap: The luxury of time to look for the right job

Immediately after graduation Francesca found herself back in her home town. Her original plan to secure a funded place at one of the Inns of Court so that she could study for the Bar had been reassessed towards the end of her degree, when it became apparent that she was not going to be offered a scholarship but would have to self-fund her law training instead. Initially she was prepared to do this and her parents were prepared to pay the associated fees, but on reflection she decided that unless she had a scholarship she would find her pathway to successful employment, if not entirely blocked, a lot more difficult to navigate:

> Basically I was adamant to go into the Bar, to be a barrister, and that was all good. And then I decided I would only do it if I got a scholarship, which was sensible because the way your CVs are looked at in Chambers, if you don't have all these awards offered you're not given a ... like you don't get a job ... If you don't have awards from uni or a scholarship from the Inns of Court then you probably won't get it. So I said to myself, I'm not going to do it if I don't get it, because the qualification only lasts five years[1] ... And I think in the very long term from where I'm sat now, I can still see myself going to the Bar but just nowhere near now.

She decided to look at other options for schemes in London where she could gain graduate employment, and perhaps enhance her CV for a future application to the scholarship programme. While preparing her applications and her online LinkedIn profile, and after a period of travel in both the United States and Europe, Francesca took up paid employment in a restaurant. She had no plan to commit to it long term because she saw the work as beneath her status:

> In the restaurant, it was so demoralizing because *I knew I was better than this* and it was just so hard to get a job. And I was applying for graduate schemes the whole time, and you were getting rejected in like 20 minutes of sending off your application. And then the job ... then I got this job in [home city], which was definitely better than what I was working on but it was still in [home city] and it wasn't something I wanted to do and it was a tiny company.

The pathway was not smooth for Francesca, despite her first-class degree achievement and her extensive experience. Like Zoe, she noted the high number of rejections, which came within minutes of sending off her application. Eventually, she moved on to a graduate job in her home city, which was related to her previous experience, but not what she was looking for in terms of work, location and opportunity. Francesca saw herself working with a larger, international or multinational company, and London was the place of opportunity in terms of career progression.

Francesca was playing the long game, trying to maximize her opportunities and overcome any perceived failings. Bourdieu explains this as follows:

> One of the most valuable sorts of information constituting inherited cultural capital is practical or theoretical knowledge of the fluctuations of the market in academic qualifications, the sense of investment which enables one to get the best return on inherited cultural capital in the scholastic market or on scholastic capital in the labour market, for example, by knowing the right moment to pull out of devalued disciplines and careers and to switch into those with a future, rather than clinging to the scholastic values which secured the highest profits in an earlier state of the market. (2010: 138)

Bourdieu reasons that not only do individuals who know the rules of the game know when to 'switch' industries, but they are also able to mobilize the various forms of capital at their disposal to enable them to achieve a maximum return on their qualifications (Bourdieu, 2010: 143). With Francesca, we can also see a practical or theoretical knowledge of how to reposition oneself in the playing field when your game has fallen short. Francesca demonstrates her feel for the game by navigating her way through, switching to a new pathway when her capitals cannot be exchanged, and tacitly finding a way to unblock her route to the sort of graduate career to which she aspires.

Conclusions

The narratives presented here, based on in-depth qualitative analysis, shed light on the textured details of class-based inequalities as they play out in university experiences and graduate transitions. Zoe and Francesca came to university with differing resources. Rather than equalizing the playing field for these young people, university appeared to provide Francesca with a greater opportunity to build upon her established forms of capitals. Meanwhile, Zoe had to struggle to generate forms of capital that would have value in a graduate labour market, particularly because of a lack of economic capital, which meant that she had little choice but to take any form of paid employment available both during and immediately after her undergraduate study. In this way, though both finished university with a good degree outcome – Zoe graduated with a 2:1, and Francesca with a first-class degree – they were not equally equipped with the necessary gold standard CV. While we recognize that a first class degree theoretically confers more value than a 2:1, we contend that this value is overwritten by the status of the institution. This is borne out by the practices of elite graduate employers (including in professions like law) targeting recruitment at the top 10–25 universities (out of 140 nationally) rather than casting their net more widely for graduates with first class degrees (Ingram and Allen, 2018). Zoe and Francesca's narratives pose a challenge to the traditional hierarchical reputational positioning of higher education institutions, for while Zoe attended a more prestigious university than Francesca she found it difficult to capitalize on this distinctive resource due to other obstacles, which included economic resources, ability to be geographically mobile, and lack of connection to London, the place where the highest paid prestigious opportunities lay. The assumption that geographical mobility is desirable or even efficacious is often overlooked when it comes to issues of employability (Finn, 2017). These narratives serve to illustrate the inequalities graduates from different backgrounds may face as they attempt to 'play the game' from unequal starting points. Bourdieu writes:

> Those who talk of equality of opportunity forget that social games – the economic game, but also the cultural games (the religious field, the juridical field, the philosophical field, etc.) are not 'fair games'. Without being, strictly speaking, rigged, the competition resembles a handicap race that has lasted for generations or games in which each player has the positive or negative score of all those who have preceded him, that is the cumulated scores of all his ancestors. (2000: 215)

Zoe struggled to keep up with the game. She believed that her degree would open doors for her future, that education was the route to a good job. However, without the extensive capitals necessary to support her, she continually struggled to find the graduate job she believed was the promise of getting a degree. Francesca, possessing a greater feel for the game, was able to move quickly to change track when her planned route appeared to be blocked. She had the luxury of time resources to consider her options, while Zoe, unable to rely on family financial support, more urgently required any form of paid work to keep her afloat. As with other middle-class students in our study, Francesca could assume financial support from her parents without feelings of guilt. This support could enable these students to have a smoother experience of higher education and focus both on their studies and on the additional activities that will ultimately position them as more 'employable'.

Unfortunately the inequalities produced by the differences in experience described in these two narratives are not easy to resolve. It is not as simple as political discourse on unleashing aspiration would have us believe. Nor is it solved by Sutton Trust or WP initiatives that encourage more working-class young people to apply to universities that position themselves as elite, such as the Russell Group. While education can be part of the solution, it is not the panacea for deep structural inequalities that facilitate the reproduction of privilege. Having particular forms of cultural and social capital enables privilege to be reproduced regardless of institution attended. Ultimately this works because these forms of capital can be acquired through economic capital, maximized through economic capital, and then, when matured, converted to greater stocks of economic capital, as can be seen in Francesca's mobilization of family economic resources to develop CV-enhancing opportunities, which increased her job prospects. Therefore, policies that focus on instilling aspiration and confidence and developing 'character' in working-class young people may well be a flawed solution to the wrong problem, because their access to economic capital is insufficient to allow these young people to mobilize cultural capital effectively. As Zoe's narrative attests, a working-class graduate may have high aspirations and high levels of confidence, have acquired cultural capital through a university degree, developed skills through paid work, and have an abundance of 'character' and resilience, but without the financial resources to enable them to buy opportunities (such as internships and London rents) they will not be in a position to convert those capitals into desired graduate opportunities.

This chapter further illuminates the policy debate on social mobility and provides evidence to support the speculation of Milburn, as the UK social mobility commissioner, on the driving forces behind unequal access to the professions. It is important not only to look at patterns of mobility, immobility and social reproduction, but also to see what may lie behind these general trends. The narrative approach we have used here demonstrates that wider social patterns are inflected differently in individual lives, and highlights the value of understanding the significance of the everyday in seeking to assess progress towards greater mobility and justice; 'possibilities for change need, at least in part, to be understood and conceived of through the small everyday acts of individuals, and the histories that have brought them to their present place' (Bathmaker, 2010: 5).

It is clear that a good degree does not automatically even the playing field. The type of university attended can add capital that is deemed to have high value, but in our study, this did not automatically create advantages for Zoe, from a working-class background, compared with her middle-class counterpart, Francesca. Knowing how to mobilize and package capitals generated at university is an essential part of the graduate job application game, and career services need to engage with students more actively in helping them to understand the shifting and fickle nature of graduate labour markets.

Family resources of capital remain important in facilitating transitions from university, and having the resources to be mobile can be crucial, particularly for 'top' professions. Some working-class students would benefit from financial support to aid their transition to elite professions, especially if the top employers are to be found in London and large metropolitan areas away from their family homes, which is itself problematic in terms of what mobility demands from graduates emotionally (Finn, 2017). However, current HE policy does not afford adequate financial provision for low-income students, leaving them with huge debts rather than assistance at the point of entering a graduate career.

There are also limited good examples of opportunities that provide support for internships and placements, meaning that the well-off can augment their stocks of capital through unpaid internships and work experience at home and abroad, while many working-class young people have to work to pay bills while at university, gaining paid work experience but in a form that is neither recognized nor valued by graduate employers.

In sum, if we are serious about improving social inequalities we need to problematize the social advantage of elites and consider ways of immobilizing unfairly gained capital. A continual focus on generating more capitals for working-class people perpetuates rather than challenges the inequality game.

Note

1 This qualification only enables the holder to be admitted to the bar within the first five years of obtaining it.

References

Abrahams, J. (2017) 'Honourable mobility or shameless entitlement? Habitus and graduate employment'. *British Journal of Sociology of Education*, 38 (5), 625–40.

Abrahams, J. and Ingram, N. (2013) 'The chameleon habitus: Local students' negotiations of multiple fields'. *Sociological Research Online*, 18 (4), 21. www.socresonline.org.uk/18/4/21.html (accessed 31 January 2018).

Archer, L., Hutchings, M. and Ross, A. (eds) (2003) *Higher Education and Social Class: Issues of exclusion and inclusion*. London: RoutledgeFalmer.

Badriotti, A. and Pappadà, G. (2011) 'Higher education and graduate employment in Europe'. *Journal for Perspectives of Economic, Political, and Social Integration*, 17 (1–2), 15–31.

Bathmaker, A.-M. (2010) 'Introduction'. In Bathmaker, A.-M. and Harnett, P. (eds) *Exploring Learning, Identity and Power through Life History and Narrative Research*. London: Routledge, 1–10.

Bathmaker, A.-M., Ingram, N., Abrahams, J., Hoare, A., Waller, R. and Bradley, H. (2016) *Higher Education, Social Class and Social Mobility: The degree generation*. London: Palgrave Macmillan.

Bathmaker, A.-M., Ingram, N. and Waller, R. (2013) 'Higher education, social class and the mobilisation of capitals: Recognising and playing the game'. *British Journal of Sociology of Education*, 34 (5–6), 723–43.

Bourdieu, P. (1986) 'The forms of capital'. In Richardson, J.G. (ed.) *Handbook of Theory and Research for the Sociology of Education*. New York: Greenwood Press, 241–58.

Bourdieu, P. (2000) *Pascalian Meditations*. Trans. Nice, R. Cambridge: Polity Press.

Bourdieu, P. (2010) *Distinction: A social critique of the judgement of taste*. Trans. Nice, R. Originally 1984. London: Routledge.

Brown, P., Lauder, H. and Ashton, D. (2011) *The Global Auction: The broken promises of education, jobs and incomes*. New York: Oxford University Press.

Browne, L. (2010) 'As UK policy strives to make access to higher education easier for all, is discrimination in employment practice still apparent?'. *Journal of Vocational Education and Training*, 62 (3), 313–26.

Ciriaci, D. and Muscio, A. (2014) 'University choice, research quality and graduates' employability: Evidence from Italian national survey data'. *European Educational Research Journal*, 13 (2), 199–219.

Clark, M., Zukas, M. and Lent, N. (2011) 'Becoming an IT person: Field, habitus and capital in the transition from university to work'. *Vocations and Learning*, 4 (2), 133–50.

Coates, H. and Edwards, D. (2011) 'The Graduate Pathways Survey: New insights on education and employment outcomes five years after bachelor degree completion'. *Higher Education Quarterly*, 65 (1), 74–93.

Devine, F. (2004) *Class Practices: How parents help their children get good jobs*. Cambridge: Cambridge University Press.

Dorling, D. (2014) *Inequality and the 1%*. London: Verso.

Finn, K. (2017) 'Relational transitions, emotional decisions: New directions for theorising graduate employment'. *Journal of Education and Work*, 30 (4), 419–31.

Ingram, N. (2009) 'Working-class boys, educational success and the misrecognition of working-class culture'. *British Journal of Sociology of Education*, 30 (4), 421–34.

Ingram, N. (2011) 'Within school and beyond the gate: The difficulties of being educationally successful and working class'. *Sociology*, 45 (2), 287–302.

Ingram, N. and Allen, K. (2018) '"Talent-spotting" or "social magic"? Inequality, cultural sorting and constructions of the ideal graduate in elite professions'. *Sociological Review*, under review.

Ingram, N. and Bathmaker, A.-M. (2013) 'Not the place for a person like me: On being middle-class at a post-1992 university in England'. Paper presented at the British Sociological Association Annual Conference, London, 3–5 April 2013.

Jacob, M., Klein, M. and Iannelli, C. (2015) 'The impact of social origin on graduates' early occupational destinations: An Anglo-German comparison'. *European Sociological Review*, 31 (4), 460–76.

Klein, M. (2016) 'Educational expansion, occupational closure and the relation between educational attainment and occupational prestige over time'. *Sociology*, 50 (1), 3–23.

Lareau, A. (2011) *Unequal Childhoods: Class, race, and family life.* 2nd ed. Berkeley: University of California Press.

Macmillan, L., Tyler, C. and Vignoles, A. (2015) 'Who gets the top jobs? The role of family background and networks in recent graduates' access to high-status professions'. *Journal of Social Policy*, 44 (3), 487–515.

Milburn, A. (2009) *Unleashing Aspiration: The final report of the Panel on Fair Access to the Professions.* London: Cabinet Office.

Milburn, A. (2012) *Fair Access to Professional Careers: A progress report by the Independent Reviewer on Social Mobility and Child Poverty.* London: Cabinet Office.

Núñez, I. and Livanos, I. (2010) 'Higher education and unemployment in Europe: An analysis of the academic subject and national effects'. *Higher Education*, 59 (4), 475–87.

Puhakka, A., Rautopuro, J. and Tuominen, V. (2010) 'Employability and Finnish university graduates'. *European Educational Research Journal*, 9 (1), 45–55.

Purcell, K., Elias, P., Atfield, G., Behle, H., Ellison, R., Luchinskaya, D., Snape, J., Conaghan, L. and Tzanakou, C. (2012) *Futuretrack Stage 4: Transitions into employment, further study and other outcomes.* Coventry: Warwick Institute for Employment Research. Online. www.hecsu.ac.uk/assets/assets/documents/Futuretrack_Stage_4_Final_report_6th_Nov_2012.pdf (accessed 4 October 2016).

Reay, D. (2005) 'Beyond consciousness? The psychic landscape of social class'. *Sociology*, 39 (5), 911–28.

Reay, D., Crozier, G. and Clayton, J. (2009) '"Strangers in paradise"? Working-class students in elite universities'. *Sociology*, 43 (6), 1103–21.

Reay, D., Crozier, G. and Clayton, J. (2010) '"Fitting in" or "standing out": Working-class students in UK higher education'. *British Educational Research Journal*, 36 (1), 107–24.

Reay, D., David, M.E. and Ball, S. (2005) *Degrees of Choice: Class, race, gender and higher education.* Stoke-on-Trent: Trentham Books.

Schomburg, H. and Teichler, U. (2006) *Higher Education and Graduate Employment in Europe: Results from graduate surveys from twelve countries* (Higher Education Dynamics 15). Dordrecht: Springer.

Skeggs, B. (2004) 'Exchange, value and affect: Bourdieu and "the self"'. In Adkins, L. and Skeggs, B. (eds) *Feminism after Bourdieu*. Oxford: Blackwell, 75–96.

Tomlinson, M. (2007) 'Graduate employability and student attitudes and orientations to the labour market'. *Journal of Education and Work*, 20 (4), 285–304.

Chapter 8

Becoming a reflexive researcher: A personal research journey

Jacqueline Stevenson

Introduction: Why Aimhigher mattered

In England, explicit policy efforts to improve the access of those groups underrepresented in higher education (HE) have formed a key element of national education policies for over 50 years (Kettley, 2007; Ross, 2003b). Throughout the second half of the twentieth century, policy interventions led to the building of new universities in the 1960s (Ross, 2003a), new polytechnics in the 1970s (Pratt, 1997), and the eradication of the binary divide between polytechnics and universities in the Further and Higher Education Act of 1992 (UK Parliament, 1992). The primary focus of these interventions was on changing the gender, class, age and ethnic profile of the HE student population, and by the late 1990s English HE had shifted from an elite system (defined as enrolling up to 15 per cent of the age group) (Trow, 1974; Trow, 2006) to a mass one (of between 16 and 50 per cent). It was under the New Labour government (in office from 1997 to 2010), however, that a sustained push was made towards achieving universal participation (of 50 per cent or more) among 18–30-year-olds (HEFCE, 2003). To help achieve this, in 1999 New Labour launched the Excellence Challenge programme, which, with a further initiative, Partnerships for Progression, evolved into the national Aimhigher programme. This ran from 2004 to 2011.

Aimhigher was given the remit to 'widen participation in higher education and increase the number of young people who have the abilities and aspirations to benefit from it' (HEFCE, 2004: 7). It operated at three levels (national, regional and subregional 'area'), with much of the funding and thus activity delivered through university-led regional Aimhigher partnerships of higher education institutions, colleges and schools (McCaig, 2010; Harrison, 2012). Although the focus of Aimhigher was on young people, the document laying out initial guidance also, crucially, concluded that 'partnerships may wish to prioritise other target groups that are under-represented in HE in their region or area' (HEFCE, 2004: 13). One of the strengths of the Aimhigher programme was, therefore, that it was able to focus on a wide range of disadvantaged, disenfranchised or underrepresented groups – unlike the current national collaborative outreach programme (NCOP) funded by the Higher Education Funding Council for England (HEFCE), for example, which is highly targeted and focused solely on supporting the most disadvantaged young people where there are gaps in participation rates (HEFCE, 2016). The latitude offered by HEFCE in 2004 was the very thing that gave Aimhigher partnerships the freedom to work with a wide range of groups based on their own local contexts and institutional criteria. This, in turn, gave rise to much of the innovative activity funded by Aimhigher regional partnerships, including in my case, work with small businesses to develop foundation degrees, work with local authority departments to support young people leaving the care system, and, crucially, work with the voluntary and community sector to support the access to HE of refugees and asylum seekers.

Evaluating widening participation projects: 2002 onwards

In 2002 I was working in a small, university-based contract research and evaluation centre, first as a widening participation project manager and then as an evaluation manager. Most of the work was externally funded, policy-related, short-term evaluations of widening participation initiatives. Aims and objectives for each evaluation were set by the funder and data collection was done through the use of structured mixed-methods approaches – primarily through the use of surveys, focus groups or semi-structured interviews. These data collection approaches allowed me to retain control over the structure of the evaluation, over my role as a researcher-evaluator, and over my relationship with those who participated in the evaluation. (I have not yet found a clear difference between research and evaluation in relation to the sorts of activities I was undertaking. The only distinction I can make here is that I use evaluation to try to determine *what* has worked, while I undertake research to gain new insights into *why* it did.)

I liked having control as this also avoided 'messiness': I could parcel up one project and move on to the next fairly effortlessly. I was not indifferent to the research or to my research participants but I did work to limit, and not embrace, my involvement in the research process. Having control also allowed me to retain a level of neutrality and objectivity that was important as the projects were invariably short term and very intensive.

To do otherwise would have been problematic for me, just like those other contract researchers who are:

> ... permanently engaged in deploying her/his self to create intimate relationships which by their very nature are 'meaningful', before moving on to a new project with a new set of colleagues and research 'subjects'. 'The project' constitutes its own bounded social world within which meaning is constructed, and [contract research staff] are required to parcel that 'meaningfulness' up and leave it, and to re-create themselves anew in another arena. They have constantly to negotiate a series of beginnings and endings ... (Goode, 2006: para. 1.2)

The constant negotiation of these new beginnings would have been difficult for me if I had not been able to 'put aside' one completed project before working on the next. Having a high level of control, neatness and boundaries was, therefore, very important to me. Despite, or perhaps because of this, I think I was (and hopefully still am!) quite a good evaluator. I was very organized and, despite my desire for control, I was also willing to continually reflect on my practice and refine my approach. I was not, however, a particularly reflexive researcher – and there is a very important difference.

As Finlay notes, reflection and reflexivity can best be thought of on a continuum: 'reflection can be understood as "thinking about" ... reflexivity taps into a more immediate, continuing, dynamic, and subjective self-awareness' (2002: 532–3). Reflexivity is therefore also better understood as being relational, embodied and emotional (Burkitt, 2012). Thus, while all researchers reflect, for positivist researchers, for example, engagement in a process of reflexivity is counterintuitive. Although I wouldn't describe myself as a positivist researcher, I was quite happy limiting my reflections to simply mulling over the process.

In late 2003, however, I was commissioned to undertake a two-year research project evaluating the efficacy of interventions designed to engage long-term unemployed adults in vocational training. This project comprised a number of smaller interventions and was funded by the EQUAL Community Initiative, financed by the European Social Fund (ESF) (European Commission, 2011). The focus of the evaluation was to identify which interventions were most successful, with the findings used to fund further initiatives. I approached the evaluation both ontologically and epistemologically as I had previously done, interested primarily in what was happening rather than why it might be happening, and working to maintain a careful level of objectivity.

The first intervention I was asked to evaluate was supported by the Big Issue Foundation and involved those who needed support to enable them to gain and sustain employment – including refugees and asylum seekers. After interviewing a number of people – who all told profoundly moving stories – I held my first interview with a refugee, a 33-year-old Egyptian called Mohammed who was selling the *Big Issue* newspaper, sold by those who are, largely, homeless and unemployed. What was notable about Mohammed was that he was a former teacher unable to practise his profession in the United Kingdom. Indeed one of the key findings from this evaluation (Stevenson, 2005) was that there were many other highly skilled asylum seekers and refugees who were either unemployed or underemployed. Moreover, for many, including Mohammed, accessing UK higher education at some point in the future offered a key route to help re-establish lives lost through the trauma of forced migration (Willott and Stevenson, 2013).

On the basis of my findings, EQUAL/ESF funded a further three research projects and Aimhigher funded four action research projects. The Aimhigher projects were specifically designed to determine barriers faced by refugees in attempting to access HE and to explore how refugees and asylum seekers could be better supported in their efforts. Aimhigher also funded guidance booklets for refugees and asylum seekers and other resources for university admissions and support staff, as well as a number of conferences and other events. Four further projects were then funded by the Yorkshire and Humberside Regional Consortium for Asylum Seekers and Refugees, the Leeds Library and Information Service, the Refugee Council and the Teacher Development Agency, and the Higher Education Academy. These 11 projects are listed at the end of the chapter.

This first interview with Mohammed thus began a research journey that has to date involved interviewing over 70 refugees and asylum seekers, including doctors, teachers, nurses, dentists, lawyers, journalists, and government workers, among others, from Libya, Sudan, Eritrea, Afghanistan, Pakistan, India, China, Egypt and many other places, and more recently from Syria.

As with previous projects I kept short field notes following each interview. The notes were not always neatly recorded: some were written up in notebooks, but others were written on scraps of paper, or on the back of my interview schedule. I discovered most of them when moving jobs and I have been able to reassemble them in chronological order. The initial notes were oriented towards the interviews I undertook, the purpose being to check and confirm the reliability of my research (reflection on action). From the start of that very first interview with Mohammed, however, my research became more complex and messy and the notes soon became accounts not just of reflection but of reflexivity. They also, over the course of a decade, evidence how my methodological and ethical approaches to research were completely transformed

Finding a new methodological approach

As soon as I began interviewing refugees I found it impossible to retain control of my semi-structured interview questions, or over my relationship to my research participants during the interview process. Rather, the interviews quickly spilt out over the neat spatial, temporal and contextual boundaries I had drawn round them: I soon had (at least to some extent) handed over choices about where the interviews should take place, and when, what to talk about, and what my role was in the research relationship! I quickly realized that I not only needed to reconsider when and where I should collect data, but also what methodological approach I should adopt and how I should analyse my data. I have often claimed that it was narrative, and storytelling in particular, however, that found me rather than the other way round. As soon as I started to interview refugees it was clear that the content of the interview would be the stories they wanted to tell me and less the data I wanted to collect. The two, of course, soon became synonymous: stories became data.

Story as data

The use of stories as research data has a long history, particularly in historical research, ethnography, cultural studies and cultural anthropology (Ollerenshaw and Creswell, 2002). Until the 1980s, however, it was little used in educational research, reflecting wider concerns over how qualitative research in general could be transferable or generalizable (Lincoln and Guba, 1985). Over the last 30 years, however, there has been a sharp increase in the collecting of stories (P. Atkinson and Delamont, 2006). This transformation can be attributed to:

> ... a change in the relationship between the researcher and the researched; a move from the use of number toward the use of words as data; a change from a focus on the general and universal toward the local and specific; and a widening acceptance of alternative epistemologies or ways of knowing. (Clandinin, 2007: 7)

For narrative researchers there is a difference between story and narrative: a story is a 'first-person oral telling or retelling of events related to the personal or social experiences of an individual' (Ollerenshaw and Creswell, 2002: 332), and it is through the process of transformation of data that story becomes narrative (Riley and Hawe, 2005). In other words, people tell stories, but narratives come from their analysis (Frank, 2000).

Across many countries, storytelling can have an important social function since it 'may accomplish social status and professional authority' (P. Atkinson and Delamont, 2006: 165). Moreover, storytelling has also long been viewed as having curative or transformative powers. Rosenthal, in her work with survivors of the Shoah (Holocaust), World War I veterans and refugees, for example, asserts that just one narrative interview 'can trigger the first curative processes' (2003: 916). Indeed, for Robert Atkinson, 'it is only through story that our truth can be told, that the meaning of life can be identified' (1995: viii). It is not unexpected therefore that for refugees, who have had their lives torn apart as a result of war, political upheaval or natural disaster, and who may have lost not only their homes and possessions but also their sense of self-worth and self-esteem, telling their stories can be important. In addition, stories can be 'a cultural device for the expression of self and experience. The narrator reconfigures him or herself with each story and with each retelling' (Warren and Karner, 2005: 24).

It is perhaps unsurprising, therefore, that refugees are willing to recount their stories despite the trauma they may have experienced, and, since so doing can be cathartic, that there were multiple times when, at the end of the interview, I was thanked for listening: 'At the end of the interview he just thanked me for listening and I felt about two inches high – he was thanking me???' (field notes, January 2008). I was, however, constantly surprised by how much detail many refugees went into and how much they were prepared to share:

> The interview just went on and on for hours, she was just talking and talking, like she couldn't stop, like someone had turned a tap on and everything was just flooding out, all these jumbled up stories, back and forward, leaping about in time, people, places, events, back and forth. (Field notes, June 2011)

I therefore learned early on to allow a lot of time for each interview, in order to let people speak for as long as they wanted. However, this meant that some interviews lasted for a long time and often covered a huge amount of ground:

That was one of the longest interviews I have done. [Name] just talked and talked about her life in DRC [Democratic Republic of the Congo] and how her parents and brothers had been killed ... The recording is 98 minutes and most of that is her talking. Should I have stopped her much earlier? (Field notes, November 2005)

In addition, telling their stories was also, for many, very emotional and this raised a number of ethical concerns for me, particularly as I was researching with 'vulnerable' communities.

Issues of vulnerability

Refugees are considered to be 'vulnerable' (Pittaway *et al.*, 2010), and/or 'doubly vulnerable' (Moore and Miller, 1999). This may be because of a particular attribute (such as age), because of previous experiences (such as trauma or abuse), or because of current circumstance (such as lacking political or economic security). Most of those I interviewed fell into the latter two categories, while the young people I interviewed for a refugee children project at the same time fell into all three. This meant I was careful from the outset to work through gatekeepers and elicit informed consent (although neither of these are without their challenges). I also took particular care to keep people's identities anonymous.

However, my assumptions about vulnerability were consistently challenged. That is not to say I was not mindful of the need to protect those I was interviewing from further harm; rather I was making assumptions about what form this harm might take. For example, one of the projects involved working with young unaccompanied asylum seekers, involving them in arts-based activities and using these in the design of a guide to accessing HE for refugees and asylum seekers (Stevenson and Willott, 2007). To ensure anonymity we gave the young people modelling clay to make images of themselves, then photographed these to go at the beginning of the book next to their names. However, when one young man, Rahimi – aged 15 and from Iran – discovered we were going to 'hide' him in this way, he told us in no uncertain terms that he wanted his real face to be shown. Rahimi described how he had been looking after his family's animals at night, at times on his own and from a very young age, and had fled the fighting in his village and made his way to safety following the death of family members. He had then made the journey to the UK and claimed asylum as an unaccompanied minor. He went on to explain that rather than being regarded as vulnerable he wanted to be recognized as a survivor. My field notes record the comment: 'Just been slapped on the wrist by a young man. Talking about keeping them anonymous when we publish the book. Really made me think about assumptions of vulnerability' (field notes, May 2006).

Further challenges to my assumptions about how to research with vulnerable adults arose during a number of the interviews, particularly being too cautious about the interview questions I might ask:

> Just done an interview and was quite taken aback. I was talking about recognizing the sensitivities of what I might ask and that he didn't have to say anything he didn't want to and that I apologized in advance if I asked anything that might be painful etc. And he just said quite crossly really, 'You ask what you want. I will tell you what I don't want to answer. Until you ask I don't know whether I will tell you or not.' (Field notes, January 2006)

I did however learn the hard way that 'the "sensitivity" of topics is relative and depended on the experience and perception of respondents' (Sin, 2005: 287). For example, one participant who talked freely about her dead sister became very distressed when talking about her mother, who was alive but whom she had not seen for many years; another talked with pride about his academic achievements but became upset when talking about his job, as this was the reason why he had had to flee his country. The interviews tended to become particularly emotional when people recounting their stories felt that I 'understood' how they felt, that we had shared experiences or status.

Rethinking positionality

The desirability of having 'insider' status – that is sharing a similar cultural, ethnic, gender or class background and identity to one's research participants – has been well rehearsed. The more the researcher is like their participants the more it is assumed that the research will offer a 'more truthful, authentic understanding of the culture under study' (Merriam *et al.*, 2001). However, the argument that the researcher is either an insider or an outsider has, of course, been refuted; rather it is now recognized that insider–outsider status operates on a continuum (Hellawell, 2006; Milligan, 2016). Nonetheless as a white British woman who has never been a forced migrant, I initially believed that I would be regarded firmly as an outsider. It quickly became apparent, however, that my outsider status or 'otherness' was determined by where I stood in relation to 'the other' – and that this was often fluid and shifting. Mostly I was a 'partial insider' in that the refugees I interviewed invariably worked to find commonalities, ensuring that what we shared became more important than what we did not. This included commonalities of gender, educational background and professional status, among others: 'We both had tears in our eyes talking about our dads and the fact that they were dead. What would they think of us? Would they be proud?' (field notes, May 2008).

However, while this allowed me to gain unexpected insights, it also led the interviews into areas that often by-passed the intended boundaries of the researcher–researched relationship: As a contract researcher, or as an evaluator, these boundaries are more clearly and carefully delineated. As a researcher involved in eliciting refugees' stories, they are not:

> Just spent an hour at the end of the interview when the tape was turned off talking about how I can help her to sort out the issues she is having with her children's schools. I was quite taken aback really because she really thought I could help. I sort of talked through what I might tell her as mother to mother but I was really concerned about whether I was overstepping the boundaries of the research relationship. Is it ok to do that once the tape is off? It's not the first time. ... Housing, education, jobs, how to get in to university ... (Field notes, February 2011).

The boundaries can easily blur, and I had to work hard to maintain some level of distance. This was particularly hard when interviews were conducted in the presence of children, grandparents and other relatives, when I was handed over babies to play with, shown photographs of home and family, and was offered copious amounts of food! At times I found the interviews both intense and exhausting:

> I felt a bit sick after that interview. Really raw, like someone's taken off a bit of my skin ... I had to gulp down glass after glass of water. I felt like I could never stop drinking like somehow I had been dried out, desiccated. Telling me about what had happened to them had actually taken something away from me ... Feels very heavy. (Field notes, July 2003)

I found using storytelling to be a very intimate form of close-up research. At times I also felt that I moved from researcher to counsellor to confessor. That is in part because stories can be sacred. As Robert Atkinson notes:

> When you ask for people's stories, and they tell you what matters most to them or they tell you the meaning of what has happened to them, it is a sacred moment that is shared. In some ways, the experience is akin to what transpires in the confessional

relationship. And what could result is very much like what is implied in the Japanese story, 'The Tale of Genji', when the character says, 'Because you have listened to my story, I can let go of my demons.' (1998: 65)

However, this process of catharsis, as described by Atkinson and Rosenthal among others, comes about to some extent because the weight of the story that is told is transferred to the listener – who then takes on, in some small way, part of this weight. This can be exceptionally painful. Using storytelling as a methodology to research with refugees is not for the fainthearted. Moreover, as this field note describes, it can be very difficult to walk away from the data:

I cannot stop thinking about Dominique's story. It haunts me. It is like a weight around my neck which I cannot take off. I have been thinking about it for days and days. I keep repeating the interview in my head, rewinding it to hear the story again, to think about what she was saying, to hear her voice, to look at her face as she was telling me her story. I feel marked by the story. And if I feel like that, what must it be like for her? (Field notes, September, 2005)

Using stories as part of an evaluation framework

Evaluation methods can help us, as practitioners, to understand 'what worked'; using storytelling research as part of an evaluation framework can help us gain new insights into *why* things worked, as well as elicit unexpected findings. These can, in turn, help to reframe and revise widening participation, or other social or educational, interventions. However, the new directions in which these stories may take the evaluator are not always positive for the overall evaluation. Two different examples can be seen in relation to my evaluation of the Free with Words project for Leeds City Council (where listening to refugees tell their stories was a wholly positive addition to the evaluation), and my co-evaluation of the Refugees into Teaching project (where it was not, to some extent, particularly helpful).

Free with Words

Free with Words was a national programme funded by the Joseph Rowntree Trust. It focused on providing access to books and reading for prisoners and young offenders and on building bridges between libraries in and outside of prison. In 2006–8, I led the evaluation of the Free with Words project being delivered by Leeds City Council's Library Service in a young offenders' institute and an adult prison, both in the Leeds area. The evaluation set out to evaluate the efficacy of the overall Free with Words intervention, as well as individual activities, and sought to determine, among other areas, whether the intervention:

1   encouraged improvements in literacy among prisoners with an increased number reading for enjoyment and sharing reading experiences;
2   encouraged family involvement in reading and reading activities between prisoners and their families.

To answer these questions both pre- and post-intervention questionnaires were completed by the participants before and after reading groups, book making activities, participation in poetry sessions, etc. The questionnaires sought to answer the specific evaluation questions. In order to explore the impact of the interventions in more detail, however, I also interviewed the prisoners and young offenders, among others. The semi-structured interview format used also, initially, focused on the evaluation questions. The impact of the intervention on the prisoners can be evidenced from this transcript except:

> I think I am 24 years old. I have been in the UK for 2 years, and in prison for 14 months. I didn't go to school at all, I worked in the market, but I learned to read and write a little Kurdish. Now I am better at reading in English than Kurdish. I read every day because I like the English language for reading and writing. Before I am released I want to be able to read and write fluently. Being here, this is my first school, it is useful for me being here in prison. I can learn to read and write in English. I enjoy these sorts of classes. I like the teacher helping me so I can learn. I like being here. All of it. I am reading *The Girl on the Platform* by Josephine Cox. I can read it but I don't understand it. (Kurdish Iraqi, 'Skills for Life' class, Leeds Prison)

However, the interviews I conducted quickly spilled over into open-ended discussions as the prisoners sought to tell their stories, not answer my research questions. In doing so, the interviews produced many unexpected findings – which would not have occurred if such an approach had not been utilized. In particular, the men talked about how they had ended up in prison, including their migration journeys, the families they had left behind or been separated from, and their struggles to settle in the UK. Consequently the interviews not only make explicit the outcome of having low levels of English literacy and language but also made clear the lack of support available to many asylum seekers:

> I arrived here [UK] and spoke no English. No English, no reading or writing English. Can't do nothing. How to get a job? Nobody helped. Can't speak it; can't write it; can't understand how to fill in forms. Can't fill in forms can't get a job ... In my country I was a teacher. Here I cannot teach. I wanted to teach but I cannot work. If cannot work, then no money. For a bit was begging, asking for money 'please help'. Not enough. Every day asking, asking, asking 'please help'. No help; no money. So I stole. To pay for things ... Now here I am learning English. (Iranian, English for Speakers of Other Languages class, Leeds Prison)

Only by hearing such stories, and those like it, have I been able to get a sense of the absolute exigencies of the lives of many refugees and asylum seekers. These findings have helped to shape not only the Free with Words evaluation but also subsequent bids for research funding, which in turn has helped to fund interventions designed to further support refugees and asylum seekers, and the place of higher education in helping them to do so. In other words, the findings have had implications far beyond the intention of either of the original evaluations.

Refugees into Teaching

Refugees into Teaching (RiT) was a national project that aimed to provide an information, guidance and training service for refugee teachers hoping to work in the UK. It was funded by the former Training and Development Agency for Schools, with the Refugee Council acting as the lead partner in the project. Our evaluation was designed to determine whether refugees enrolled on the scheme were accessing sufficient information, advice and guidance to enable them to understand routes into teaching and/or gain the experience they needed to make this transition. An integral part of the evaluation was to interview refugees to elicit their experiences of the RiT scheme and make recommendations for improvements.

A semi-structured interview schedule was developed, designed to answer the evaluation questions. Again, however the refugees' stories spilled out and over any intended interview questions as they spoke of their experiences of participating in the RiT scheme. There was a huge level of frustration, at times bordering on anger, about the alleged failure of the scheme to deliver what the refugees wanted – which went, however, well beyond the intentions of the scheme. What became clear from the refugees' stories was that they had multiple disadvantages to overcome if they were to make the transition into teaching. While many of these were beyond the gift of the RiT scheme, they coloured and shaped how the refugees thought about their experiences. In other words, the criticism the refugees had of the broader lack of support they were accessing was redirected towards the scheme – simply because we were allowing them to express their frustrations. So what came out of the interviews were stories of rejection, failure and disenchantment, all directed towards the RiT scheme. In reality, much of what the refugees were expressing resulted from the lack of support being offered by other bodies (such as social, health, housing or financial services, etc.).

It was very difficult, however, to pick out where such frustrations with RiT were actually valid and where they were not. For that reason the overall evaluation was coloured by a certain level of negativity that was quite pervasive. At the same time, the stories we were told were so moving and so poignant that it motivated us to push for additional research and the funding of other interventions. So there were broader benefits from using storytelling as part of the evaluation.

Final reflections: Becoming a reflexive researcher

My decade of researching with refugees has been a humbling experience. I have been privileged to hear accounts of extraordinary resilience and survival, and have also been treated with warmth, dignity and respect. Over time I have, as my field notes I believe testify, moved from being a reflective to a reflexive researcher, engaged in 'critical thought and careful consideration followed by action rooted in understanding' (Tanaka *et al.*, 2013). Becoming a (meta)reflexive researcher has also required me to:

- disclaim the neutral observer status;
- be brave: and allow for self-vulnerability, emotion, challenge;
- recognize the place of ethics-in-practice not ethics-in-process;
- reposition and relinquish power;
- accept personal responsibility.

By eliciting and drawing on individuals' stories, I and other researchers are able to offer more richness and depth to what can be known than may be available through other forms of data collection. Indeed as Connelly and Clandinin write, narrative research 'brings theoretical ideas about the nature of human life as lived to bear on educational experience as lived' (1990: 3). This in turn can help to better inform national policy and institutional practice.

However, the days of Aimhigher and the 'looseness' of the Aimhigher programme are long gone. The focus of the current state-funded interventions, such as the NCOP, is firmly on young people from wards with the lowest progression rates into HE. The possibilities of funding the sorts of projects I worked on a decade ago are remote. Moreover, there is an increasing pressure on those funding outreach activities to evaluate them using randomized control trials or quasi-experimental designs. Our concern, as we have written elsewhere, is that 'what really matters is to know why something works' (Clegg *et al.*, 2016: 2). Narrative approaches, and storytelling research in particular, can help to do exactly that.

The projects

1 *Study Skills research*, ESF/EQUAL 1 (2004–5)
2 *Gender and Dissemination*, ESF/EQUAL 1 (2005)
3 *Overcoming the Barriers*, ESF/EQUAL 1 (2005)
4 *Refugee Barriers to Higher Education*, Aimhigher West Yorkshire (2005)
5 *Refugee research*, Aimhigher West Yorkshire (2006)
6 *Aspiration Raising for Refugee Children*, Aimhigher Yorkshire and Humberside (2006)
7 *Refugee Women: Access to Employment*, Yorkshire and Humberside Regional Consortium for Asylum Seekers and Refugees (2006)
8 *Refugee project continuation*, Aimhigher Yorkshire and Humberside (2006)
9 *Free with Words*, Leeds Library Service (2006–8)
10 *Refugees into Teaching*, Refugee Council/Teacher Development Agency (2007)
11 *Promoting students' 'resilient thinking' in diverse higher education learning environments*, Higher Education Academy (2011–13)

References

Atkinson, P. and Delamont, S. (2006) 'Rescuing narrative from qualitative research'. *Narrative Inquiry*, 16 (1), 164–72.

Atkinson, R. (1995) *The Gift of Stories: Practical and spiritual applications of autobiography, life stories, and personal mythmaking*. Westport, CT: Bergin and Garvey.

Atkinson, R. (1998) *The Life Story Interview*. Thousand Oaks, CA: Sage.

Burkitt, I. (2012) 'Emotional reflexivity: Feeling, emotion and imagination in reflexive dialogues'. *Sociology*, 46 (3), 458–72.

Clandinin, D.J. (ed.) (2007) *Handbook of Narrative Inquiry: Mapping a methodology*. Thousand Oaks, CA: Sage.

Clegg, S., Stevenson, J. and Burke, P.-J. (2016) 'Translating close-up research into action: A critical reflection'. *Reflective Practice*, 17 (3), 233–44.

Connelly, F.M. and Clandinin, D.J. (1990) 'Stories of experience and narrative inquiry'. *Educational Researcher*, 19 (5), 2–14.

European Commission (2011) 'About EQUAL'. Online. http://ec.europa. eu/employment_social/equal_consolidated/about.html (accessed 10 December 2017).

Finlay, L. (2002) '"Outing" the researcher: The provenance, process, and practice of reflexivity'. *Qualitative Health Research*, 12 (4), 531–45.

Frank, A.W. (2000) 'The standpoint of storyteller'. *Qualitative Health Research*, 10 (3), 354–65.

Goode, J. (2006) 'Research identities: Reflections of a contract researcher'. *Sociological Research Online*, 11 (2). Online. www.socresonline.org.uk/11/2/ goode.html (accessed 10 December 2017).

Harrison, N. (2012) 'The mismeasure of participation: How choosing the "wrong" statistic helped seal the fate of Aimhigher'. *Higher Education Review*, 45 (1), 30–61.

HEFCE (Higher Education Funding Council for England) (2003) *HEFCE Strategic Plan 2003–2008*. Bristol: Higher Education Funding Council for England.

HEFCE (Higher Education Funding Council for England) (2004) *Aimhigher: Guidance notes for integration*. Bristol: Higher Education Funding Council for England.

HEFCE (Higher Education Funding Council for England) (2016) 'Gaps in young participation in higher education'. Online. www.hefce.ac.uk/analysis/yp/ gaps/#d.en.91628 (accessed 10 December 2017).

Hellawell, D. (2006) 'Inside-out: Analysis of the insider-outsider concept as a heuristic device to develop reflexivity in students doing qualitative research'. *Teaching in Higher Education*, 11 (4), 483–94.

Kettley, N. (2007) 'The past, present and future of widening participation research'. *British Journal of Sociology of Education*, 28 (3), 333–47.

Lincoln, Y.S. and Guba, E.G. (1985) *Naturalistic Inquiry*. Newbury Park, CA: Sage.

McCaig, C. (2010) 'Access agreements, widening participation and market positionality: Enabling student choice?'. In Molesworth, M., Scullion, R. and Nixon, E. (eds) *The Marketisation of Higher Education and the Student as Consumer*. London: Routledge, 115–28.

Merriam, S.B., Johnson-Bailey J., Lee, M.-Y., Kee, Y., Ntseane, G. and Muhamad, M. (2001) 'Power and positionality: Negotiating insider/outsider status within and across cultures'. *International Journal of Lifelong Education*, 20 (5), 405–16.

Milligan, L. (2016) 'Insider-outsider-inbetweener? Researcher positioning, participative methods and cross-cultural educational research'. *Compare: Journal of Comparative and International Education*, 46 (2), 235–50.

Moore, L.W. and Miller, M. (1999) 'Initiating research with doubly vulnerable populations'. *Journal of Advanced Nursing*, 30 (5), 1034–40.

Ollerenshaw, J.A. and Creswell, J.W. (2002) 'Narrative research: A comparison of two restorying data analysis approaches'. *Qualitative Inquiry*, 8 (3), 329–47.

Pittaway, E., Bartolomei, L. and Hugman, R. (2010) '"Stop stealing our stories": The ethics of research with vulnerable groups'. *Journal of Human Rights Practice*, 2 (2), 229–51.

Pratt, J. (1997) *The Polytechnic Experiment, 1965–1992*. Buckingham: Society for Research into Higher Education and Open University Press.

Riley, T. and Hawe, P. (2005) 'Researching practice: The methodological case for narrative inquiry'. *Health Education Research*, 20 (2), 226–36.

Rosenthal, G. (2003) 'The healing effects of storytelling: On the conditions of curative storytelling in the context of research and counseling'. *Qualitative Inquiry*, 9 (6), 915–33.

Ross, A. (2003a) 'Higher education and social access: To the Robbins Report'. In Archer, L., Hutchings, M. and Ross, A. (eds) *Higher Education and Social Class: Issues of exclusion and inclusion*. London: RoutledgeFalmer, 21–44.

Ross, A. (2003b) 'Access to higher education: Inclusion for the masses?'. In Archer, L., Hutchings, M. and Ross, A. (eds) *Higher Education and Social Class: Issues of exclusion and inclusion*. London: RoutledgeFalmer, 45–74.

Sin, C.H. (2005) 'Seeking informed consent: Reflections on research practice'. *Sociology*, 39 (2), 277–94.

Stevenson, J. (2005) *Longitudinal Tracking Study: Final project report*. Prepared for EQUAL e-Employability Development Partnership, Leeds.

Stevenson, J. and Willott, J. (2007) 'The aspiration and access to higher education of teenage refugees in the UK'. *Compare: A Journal of Comparative Education*, 37 (5), 671–87.

Tanaka, M., Stanger, N., Tse, V., Farish, M. and the TI Research Team (2013) *Transformative Inquiry*. Victoria, BC: University of Victoria, 108–11. Online. www.transformativeinquiry.ca/downloads/files/transformativeinquiryv4.pdf (accessed 10 December 2017).

Trow, M. (1974) 'Problems in the transition from elite to mass higher education'. In *Policies for Higher Education: General report on the Conference on Future Structures of Post-Secondary Education*. Paris: Organisation for Economic Co-operation and Development, 51–101.

Trow, M. (2006) 'Reflections on the transition from elite to mass to universal access: Forms and phases of higher education in modern societies since WWII'. In Forest, J.J.F. and Altbach, P.G. (eds) *International Handbook of Higher Education* (Springer International Handbooks of Education 18). Dordrecht: Springer, 243–80.

UK Parliament (1992) Further and Higher Education Act, c. 13. London: HMSO. Online. www.legislation.gov.uk/ukpga/1992/13/contents (accessed 10 December 2017).

Warren, C.A.B. and Karner, T.X. (2005) *Discovering Qualitative Methods: Field research, interviews, and analysis*. Los Angeles: Roxbury Publishing Company.

Willott, J. and Stevenson, J. (2013) 'Attitudes to employment of professionally qualified refugees in the United Kingdom'. *International Migration*, 51 (5), 120–32.

Index

A levels 40, 60, 66; 'difficulty' 65; facilitating A levels 79; institutional decision making 80; predication 70, 81; reform 80; subject choice xvi, 79; taxonomy 63; use in selection 66, 67

Abrahams, Jessica 44

Access Agreement 38, 57, 167

action research 7, 10, 53, 156

affective 11, 14, 114-15, 123; association 123; eduscapes 111; learning xvi, 111; processes 111; space 112

African; African American women 118; African Caribbean men 126; African Caribbean students 115,116, 123; Black African men, 121

agency; external 5; choice 24; individual 36; lack of 127; religious 124-5; strategic 36; structure and agency 25, 37

Ahmed, Sara 113, 128, 123, 124

Aimhigher 2, 4, 35, 153-4, 156

allodoxia 140

Archer, Louise 3, 12, 28, 40, 43, 88, 92,133

Archer, Margaret 24, 43

Ashley, Louise 59, 68

asylum seekers 156, 159, 164

atheoretical 3, 12, 15, 22

attainment 39, 88, 89; A Level 81; gap 2, 99; GSCE 40; parents 99, 104, 106, 107; prior, 63, 65, 66, 67, 79, 81, 82; raising 39, 50; university choice 136, 145

Atkinson, Robert 158, 161

Aveling, Nado 121

Badriotti, Augusta 135

Ball, Stephen J. 39, 40, 117

Bar 59, 68; Bar Standards Board 59

Bathmaker, Anne-Marie 135, 138, 140, 142, 144, 146, 148, 149

Bengry-Howell, Andrew 22

Bhaskar, Roy 23-4

bilingualism 122

BiS (Department for Business, Innovation and Skills) 33, 59, 60

black and minority ethnic students 112-13; assumptions about 115-16; categorizations 16, 115; equity 127; exclusionary practices 117-18, 121; external materiality 115; institutional 'flashpoints' 111, 115, 125; retention 120, 122

black and postcolonial ethnicized women 114

black feminist theory 114

BMA (British Medical Association) 66

Bourdieu, Pierre 13,16; academic capital 51, 116-117; adding/acquiring capital 149; concepts/conceptual tools/ theories 36-7, 134, 137; economic capital 137-8, 141, 148; family capital 135, 137, 149; field 36-8, 41, 44, 46, 49, 51, 54, 119, 126, 135-7, 146-7; game 37, 50, 135, 140, 142, 146-7, 149; habitus 37-38, 40, 42-5, 49, 52-3,117, 126, 135, 137,139; human capital 96; hypermobilization of capital 144; identity capital 96; intellectual and skills capitals 45, 50-51; reproduction of privilege 148; science capital 43; social and cultural capitals 22, 35-7, 39-40, 42-3, 136, 144, 146; symbolic (value) 36, 38, 139, 142

Brah Avtar 114

Britton, Jack 59

Browne, Liz 137

Buke, Ciaran 36

Burke, Penny Jane 6, 11-13, 20-21, 42-4, 106

Butler, Judith 115

Bygstad, Bendik 26

Casey, Kathleen 117-18

causation 7, 24

Centre of Excellence for Equity in Higher Education (CEEHE) 11, 21

Chen Huey-Tsyh 25

Chevalier, Arnaud 59

circle of knowledge 20

Ciriaci, Daria 135

class 134, 153, 160; background 134, 139, 149; classed processes 137; dominated/dominant class 140; experience 138, 143; inequality 134, 146; middle-class 116, 134, 135, 137, 140, 143, 144, 147, 149; social class 134, 137; working class 137, 138, 139, 140, 148, 149

classics 46

Clegg, Sue 5, 22, 26

Collins, Patricia Hill 114, 118

colonizing; research 12, 13

Combahee River Collective 114

contract research 154-5

Crenshaw, Kimberle 114

critical, critical action 11, 17, 42; critical consciousness 122; critical race theory 113; critical reflection 17, 42; critical theory 115

Crozier, Gill 22

culture 7, 40, 44, 53, 90, 92, 112, 119, 120, 125, 127; cultural identity 111

David, Miriam 117

Davis, Angela 114

deficit model 15, 28, 36,106

democratic 15

dentistry 69, 70, 71, 72, 73, 78, 79, 80, 81, 82

Index

Index